A Birder's Guide

to

Wyoming

A BIRDER'S GUIDE

TO

WYOMING

by
Oliver K. Scott
1993

American Birding Association, Inc.

Library of Congress Catalog Card Number: 92-74478

ISBN Number: 1-878788-02-7

First Edition

1   2   3   4   5   6   7   8

Printed in the United States of America

Publisher

ABA / William J. Graber, III, Chairman, Publications Committee

Series Editor

Paul J. Baicich

Associate Editors

Cindy Lippincott and Bob Berman

Copy Editor

Hugh Willoughby

Layout and Typography

Bob Berman; using Ventura Publisher, Windows version 4.0

Maps

Cindy Lippincott; using CorelDRAW version 3.0

Cover Photography

front cover: *Sage Grouse*; Herbert Clarke
back cover: *Black-backed Woodpecker*; D. Parker Backstrom

Illustrations

Shawneen Finnegan
Charles H. Gambill
Gail Diane Luckner
Cliff Scott

Distributed by

American Birding Association Sales
PO Box 6599
Colorado Springs, Colorado 80934-6599 USA

(800) 634-7736 (US & Canada) or (719) 578-0607
fax: (800) 247-3329 (US & Canada) or (719) 471-4722

Dedicated
to
the memory of

LUDLOW GRISCOM

whose inspiration helped produce this work

EDITOR'S PREFACE

A few years ago the American Birding Association secured the rights to the guides put out by the late Jim Lane. It was the organization's intention to revise all of Jim's guides and publish them for broad distribution. ABA is now in the midst of pursuing that goal. The Association also wished to bring out brand new birdfinding guides. This volume marks the third **ABA Birdfinding Guide**, but the first that is a completely new work.

It is with no small pride that ABA presents this volume, **A Birder's Guide to Wyoming**, for it covers a state that begs for exploration, and is written by a man who knows the birdlife of the state intimately.

Though the Great Parks of Wyoming—Grand Teton and Yellowstone—are visited regularly by those whose interests include birds, much of the rest of Wyoming is not heavily birded by outsiders. This is at least partially true because there has never been a birdfinding guide to cover the whole state in a coherent manner. The birders of Wyoming, a hardy troupe, are blessed with numerous sites for productive birding. The number of birders in this eighth-largest state, however, is not large, in keeping with the population of Wyoming, the state with the lowest human population in the U.S. This book is intended to advance bird study in Wyoming and essentially put Wyoming on the birding map.

Dr. Oliver K. Scott is the ideal man to write this book. He has spent well over four decades studying the birds of Wyoming. He has loved the state's environment and worked to protect it. As you read the text you will also find that he clearly has strong opinions about the state's environmental riches and their uses. What is important is not simply that he has written a book which reflects his interests and his concerns, but that he has written a book which will introduce birders throughout North America—and the world—to the fascinating birding potential of "The Cowboy State." Doctor, rancher, and conservationist, Oliver Scott has made an imprint on the state, and the American Birding Association is pleased to present his book to the birding public. Use it and enjoy it.

Paul J. Baicich
Series Editor, ABA Birdfinding Guides

ACKNOWLEDGEMENTS

The development of this book is very much an outgrowth of my experiences in Wyoming since 1948 and those of people with whom I've birded over the years. I am, indeed, deeply indebted to a number of these people. First off, I am very thankful for the Casper gang. The dean of the group is Lucy Rognstad, who took my first junior-college evening course and has become a first-rate birder. She also helped to search a decade of records from *American Birds* for me. Then there is Bud Stratton, a sharp-eyed birder who is a botanist by training and an excellent merchandiser by avocation, who helped with the evening bird-course. Bud now teaches the course himself very well. Then there was Fred Broerman, who was here for a year or two and is now a real expert on the Spotted Owl.

Outside of Casper I first visited Sheridan and am indebted to the late Tom Kessinger and the late Platt Hall, who showed me around that area. Then the late Florence Spring retired to Big Horn after presiding over the Casper club and starting two chapters of National Audubon. The first interest of all of these groups was birds.

Helen Downing is the current chief birder in the Sheridan area. She has helped me innumerable times and now has published her own records for the area.

Among folks in Cheyenne, I am grateful for the assistance of Fred Lebsack, and before Fred there was Steve Streeper, an ex-Casper boy.

It was a great day when Forrest Luke from Rock Springs showed up. He was helped by Marie Adams, formerly of Green River and now of Evanston. Forrest lives near the juniper country of southwest Wyoming. I had poked around there a good deal before Forrest arrived, but he has been most helpful and has gathered other birders like Rick and Janis Steenberg, Jo Larson, and others. Bert and Meg Raynes in Jackson Hole have kept tabs on the surrounding birdlife there.

I have never done very well with the personnel of the Great Parks, Teton and Yellowstone. As soon as I get acquainted with a good birder, he or she usually get promoted away. Over the years I have been in most of the nooks and crannies of these National Parks except for northern

Yellowstone, where Ed Harper has skillfully taken over the text in this book. (Ed was also very helpful with the Beartooth section of the Cody chapter.)

I cannot forget Sam Fitton and his wife Terri, good friends, excellent birders, and good advisers. Sam is also an owl-caller *extraordinaire*, with a complete repertoire. In the short time Sam was assistant to the non-game biologist of the State Game and Fish, he did more for birding than anyone else had done in years; his work included setting up a rare-bird committee.

Then there are Jim Gaither, Jim and Verna Herold, Wilmer and Ann Hines, Frank and Lois Layton, Gloria and Jim Lawrence, Chris Michelson, K.C. and Bobbie Roberts, Bob South, and a host of others who have been most helpful.

Most of the people mentioned here have influenced the text or actually reviewed portions of it. Others who helped by reviewing portions of some of the text have been Tom Allen, Jocelyn Lee Baker, George Cardon, Katy Duffy, Virginia Maynard, Terry McEneaney, John McGough, Carol Orr, Bill Schreier, and Nathaniel R. Whitney. To all these folks I am very grateful.

Artwork in this volume is by Shawneen Finnegan, Charles H. Gambill, Gail Diane Luckner, and Cliff Scott. Their works and the cover photographs by Herbert Clarke and D. Parker Backstrom are much appreciated.

I am also grateful to Paul J. Baicich, who is editor of the ABA birdfinding guide series; to Cindy Lippincott, who made the fine maps and also assisted in editing tasks; to Bob Berman for his technical skills; to Hugh Willoughby for copy-editing; and to the board and staff of the American Birding Association for their support.

I especially wish to recognize my wife, Deborah, whose patience has been outstanding for many decades.

There is no way, however, that errors have escaped this volume. Since this book is intended to be revised in the future, I hope that you will advise me when you find any errors or omissions.

Oliver K. Scott
5120 Alcova Route, Box 16
Casper, Wyoming 82604
October 1992

Townsend's Warblers
Shawneen Finnegan

American Birding Association Code of Ethics

We, the Membership of the American Birding Association, believe that all birders have an obligation at all times to protect wildlife, the natural environment, and the rights of others. We therefore pledge ourselves to provide leadership in meeting this obligation by adhering to the following general guidelines of good birding behavior.

I. Birders must always act in ways that do not endanger the welfare of birds or other wildlife.

In keeping with this principle, we will

- Observe and photograph birds without knowingly disturbing them in any significant way.
- Avoid chasing or repeatedly flushing birds.
- Only sparingly use recordings and similar methods of attracting birds and not use these methods in heavily birded areas.
- Keep an appropriate distance from nests and nesting colonies so as not to disturb them or expose them to danger.
- Refrain from handling birds or eggs unless engaged in recognized research activities.

II. Birders must always act in ways that do not harm the natural environment.

In keeping with this principle, we will

- Stay on existing roads, trails, and pathways whenever possible to avoid trampling or otherwise disturbing fragile habitat.
- Leave all habitat as we found it.

III. Birders must always respect the rights of others.

In keeping with this principle, we will

- Respect the privacy and property of others by observing "No Trespassing" signs and by asking permission to enter private or posted lands.
- Observe all laws and the rules and regulations which govern public use of birding areas.
- Practice common courtesy in our contacts with others. For example, we will limit our requests for information, and we will make them at reasonable hours of the day.
- Always behave in a manner that will enhance the image of the birding community in the eyes of the public.

IV. Birders in groups should assume special responsibilities.

As group members, we will

- Take special care to alleviate the problems and disturbances that are multiplied when more people are present.
- Act in consideration of the group's interest, as well as our own.
- Support by our actions the responsibility of the group leader(s) for the conduct of the group.

As group leaders, we will

- Assume responsibility for the conduct of the group.
- Learn and inform the group of any special rules, regulations, or conduct applicable to the area or habitat being visited.
- Limit groups to a size that does not threaten the environment or the peace and tranquility of others.
- Teach others birding ethics by our words and example.

TABLE OF CONTENTS

INTRODUCTION

Wyoming is a state of awesome beauty, of grandeur and wilderness. It is a land of spectacular mountains, vast evergreen forests, expansive sagebrush and prairie country, and enough lakes, streams, and rivers to please almost anyone. In all, Wyoming is one of the most impressive outdoor recreation areas in the country.

It is a huge, almost-square plateau, tipped up in the south and down in the north and northeast. The plateau is pierced by at least nineteen mountain ranges. Of course, many an American has mountain images of Wyoming, with visions of the Great Parks—Yellowstone and Grand Teton—conjured up whenever the state's name is mentioned.

Though all of the state's mountain ranges belong to the Rocky Mountain system, their discontinuity produces different breeding birdlife from one coniferous-dominated range to another. And in Wyoming there is almost always a mountain range in the distance.

The state is also the ridgepole of much of the nation. Many of the great rivers of the continental United States have their headwaters in Wyoming. The Green is the principal tributary of the Colorado. The Snake heads west to join the Columbia River on its course to the Pacific. The mighty Missouri gathers up a lot of tributaries from the high ground of Wyoming, such as the Madison, Yellowstone, Powder, Belle Fourche, Cheyenne, and Niobrara. Then there is the meandering North Platte River, whose headwaters are in Colorado but which gets much of its water from Wyoming.

Along with these watercourses are wooded areas often dominated by willow, Western Box Elder, and cottonwood. Riparian birdlife here—both resident and migrant—can be very interesting.

Wyoming's open country—prairie grassland and sagebrush—is vast. These impressive expanses constitute the predominant physiographic features of the state. Mile after mile of sagebrush, greasewood, and grasses greets the traveling birder. The Antelope (or Pronghorn) shares this habitat with many of Wyoming's most characteristic birds. Some of these areas can be rather impressive. The desert-like qualities of the Great Divide Basin (sometimes called the Red Desert) make for hard scenery, indeed. Yet Wyoming's foothills, hogbacks, and buttes—sometimes with juniper associations—still demand attention from birders.

Otto McCreary published a comprehensive study of the birds of Wyoming, first a 133-page effort in "mimeoprint" (1937), reproduced later in pamphlet form (1939). Those were the days when the identification of subspecies was important. In the fifty-odd years since that time there have been mighty changes in Wyoming. Our road system has expanded tremendously and so has our birding coverage. One can easily go places now that were almost impossible to reach by vehicle fifty years ago. For example, in 1984 Sam Fitton published a paper in *Western Birds* on the southwest juniper country, a region that was entirely out of bounds to McCreary. Even now, though, there have been few publications on Wyoming birds, though the bibliography at the end of this section lists some recent advances.

Fifty years ago practically marked the heyday of the homesteader in Wyoming. But today, for economic reasons, there are almost no homesteads left. Consequently, the population of Wyoming has not increased as significantly as that of other western states. Now we have the smallest population of any state (475,000 people), although in geographic size we are eighth largest (97,914 square miles).

To survive economically, Wyoming ranches have had to grow bigger. Some of these ranches are over 100,000 acres in size. However, when it comes to productivity, that is an entirely different matter. For instance, I have a 23,000-acre ranch, but in productivity it is equal to about 300 acres in Iowa—which means that it is a somewhat marginal operation. The bigger family unit of 64,000 acres in Wyoming is about equal to 1,000 acres in Iowa. Some 64,000 acres makes for a good-sized ranch, but one which is by no means unusual in the state. The homesteaders took the best land and particularly sought the land by watercourses and springs, because they knew that they could use the remainder of the land for free grazing. Now, however, one has to pay a fee for grazing-rights on federal lands. There has always been a fee for grazing on state lands.

The state was granted the 16th and 36th sections in every township for the benefit of the schools. (A section is a square mile in size, and a township is merely a unit of thirty-six of these sections of land. A township really has nothing to do with a town.) The railroads were also given land—to induce them to route their tracks across Wyoming. The Union Pacific, for example, got 20 miles of alternate sections on either side of the tracks, organized like a checkerboard. This deprived the state of a lot of land, so it got whatever was available elsewhere that was worth something in order to make up for what it had lost to the railroads.

With so much land available it followed that the fees charged for grazing-rights were minuscule. The value of what was under the surface, however, was enormous—with tremendous revenue reverting to the state. Wyoming ranks sixth in oil production, first in coal output, first in production of trona (the ore for soda ash, used in the manufacture of detergents, glass products, baking soda, and other basics), first or second in uranium production, and has as-yet untapped but mind-boggling reserves of natural gas. The result is that Wyoming may have the wealthiest state government in the United States. The legislature, wisely, has squirreled away these funds so that a large portion of the state's expenses are now funded by the interest on these monies. (Consequently, there is no income tax in the state, and property levies are comparatively small.)

The ownership of land in Wyoming is the darndest hodge-podge you will ever see. The federal government land looks as if someone spilled ink on the map and then scattered it in tiny bits everywhere. The state ownership is a little more orderly but follows much the same pattern. This means that private ownership has to be similarly haphazard. In general, the federal government owns about 20 percent of the land in the eastern third of the state, about 50 percent in the middle third, and 80 percent in the western third.

What does all this mean to the average birder? It means that in the mountainous, hilly, and strictly sagebrush lands of the state, you have as much right to wander around as anybody else—providing, of course, that you don't eat the grass. The grazing-rights are leased. The government agency controlling some 17.8 million acres, or more than one-quarter of the state's acreage, is the Bureau of Land Management (BLM). Although they lease what they can, there are still tremendous areas across the state belonging to the federal government—BLM—that are essentially unleasable. (This is particularly true of the area north of Powder Rim.) The BLM elsewhere in the state has much more land that is leased. Due to the current paucity in cattle numbers, about 20 percent of the leasable land is not leased. In the short run, it may be a good thing to give the grassland a rest, but should this practice continue over the long haul, there is increasing evidence that it would be a disaster for the grasslands. Grasslands need some grazing by big sharp-hoofed animals like the Buffalo (or Bison), Elk, Bighorn Sheep, and even the beloved cow that can kick up some dust, thereby planting the grass seeds. Wild animals keep moving all the time. There is now a growing realization that cattle have to recreate the same kind of movement to improve the range, which will help to keep the ranching operations profitable.

I present these points—on the land, ranching, and changes in Wyoming over the years—not as digressions in this birdfinding book, but as points that might help birders to appreciate and understand this state better as they travel through it.

BIRDING BEHAVIOR

In this work I have avoided giving directions to birding areas on private lands as much as possible; this is really not hard to do in Wyoming. Whereas over most of the continent one has to ask permission to bird on private land, in Wyoming this is not a real problem because so much of the land belongs to the federal or state governments. On county roads you will find cattle-guards between one holding and another, so you should not have to open a gate. Should you go through a gate, however, be *sure* to leave it as you found it.

This leads us to the applicability of the "American Birding Association Code of Ethics" while birding in this state. Opposite the Table of Contents of this book is a copy of these guidelines. I recommend that those who use this book familiarize themselves with the tenets of the code. Generally, the code indicates that birders should:

1. Always act in ways that do not endanger the welfare of birds or other wildlife;
2. Always act in ways that do not harm the natural environment;
3. Always respect the rights of others;
4. Assume special responsibilities when birding in groups.

The first rule in the ABA Code of Ethics—on the welfare of the birds themselves—needs some special emphasis here. Today there are increasing concerns over possible harassment of nesting and rare birds, as well as excessive tape-use in the field. Nesting birds can be easily disturbed. If adult birds are frightened off the nest by you, you are clearly *pushing too hard*. If an adult bird is alarmed by your presence, circling you at the nesting area, you are again *pushing too hard*. Unattended nestlings will succumb readily to predators or exposure to heat, cold, or wet weather. In this book I have sometimes avoided specific details on owls, Trumpeter Swans, diurnal raptors, or other sensitive species. Where I have given detailed directions to some well-known sites, I advise using care. The same warning goes for tape-recorder use. The excessive use of tapes that results in the agitation of owls, of secretive species, and, especially, of endangered species is certainly inappropriate.

Birders should also be aware that there is a regulation enforced within Yellowstone and Grand Teton National Parks which forbids the use of audio attractants—artificial or otherwise—to lure wildlife. This regulation (under provisions of 16 U.S.C., Section 3, and Title 36, Code of Federal Regulations, Section 2.2) provides for a stiff fine for violators.

THE BIRDING SCENE

Perhaps the most gratifying change in the fifty-odd years since Otto McCreary's publications has been the growth in numbers of competent birders in Wyoming. When I arrived in Casper with my family in 1948 for the practice of Pediatrics, I could not find another birder anywhere. After some years of frustration, in 1953 I offered a course in bird identification at the night school of the local junior college, and we were off and running.

Gradually I found birders elsewhere, but to do so in the nation's least-populated state was no small task. The acknowledgements section in this book enumerates many—though not all—of those birders who were crucial to the growth of birding in the state.

One of them, Sam Fitton, started a Wyoming Bird Records Committee in 1989. This has been an important achievement for birders in the state. The Wyoming Bird Records Committee can now review important sightings and approve what is accepted. Fortunately, today we have the personnel to do the job right. You can help the Committee by sending any reports of rare birds seen in the state to: Secretary, Wyoming Bird Records Committee, c/o Game and Fish Department, 260 Buena Vista, Lander, WY 82520.

Now that we have people interested in birds throughout most of the state, we are learning more about the distribution of birds in Wyoming. There is now a statewide "Rare Bird Alert" run by the Murie Audubon Society, with an emphasis on the Casper area (307/265-BIRD).

The birding scene, like much of Wyoming itself, is informal. Wyoming is not called "the Cowboy State" for nothing. Blue-jeans, western-style shirts, and sturdy boots are very much in order while in the field. The important thing is to be practical and comfortable. Hats are quite practical. Shorts in the summer, however, are impractical, because of exposure to insects, brush, and often a burning sun. Even in summer, be sure to carry warm clothes and the standard emergency gear if you are going into the mountains for any reason. Early and late blizzards are not unknown, and I have seen snow in Yellowstone during virtually every month of the year. Between the months of September and May it is wise to carry warm clothes in your vehicle, even if you don't plan to leave the road much. The winter months themselves can be highly challenging, with below-zero temperatures, high winds, and deep, drifted snow in places. A ground-blizzard has to be experienced to be believed.

At high altitudes be conscious of possible acute mountain sickness (AMS), though it is not likely below an elevation of 7,500 feet. The symptoms are headaches, loss of appetite, shortness of breath, rapid pulse rate, insomnia, and/or lethargy. If symptoms are severe, you should turn around, start descending, and seek care. A quick descent often ends the suffering.

Of course, Wyoming is big game country, too, and there are potential hazards related to large animals. It is wise to keep a safe distance (say, 100 yards), from large mammals—Buffalo, bears, and Moose. And it is also wise to remember that the Grizzly horror stories from the Great Parks are often preceded by stories of foolish tourists.

Be aware of the hunting seasons. They usually range from September through November for different game. Take precautions; you are in the field with binoculars while other folks have guns.

Prairie Rattlesnakes can be found in rocky, isolated areas. They are small and are rarely a problem. However, it is smart to avoid putting your hand where you can't see. And then there are ticks. The tick season can start as early as March and will go into June. Use caution since Rocky Mountain spotted fever can be carried by the wood tick. Spray yourself and your clothing, and always check clothing and body after being out in the field during this season. Mosquitoes can be bothersome, especially in July, with deerflies and gnats prevalent in midsummer. There is some poison oak and poison ivy in areas of higher moisture, so beware.

WHEN TO COME TO WYOMING

I am often asked by birders about when to come to the state. Almost anytime will do. In winter lots of the mountain roads are closed along with most of Yellowstone Park (though snowmobiling is still possible), and winter travel over the state can be a bit dicey at times. However, our winter birds can be interesting with Snow Buntings, Common Redpolls, and big flocks of Bohemian Waxwings and Rosy Finches.

Spring is always stimulating. Birding in April, May, and June can bring excitement with the possibility of eastern vagrants as well as the arrival of summer residents in full dress. When snows melt off the mountain ranges in June, the rivers may flood.

Most people visit Wyoming in summer and some popular areas can be uncomfortably packed. Still, the birds will please you. Such stunning passerine summer residents as Western Tanager, Lazuli Bunting, and Lark Bunting make any day enjoyable. Our summer climate tends to be delightful since it doesn't get too hot and there is plenty of sunshine. Summer nights can be cool, though. Practically the only moisture in summer comes from thunderstorms. The Wyoming Plateau is semi-arid and gets drier to the south, but the mountain ranges gather lots of moisture.

The fall passerine migration is likely to be more interesting that the spring one. Of course, this is certainly true for shorebirds, with the migration peaking during the last two weeks of August and again during the first two weeks in October. The waterfowl start up in September. The rarer species are more likely in fall than in spring.

ACCOMMODATIONS

Tourism is now Wyoming's second-largest industry (following mineral extraction), and accommodations can be found almost everywhere. Campgrounds are actually too numerous to list in this book. Many of the places to see birds that are mentioned in the text are campgrounds. All towns of any size have at least one, and usually several. Motels abound, and dude ranches can be either open to everyone, or very exclusive, requiring a year's advance reservations. Most of the dude ranches are in the Big Horn Mountains or the mountains of the northwest near the Great Parks, Grand Teton and Yellowstone, but really they are almost everywhere in the mountain country. They offer riding, pack-trips, fishing, and loafing.

Many Wyoming towns have rodeos sometime during the summer, and on most weekends there are several going. In the last full week in July Cheyenne has the biggest rodeo of them all—the "Cheyenne Frontier Days." Overall, Wyoming is very recreation-oriented, and birders should delight in its outdoor offerings.

WYOMING INFORMATION

For information on Wyoming, one can write to the Wyoming Travel Commission at I-25 and College Drive, Cheyenne, WY 82002, or call them at 307/777-7777. The Commission has a free *Wyoming Vacation Guide* that has all kinds of helpful information for the visitor. It is regularly updated.

You might also want to contact the Wyoming Game and Fish Department. This is an independent department of the Wyoming state government with Commissioners appointed by the Governor. The Commissioners represent hunting and fishing interests; these are much-sought-after appointments. Game and Fish is Big Business in Wyoming. The Department has a huge budget, much personnel, and has done a remarkable job with game animals—from Elk to Wild Turkeys. The Department is also to be commended for their consistent stand against the introduction of exotic species to the state. However, the small non-game department (whose activities would be the birders' major interest) in Lander, 250 miles from Cheyenne, is almost an afterthought. Of course, it is the hunting and fishing license fees which provide the department with funds.

For publications and other materials, write to the Wyoming Game and Fish Department, 5400 Bishop Boulevard, Cheyenne, WY 82006; phone: 307/777-4600.

They also have a checklist of Wyoming birds. You will find this list to be a little unusual. No one proofread it, and as you peruse it you will find that you are reading the same birds over again. The list also contains a number of species that the Wyoming Bird Records Committee thinks should not be there, but perhaps this is a minor problem. The Game and Fish Department thought their checklist so fine that they printed 30,000 of them. The whole matter is probably indicative of the Wyoming Game and Fish's attitude toward non-game birds.

Good maps of land ownership can be had at Bureau of Land Management offices and most sporting-goods stores throughout the state. For most birders, though, I doubt that these are necessary. Still, if you want to plan ahead, contact the BLM at Box 1828, Cheyenne, WY 82003; phone: 307/772-2334.

For details on the larger properties of the US Forest Service in Wyoming you can contact the following offices:

Bighorn National Forest
  1969 South Sheridan Avenue
  Sheridan, WY 82801   307/672-0751

Black Hills National Forest
  Ranger Station
  PO Box 680
  Sundance, WY 82729   307/283-1361

Bridger-Teton National Forest
  Box 1888
  Jackson, WY 83001   307/733-2752

Medicine Bow National Forest
  605 Skyline Drive
  Laramie, WY 82070   307/745-8971

Thunder Basin National Grassland
  Douglas Ranger Station
  809 South 9th
  Douglas, WY 82633   307/358-4690

Shoshone National Forest
  PO Box 2140
  Cody, WY 82414   307/527-6241

The US Forest Service Regional office in Colorado (PO Box 25127, Lakewood, CO 80225) can also supply you with maps of all of these National Forests for $3.00 each.

Other areas of birding interest (Grand Teton National Park, Yellowstone National Park, Devils Tower National Monument, Flaming Gorge National Recreation Area, and Bighorn Canyon National Recreation Area) are treated individually in the main text.

HOW TO USE THIS BOOK

The purpose of this book is to help birders to find the varied birds of Wyoming and to become acquainted with the better birding-sites in the state. This book should be valuable for both the Wyoming visitor and the Wyoming resident.

I have organized this work into 19 chapters of varying lengths and consisting of three broad routes from east to west. The three routes could be turned around and run in the opposite direction. Or one could simply sample one or more of the chapters without regard to any particular order. The route maps (on the next page and also inside the covers) should help to clarify the three routes as outlined below.

The first route follows Interstate 80 west from Cheyenne through Evanston, along much of what was historically known as the "Overland Trail" and along the route of the first transcontinental railroad. This route has slight side trips north to Farson and Pinedale, as well as to Cokeville and Afton. The second route follows US 26 from Torrington through Casper, on over the Wind River Range at Togwotee Pass (pronounced TOE-got-ee) and up north through the Great Parks (Grand Teton and Yellowstone). The third route is over Interstate 90 from the Black Hills of South Dakota to north of Sheridan, where you turn west onto US 14 over the Big Horn Mountains to the Big Horn Basin (a high, dry desert) and on to Cody.

Each chapter should take you through one or more areas of prime birding. Most of these chapters are divided into individual sections, each of which guides you mile-by-mile from site to site, sometimes bird to bird. You can find the birds mentioned *in the proper season*. (This may mean making reference at times to the Annotated Checklist.) This format is probably the most helpful to birders, and is the feature that makes birdfinding guides so useful. Some of these chapters take you through some remote routing, so be conscious of the gasoline situation and check your gauge regularly.

There is a useful statewide map on the inside back cover; each chapter has at least one map. The maps are an essential part of each chapter, helping to supplement or clarify the textual directions. Some of the chapter maps are more crucial to the accompanying text—say, the maps for Ocean Lake or Goshen Hole—than others. Section lines are shown in a few of the maps; they can be easy to get used to, organized as they are on simple mile-square grids.

The annotated checklist is the other major part of this volume. The order and the nomenclature for the checklist are from the *ABA Checklist: Birds of the Continental United States and Canada* (4th edition, 1990). This Wyoming annotated checklist should give you the kind of information which you need about Wyoming birds on a species-by-species basis. When going through the annotated checklist, you can refer back to the birding-sites written up in the birdfinding chapters. In all, your Wyoming birding should be made easier and more enjoyable through use of both major parts of this volume.

Birdfinding Routes

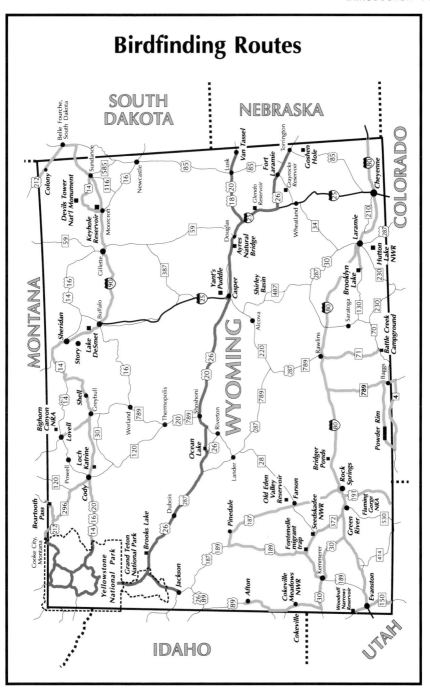

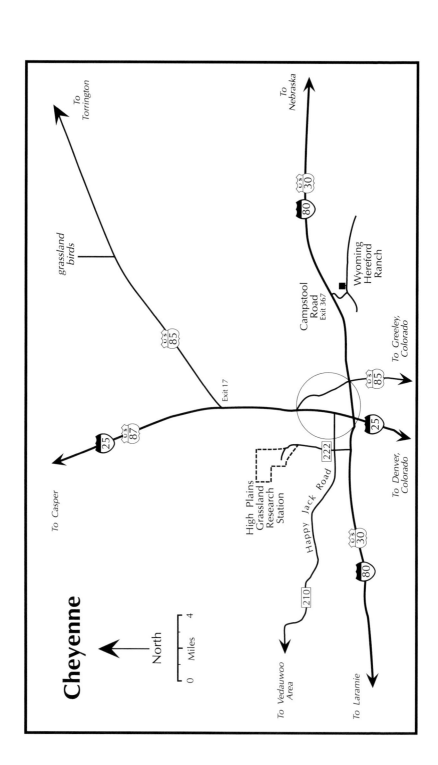

1. CHEYENNE AREA

Cheyenne is located in the middle of the region's high grasslands, just east of the Rocky Mountains. Its beginnings originate with the Union Pacific Railroad's decision to build a terminal there in 1867. Soldiers, railroaders, mule-skinners, telegraph crews, and stage-drivers mingled, and soon made the town the logical place to serve as the territorial capital. Today, with a population of 51,000, it serves as the state's capital, as well as being a commercial center. Cheyenne also has Wyoming's only U.S. military installation, Francis E. Warren Air Force Base. (The base maintains the many missile siloes scattered across southeastern Wyoming).

In many visible ways Cheyenne has not lost its Western roots. Cowboy boots, string ties, and western rodeos are all found in Cheyenne. In fact, the world's largest outdoor rodeo, the "Cheyenne Frontier Days", is a point of pride—and a major source of income—for the city. But for folks from Wyoming, there is little particularly "Western" in Cheyenne, with many features geared toward the tourist trade. It is a still a prim and tree-lined small city. And in many other ways Cheyenne has modern qualities—a symphony, art galleries, and a botanical garden, for example. For birders, there is the Wildlife Visitors Center run by the Wyoming Game and Fish Department at Interstate 25 and Central Avenue (exit 12), not far from Lions Park. This facility may have useful wildlife information, maps, and other literature helpful to the Wyoming visitor. (Open seven days a week from Memorial Day through Labor Day, weekdays during the remainder of the year.)

For birders Cheyenne also has grassland birds close to the city limits and a series of oases, often remarkable for migratory passerines. Cheyenne is the gateway to Rocky Mountain birding for a traveler westbound on Interstate 80.

1. **Lions Park.** Cheyenne itself is an oasis of trees in the high-plains grassland. The older parts of town are excellent in migration for landbirds. The best birding area in the city is Lions Park and Sloan's Lake. To get there, turn off westbound Interstate 80 at the Central Business District (exit 362) and go north on US Highway 85/87 (one-way Warren Avenue) 2.6 miles through the heart of Cheyenne. Turn left onto 8th Avenue, then right after 0.4 mile into the park. There are several parking lots. The public will come pouring in by 8am, particularly on weekends, so be there at sun-up. The thing to do is to walk around the lake, especially visiting both conifer and deciduous trees at the north end. The lake itself will have a few gulls, both Ring-billed and

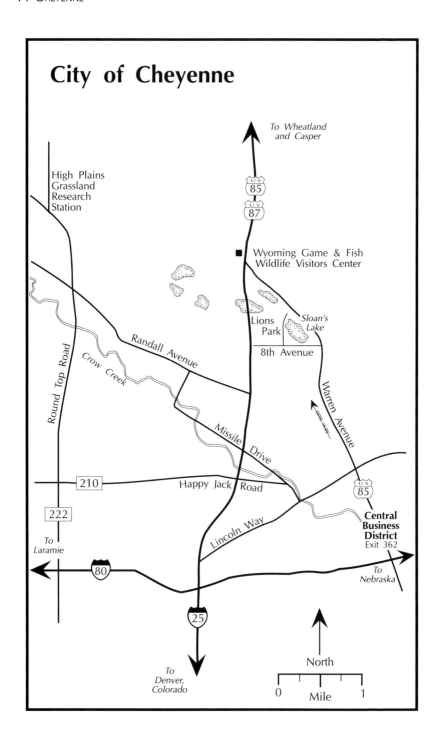

City of Cheyenne

To Wheatland
and Casper

High Plains
Grassland
Research
Station

US 85

US 87

■ Wyoming Game & Fish
Wildlife Visitors Center

Lions
Park

Sloan's
Lake

8th Avenue

Randall Avenue

Round Top Road

Crow Creek

Missile Drive

Warren Avenue

ONE WAY

210

222

Happy Jack Road

US 85

Lincoln Way

**Central
Business
District**
Exit 362

To
Laramie

80

To
Nebraska

25

To
Denver,
Colorado

North

0   Mile   1

California, as well as Eared, Pied-billed, and Western Grebes. There are likely to be a few eastern warblers here in mid-May, such as Chestnut-sided, Black-throated Blue, or Magnolia Warblers. You may also find western warblers such as Townsend's and the common MacGillivray's. Northern Waterthrush has been regular here. During the latter half of May there will be Western Tanagers and Black-headed Grosbeaks, and from early May, Northern (Bullock's) Orioles and Lazuli Buntings will show up. In May, both Green-tailed and Rufous-sided Towhees are here, along with the possibility of many other migrant passerines.

2. **Grassland birds.** Go back to Warren Avenue, turn left, and continue north 1.2 miles to its junction with Interstate 25. Go north 4.4 miles on Interstate 25 and then bear right onto US 85 (exit 17). US 85 passes through the high grasslands for 40 miles or more. Chestnut-collared and particularly McCown's Longspurs are common, but McCown's more so. Since US 85 is a high-speed highway (most Wyomingites think that if they can't drive 65 mph or more, they have been deprived of the right to live), the best thing to do is to take one of the side roads to the north where you can stop to look for birds without creating a traffic hazard. One of the better side roads starts 9.8 miles northeast of the junction with Interstate 25. Although it is apparently not named, a sign at the intersection (*The Berrys, 3 miles, Registered Hereford Bulls*) will let you know that you're on the right road. During the second half of May, look for Baird's Sparrows here. There are occasional Mountain Plovers, but the best place to see these is the Laramie Plains (see Chapter 2). Remember that all of these grassland-nesting species require native grasses. Don't bother to look for them where the prairie has been plowed up for wheat strip-farming. The difference is very obvious.

3. **Wyoming Hereford Ranch.** This is another excellent oasis for migrant passerines. Retrace your route to where you left Interstate 25 (exit 17) and drive south 9.0 miles to its intersection with Interstate 80. Get on Interstate 80 eastbound for 8.0 miles to the second interchange, Campstool Road, which is marked "Wyoming Hereford Ranch" (exit 367). The ranch is a special pedigree registered bull-raising operation. It is not like the usual commercial ranch. Most visitors come to see a registered Hereford bull operation; we birders come for quite different reasons!

As you exit Interstate 80, turn right and follow the paved road 1.1 miles across a meadow to the ranch entrance, a lane with big trees on each side. This is private land. You will know that this is the right place when you come to a large monument to a bull—a Hereford bull. You ought to get permission to look around at the headquarters building on the left, but if no one is there ask any staff you see. They have been very nice to visitors.

Established in 1883, the Wyoming Hereford Ranch used to be the foremost breeder of Hereford bulls. Today the ranch is so close to rapidly expanding Cheyenne that its land value has gone up. It has been through a series of owners who have sold off much of the land and some of the breeding stock; it is now not as famous as it used to be.

The area near headquarters, the entrance driveway, and the road extending to Crow Creek are all excellent for migrants in May. A Worm-eating Warbler was seen here in May 1989. Townsend's Warbler has been seen here a number of times in the spring, although it is usually only a fall migrant. Around headquarters is a favorite area for thrushes; these are mostly Swainson's with an occasional Veery mixed in. Lazuli Buntings are regular migrants, and some will nest here. Blue Grosbeaks are often seen during migration. Over the years this has been the best place near Cheyenne for migrants. When returning, take the first road to the left and drive up 0.5 mile through the meadows, which have Bobolinks. Go as far as a locked gate. Return to Interstate 80 and turn west.

4. **High Plains Grassland Research Station**. This is another oasis northwest of Cheyenne. It is fairly extensive but lacks much water. There have been some interesting migrants here, but they are relatively few and far between. The facility is run by the US Department of Agriculture in a cooperative arrangement with the University of Wyoming. It used to be called the "Horticultural Station", and various valuable strains of grains and grasses have been developed here. The management has recently become a little fussy about visitors so you ought to call them before you come: 307/772-2433. You may need to obtain a permit. The trouble is that on the grounds there are residences which have nice thickets of brush around them as well as fine trees. Birders have gone around with binoculars, appearing to peer into windows, and the residents have objected. The residences are now out-of-bounds for birders, but there are many other areas to bird. The Station has many planted conifers on the north side and deciduous trees on the south side. The south side has the more interesting birds. In May one can usually find an eastern warbler such as Blackpoll, Black-and-white, Magnolia, or Chestnut-sided, all rare in Wyoming. On my first visit to the Station years ago, I found my first Summer Tanager for Wyoming. In migration this facility attracts most of the common passerines, especially flycatchers.

To get there, go west on Interstate 80 to its junction with Interstate 25. (This is the interchange just west of the Central Business District.) Turn right onto Interstate 25 for 1.6 miles to the second interchange, Missile Drive (exit 10B). Get off the Interstate and go a short distance west on Missile Drive; then bear left for Happy Jack Road (Route 210). This is the old road to Laramie. (It was named after Jack Hollingsworth, a local character who had a ranch in the foothills beyond Cheyenne in the 1880s. In accord with the usual Wyoming wry humor, however, Happy Jack probably never cracked a smile.) Go west on this road for 2.3 miles and turn right onto Round Top Road (Route 222). Drive north for another 2.3 miles. Then take a left jog after crossing the railroad tracks and continue north. A shelterbelt on the west side of the road here is a great place for kingbirds, particularly Western but occasionally Cassin's. This is also a great place to look for Northern Mockingbirds. Continue north for 1.0 mile and you will come to the entrance of the Research Station on the left (Hildreth Road). The group of trees at the entrance can be rather productive. Bird the trees on both sides of the road as far as the fork in the road. The bulk of the deciduous trees are on the left here while the conifers are on the right. After visiting the Research Station, go back to Cheyenne.

A rock formation at Vedauwoo   Paul J. Baicich

5. **Vedauwoo.** Just after the Civil War, General Grenville Dodge, exploring for a way for the railroad to get over the Rockies, found a tongue of land that started in the plains and with steady and excellent grades ran to the top of the mountains. At the bottom of this tongue of land, known as Sherman Hill, stands Cheyenne, and near the top you will find the Vedauwoo Glen Picnic Area in the conifers. The area takes its name from the local Indian word meaning "earthbound spirits," clearly a reference to the strange rock structures in the area which were believed to have been formed by the lively spirits of men and beasts. Both the railroad and Interstate 80 go over this tongue of land. This is part of the Laramie Range, a continuation of Colorado's Front Range, but not so formidable. Nevertheless, in winter this stretch of highway can be rough with high winds and ground-blizzards leading to no visibility.

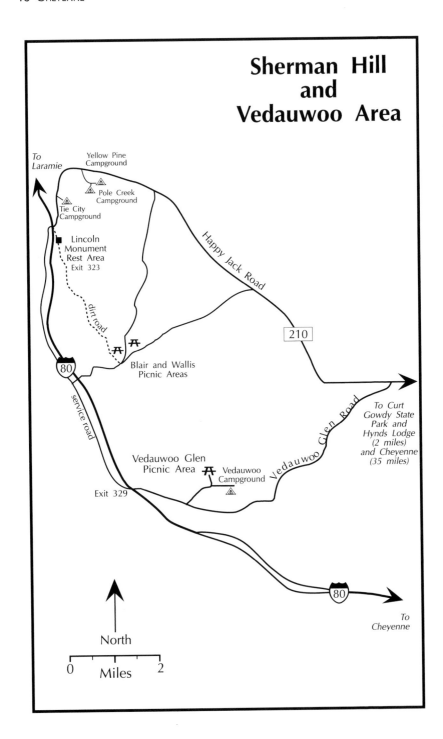

Sherman Hill
and
Vedauwoo Area

From the interchange with Interstate 25 (exit 8B) in Cheyenne, it is 30.2 miles on Interstate 80 to the Vedauwoo Road interchange (exit 329). Get off here and go right. You are in the Medicine Bow National Forest. Follow the signs 1.0 mile to the picnic area on the left. This and the surrounding country will give the newcomer many of the Rocky Mountain birds. Clark's Nutcracker, Steller's Jay, Mountain Bluebird, and Mountain Chickadee can be found in the picnic-grounds or on the loop that follows. As you come out of the Vedauwoo Area, take a left around some interesting rock formations onto Vedauwoo Glen Road. Follow this dirt road for 6.1 miles north to Happy Jack Road across creeks, meadows, and woods. In the aspens look for Red-naped Sapsuckers. In the alder-choked creeks look for Willow Flycatchers. Turn left onto Happy Jack Road. (Alternately, at dusk you can turn right here for 2.6 miles to Curt Gowdy State Park and, after a left turn, go past Hynds Lodge. Here there are dry hillsides where you can wait for Common Poorwills to come out.)

If you are coming from the High Plains Grassland Research Station in Cheyenne and want to avoid the interstate on your way to the Vedauwoo area, go back to Happy Jack Road (Route 210) and turn right (west) toward Laramie. After 21 pretty miles, you will reach Curt Gowdy State Park and can follow the birding directions above and below.

After traveling for 4.7 miles on Happy Jack Road, you will come to a road on the left leading to two fine picnic-grounds at the bottom of the valley. (The highway sign here reads *Blair-Wallis*.) These two picnic areas, each 4.0 miles off Happy Jack Road, are spots for some of the same birds as the Vedauwoo area. (You can continue, if you wish, on a dirt road through the Blair-Wallis Area on to the visitor center and the Interstate as described farther along in the text.) Farther along Happy Jack Road there are three more campgrounds that are fine for birds (Yellow Pine, Pole Creek, and Tie City). Yellow Pine and Pole Creek are part of the Happy Jack Recreation Area and are one mile off to the left, some 4.3 miles from the Blair-Wallis turnoff. Yellow Pine is good for Willow Flycatchers and Red-naped Sapsuckers. Also, along the stream but not in the willows, one can look for Cordilleran Flycatchers. Dusky Flycatchers will be higher on the dry hillsides on the edge of the woods. There should be Townsend's Solitaires as well. Some 1.1 miles on Happy Jack Road beyond the Happy Jack Recreation Area is the turnoff for the Tie City campground. After 0.9 mile more you will be back on Interstate 80 (exit 323) at the summit of Sherman Hill. This is the highest elevation on Interstate 80, some 8,640 feet. The visitor center is dominated by a statue of Abraham Lincoln. Now you are only 10 miles from Laramie. To confuse you, Cheyenne is the county seat of Laramie County as well as the state capital. Laramie is the county seat of Albany County and the site of the University of Wyoming.

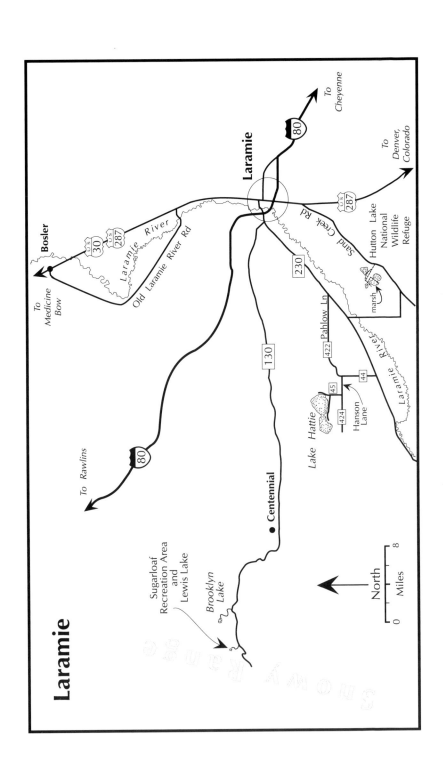

Laramie

2. LARAMIE AREA

Laramie lies at the lower end of the Laramie Plains. It is bounded on the west by the Snowy Range and on the east by the Laramie Range. It is high, over 7,000 feet. Its origins are similar to Cheyenne's, having been essentially the byproduct of the route of the Union Pacific Railroad in the late 1860s. With a population of 25,000, Laramie is the state's third-largest city.

This area harbors the largest number of nesting Mountain Plovers in the nation as well as many McCown's Longspurs, which, in places, outnumber the Horned Larks. The town itself has the University of Wyoming, the state's only university and four-year college. The University was founded in 1886, four years before Wyoming became a state. The most interesting birding places in the Laramie area are:

1. **Hutton Lake National Wildlife Refuge**. This is a fine, small refuge of almost 2,000 acres, but it appears to be sorely neglected. It consists of five small lakes surrounded by marsh and upland. The largest of these lakes is about a half-mile across. Although I have been there many times, I have yet to meet any federal personnel there. The refuge, administered from Walden, Colorado, is not currently staffed.

To get to Hutton Lake take US Highway 287 south from the interchange with Interstate 80 (exit 313) for 1.3 miles and then turn right onto an unmarked road for 0.4 mile. At the T-intersection with Fort Sanders Drive turn left and drive 0.7 mile; then turn right over the tracks onto Sand Creek Road. Turn left to continue south on Sand Creek Road. (The gravel road surface improves after the first mile.) The road goes around the south end of a huge cement plant and through grassland, a fine area for Mountain Plover. You may also find grassland sparrows, longspurs, and Ferruginous Hawks along the way. After 8.1 miles you reach the entrance to Hutton Lake National Wildlife Refuge. The two-rut track into the refuge is not what you might expect. It is marked only by a 4-foot-high wooden post with the numbers "791" on it; the brown National Wildlife Refuge sign is visible (with binoculars) 0.5 mile off to the right. The track is poor but passable; take care not to drive into one of the numerous prairie-dog burrows along the way.

The first fork in the "road" leads to Creighton Lake. It is deep and usually has the most-interesting ducks. In October it often has scoters, and in migration it will have the usual ducks—Green-winged Teal, Mallard, Northern Pintail, Northern Shoveler, Gadwall, American Wigeon,

Canvasback, Redhead, Lesser Scaup, Common Goldeneye, Bufflehead, and Common Merganser. There also will be Eared and Western Grebes, Canada Geese, and Double-crested Cormorants. Continue on toward the small group of buildings, turning left (south) onto another track just short of them. Soon you will cross a dike (little Lake George will be on your right), and a bit farther you will come to the west end of one of the best marshes in Wyoming. When the marsh has water, there are lots of nesting ducks, Black-crowned Night-Herons, Forster's Terns, and an occasional American Bittern, plus the inevitable American Coots.

Backtrack across the dike and take the first track leading right (east) to another viewpoint at the east end of the marsh. You may drive on another dike here that separates the marsh from a large lake to the east, but approach carefully and check the marsh and lake first because your passage across this dike will spook the birds. The shallow water on the right has ducks, including all three teal (Green-winged, Blue-winged, and Cinnamon) and plenty of shorebirds. These will include American Avocet and Baird's Sandpiper. The large lake to the east will have more of the same species. One gets to it by taking the track that leads off to the south from the south end of the dike. It has the bulk of the birds in the refuge. Hutton Lake is relatively small, but it is the best part of the Laramie Plains as far as waterbirds go. There has been a long list of Wyoming rarities observed here, such as adult Little Blue Heron, Peregrine Falcon, and Common Moorhen.

2. **Lake Hattie Reservoir.** Now return to Sand Creek Road, turn right, and continue on through grasslands. After 4.5 miles the road splits; take the right-hand fork and drive west, then north through low land. (You may find nesting Wilson's Phalaropes in wet areas during breeding-season.) You will cross the Laramie River with its riparian habitat of brush and trees, the home of Lazuli Buntings and Red-tailed Hawks. The country which you have driven through on these gravel roads is the habitat of the Ferruginous Hawk. After crossing the Laramie River you come to a paved highway in 1.0 mile, State Route 230. Turn right toward Laramie for 2.1 miles, then hard left onto Route 422 (Pahlow Lane). Follow this road for 6.8 miles to the marked turnoff at Hanson Lane (Route 424) for Lake Hattie, and drive another 2.9 miles to the reservoir. There are a number of ponds and small reservoirs along the way where you may find Caspian Tern, White-faced Ibis, Snowy Egrets, lots of ducks, and Wilson's Phalarope.

In spring and fall, there are great concentrations of Redheads on Lake Hattie, at times thousands of them. Just why they congregate here is not clear. The reservoir's water-level has been low recently, creating large mudflats. Scope for shorebirds, gulls, and American White Pelicans.

3. **Old Laramie River Road.** On this grassland you are just about in the center of the best Mountain Plover nesting-grounds on the Laramie Plains. Return to Laramie on Route 230. From Laramie take US Highway 30 (which

Mountain Plover
Charles H. Gambill

overlaps with US Highway 287) and drive north 20.0 miles to the virtual ghost town of Bosler. Turn west (left) across the tracks at the south end of town and go south on what is actually the old Laramie River Road. This old county road roughly parallels the river at a considerable distance and goes through excellent Mountain Plover country. Besides looking for Mountain Plover, you should be able to find grassland sparrows, longspurs (mostly McCown's), and an occasional Ferruginous Hawk or Golden Eagle. After 16.9 miles, the road goes back to US 30/287. This intersection is 6.3 miles north of Laramie.

There may be some unusual hazards on this route. The last time I went over it, there was a herd of Buffalo, also known as Bison by out-of-staters, that sat on the road blocking a cattle-guard. By staying in the car and driving slowly toward the herd, I quietly convinced the Buffalo to move off the road, and I got over the cattle-guard without incident. There are a number of private herds of Buffalo in Wyoming at the present time, and they are increasing. Since there have been disastrous slumps in the cattle business, a number of operators have diversified into Buffalo, which offer more economic benefits. Normally, the Buffalo is a docile animal and if you behave yourself and stay in the car you have little to worry about. But the Buffalo is an unpredictable animal, and being a fool with a Buffalo threatens your life. Many more people have been killed or seriously injured in Yellowstone National Park by the Buffalo than by the Grizzly, and not all the fools are dead yet.

There's a story in Wyoming about a fellow who got a young Buffalo and took it around to rodeos and county fairs. The Buffalo was quite a sensation, but one night, without warning, it turned on the fellow and killed him.

4. **Brooklyn Lake in the Snowy Range**. Get back to Laramie on US 30/287 and take westbound Interstate 80 to the next interchange (Route 230). Take this road west for less than one mile and turn right onto Route 130. This takes you 27 miles to Centennial, a small town at the foot of the Snowy Range and the hub of outdoor recreation activities in the range. There are hummingbird feeders at Centennial, and one can find Rufous Hummingbirds in July and early August as well as the more common Broad-tails. A little bit beyond Centennial you will enter the Medicine Bow National Forest. The road ascends the mountain range 7.9 miles from Centennial to USFS Road 317, the turnoff to Brooklyn Lake. (Most years Route 130 through the National Forest is snow-bound until about Memorial Day and may close again around late October. And the Forest Service road from Route 130 to our destination at Brooklyn Lake is open from about July 15 to late October. You may want to check accessibility with the Forest Service at 307/745-8971.) USFS Road 317 is a well-marked road, and it is only 1.7 miles from Route 130 to the lake and its popular campground. The lake, at a very high elevation of around 10,000 feet, has a stand of big spruce around it. In late summer I don't think I have ever missed seeing Pine Grosbeak by the lake. There is a road around the lake, and, if snow doesn't prevent it, it is a nice mile-long walk or drive. Gray Jays are often looking about the campground. Cordilleran, Olive-sided, and Dusky Flycatchers are common through July. Three-toed Woodpecker should be looked for. Williamson's Sapsucker is rare. Look for Clark's Nutcracker, Mountain Chickadee, Yellow-rumped (Audubon's) Warbler, Pine Siskin, Cassin's Finch, and even Northern Goshawk here.

5. **Lewis Lake**. After visiting Brooklyn Lake, go back to Route 130 and turn right. In the next mile Bill Hayes, in 1988, found a nesting Boreal Owl. Many of us saw the adult feeding a juvenile. After 3.4 miles turn right into the Sugarloaf Recreation Area. It is well-marked. (The same dates for open roads mentioned for Brooklyn Lake also pertain to the Sugarloaf Recreation Area.) Go 1.1 miles to the parking lot at Lewis Lake. There is a well-traveled trail from this point up Medicine Bow Peak (El. 12,013 ft.) at the top of the Snowy Range. The trail skirts the left side of Lewis Lake, and since you are practically at timberline at the lake you get up to the alpine zone right away. There are American Pipits everywhere, along with the brown-capped subspecies of the Rosy Finch which is the real rosy finch. (That is, it is rosy whereas the other subspecies are maroon and black.) There have been

White-tailed Ptarmigan here, but the claim is that they haven't been seen since 1978. I must confess that the last time when I saw them at this location was in 1974. However, they may well be here, and it may still be worthwhile looking for them.

One can walk this range from Medicine Bow Peak to the southwest and come down at the south end of Marie Lake. It is only about 5 miles, and the trail is well-marked. It is a good place to see hawks—accipiters and falcons. If you take a walk up the peak, make sure that you do it in the morning. Afternoon thunderstorms are very common in the Snowy Range, and you do not want to be caught above timberline during an electrical storm.

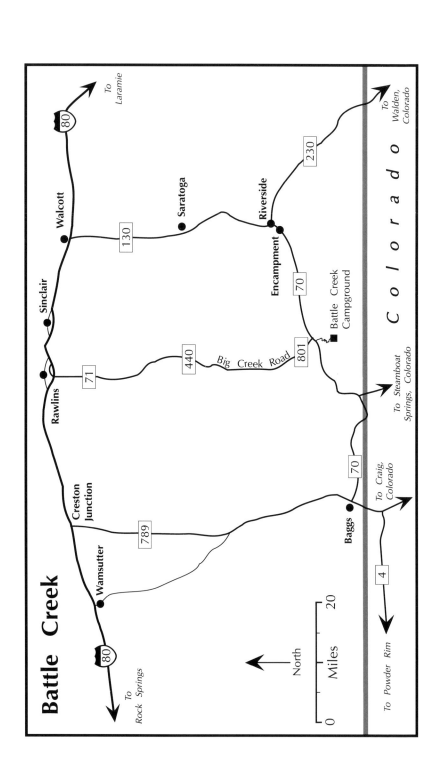

Battle Creek

To Laramie

80

To Rock Springs

Walcott

Sinclair

Rawlins

Creston Junction

Wamsutter

80

71

130

440

Big Creek Road

789

Saratoga

Riverside

Encampment

70

801

Battle Creek Campground

Baggs

70

4

230

To Walden, Colorado

To Steamboat Springs, Colorado

To Craig, Colorado

To Powder Rim

Colorado

North

Miles

0   20

3. BATTLE CREEK CAMPGROUND

Battle Creek Campground is a lovely spot in almost the middle of the Sierra Madre Range in south-central Wyoming. You can get there easily from Rawlins, Encampment, or Baggs. (It is 31.5 miles from Baggs to the entrance for the campground or 25.5 miles from Encampment to the entrance for the campground. Our route, however, is designed to originate from Rawlins just off Interstate 80.)

From westbound Interstate 80 in Rawlins exit at Higley Boulevard (exit 214). Turn immediately right and then left. (These directions will have you leave Rawlins almost immediately, so you may want to check your gas-gauge before continuing on this long trip.) You are on Frontage Road, or Wyoming Route 71. Frontage Road runs parallel to Interstate 80 and goes under the Interstate in 1.4 miles. Begin your mileage count here for the rest of the trip down to Route 70.

Wyoming Route 71 heads south and climbs up through grassy hills and along ridges for another 23.1 miles to the end of the pavement. You may want to check for Sage Thrashers, Sage Sparrows, and Horned Larks on this stretch. A gravel road continues, and at 31.3 miles from the Interstate underpass the road becomes Route 440 and at 43.1 miles becomes Route 801, a Forest Service number. Here it is also called Big Creek Road. This is where the grassland stops and the forest begins. You have entered the Medicine Bow National Forest. Bear left at the next junction and continue driving up through alternating mature conifers and deciduous woods. You may wish to pause here for woodpeckers, Mountain Chickadees, White-breasted Nuthatches, Dark-eyed Juncos, and other common birds. When you encounter a good overlook for Deep Creek (at 45.1 miles), you might want to check the area for Olive-sided Flycatchers. At 51.9 miles the road narrows to little more than one wide lane with no verges for a two-mile-long stretch of private property—a truly enchanting area with towering aspens crowding in to form a tunnel through the grove. Finally at 53.0 miles from Rawlins you join Route 70. Turn right for 0.3 mile to a left-hand turn-off onto the road to Battle Creek Campground.

The campground is 2.2 miles down this road. The road is narrow and with steep switchbacks. (You might hesitate to attempt this road with a travel

Battle Creek Campground from access road   Paul J. Baicich

trailer, although many people do take trailers down to camp.) Battle Creek Campground is small and rather primitive, but there are plenty of camping-spaces along the cottonwood-lined creek. There are Scrub Oaks here, and Band-tailed Pigeons have been found in late August and early September a number of times. So far this occurrence has been unique for Wyoming. The sides of the valley have Dusky Flycatchers, both Green-tailed and Rufous-sided Towhees, lots of Lazuli Buntings, Western Tanagers, Black-headed Grosbeaks, some Red-naped Sapsuckers, and in September,

Mountain Chickadee
Charles H. Gambill

Battle Creek Campground   Paul J. Baicich

Steller's and Gray Jays. This spot attracts many of the more common birds as well. There are dirt roads which extend westward from Battle Creek Campground. Some of them run back up to Route 70. These roads may provide some interesting birding.

In general, the birds of the Sierra Madre Range are not well known yet, however. This area certainly deserves further exploration.

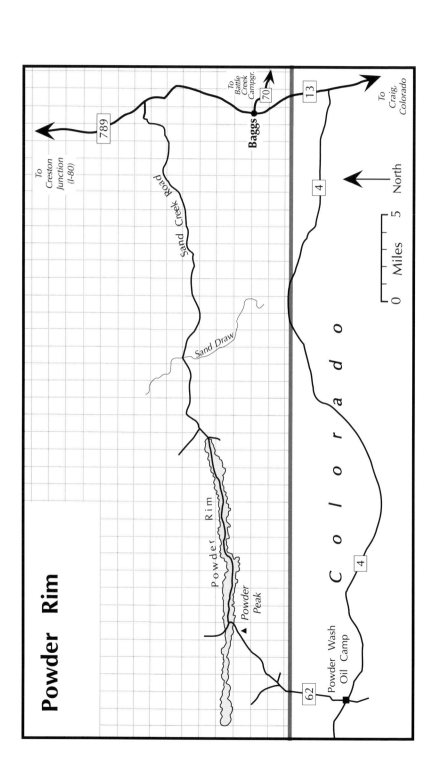

Powder Rim

4. POWDER RIM

Powder Rim is an east-west ridge with juniper growth just north of the Colorado line west of Baggs, Wyoming. It is a very remote place. If you go there, you may not see anybody else. Powder Rim is in the lower part of the biggest empty space on the Wyoming map. Its interest bird-wise is that it has most of the juniper species characteristic of southwestern Wyoming. The best of the juniper habitat is around Powder Peak, the highest point of the western part of the rim. Your efforts to get to the vicinity of the Peak, especially to the south, should be rewarded.

There are two ways to get there. Neither route is particularly easy, and in both cases you should watch out for sandy spots where you could get stuck. In general this area is no place for any low-slung car. An ideal car for the back country roads and tracks is the old VW Bug, which has high clearance and a short wheel-base.

One way to get there is to take the first paved road to the west on Colorado 13, which is 1.8 miles south of the Colorado-Wyoming border, which, in turn, is just 2.4 miles south of Baggs on Wyoming 789. This road is Moffat County Road 4, and after 39 miles you come to Powder Wash Oil Camp. (The last 13 miles are unpaved, but it is a good road nonetheless.) From the oil camp turn right onto Moffat County Road 62 and drive north. You will have to bear right at 0.8 mile, and you will cross back into Wyoming after another 2.6 miles. (You are going through an oil patch, and the best roads and the most heavily used ones are likely to take you to an oil-well site. These roads usually come in at right angles to the main road.) Just 0.6 mile after getting into Wyoming turn right for a hundred yards. The road splits; bear left and go straight ahead up Powder Rim. It is only 4.0 miles after the road splits to the base of Powder Peak, which dominates the country here.

In the juniper—here and elsewhere on the route—one should find Gray Flycatcher, Scrub Jay, Plain Titmouse, Bewick's Wren, Blue-gray Gnatcatcher, and Black-throated Gray Warbler. From this spot you continue another 1.1 miles up the rim and bear right (eastward) along the rim.

Another way in to Powder Rim is to go 7 miles north of Baggs on Route 789 and turn west (left) onto a dirt road well marked as Sand Creek Road. Lately, this has been the easier route, but conditions change. Bear left at 10.3 miles and after 17.2 miles (from Route 789) you come to Sand Draw, which is usually dry. Get out and test the crossing to make sure that the ground is hard enough. It most often is, even if wet. If you get into trouble here, someone might come along soon—and then again it might be a week or a month. There used to be a bridge here, but that washed out years ago. After crossing the wash, you gradually climb Powder Rim. Be careful; the road in this region is very erodible. (One evening I was coming along here and saw a dip over part of the road. It turned out to be a trench from some infrequent rain, and the trip stopped abruptly right there with a crash. My car and my ego were damaged. Fortunately, there was a sheep camp not far away, and the man there was going to town the very next day. So, I got out of it with only $700 expenses.) At 24.1 miles from Route 789, just before you get to the rim, there is a fork in the road. Bear left. When you get on the rim—from either route described here—stay on the rim. Shortly the road will go off the rim to the south. Take the track straight ahead up the rim; it should be obvious. As you drive west along Powder Rim, there are breathtaking views both north and south, with almost nothing of the works of man in sight; even at night there are no lights.

There are usually wild horses here, and horse manure can almost cover the country. Unfortunately, there has been much damage to the grass due to wild horses. These exotics are just lazy-rancher horses gone wild, and they are destroying the country. They can overgraze worse than any other animal. Cattle can be controlled, and the BLM (Bureau of Land Management, which is the country's largest landholder) is beginning to take an interest in the range

Rock Wren
Shawneen Finnegan

Approaching Powder Peak from the south   Paul J. Baicich

and is steadily improving the control of cattle. Due to sentimentalist pressure on Congress, however, controlling the wild horse has become prohibitively expensive. The result is disaster. Those who have caused this problem should be forced to come west and see the havoc that they have created. There have been many thousands of wild horses scattered in small groups throughout the area north of Powder Rim, which is often called the Wamsutter Basin. These groups have been made up of a stallion and a few mares and their young progeny. At great expense the BLM has recently cut down on the number of wild horses—which are still there, however, with a steady 20 percent increase per year. This will necessitate additional expensive round-ups in the future, so the BLM has developed another permanent job for itself.

After traveling 32.7 miles west from Route 789 and on Powder Rim, one comes to a side track north just beyond an old water-tank. In the juniper just off the end of this road Sam Fitton showed me the nest of a Long-eared Owl. In general in the juniper country if an owl is smaller than a Great Horned, it is a Long-ear until proved otherwise. At 35.5 miles, you come down to the vicinity of Powder Peak, a fine spot for finding the birds of the area.

In the sage along the rim Green-tailed Towhees are very common. Somewhere along the rim there will be Ash-throated Flycatchers. They nest in tree holes, of which there are many. The rare birds to look for are Bushtits and Scott's Orioles. Sam Fitton found the first Scott's Oriole nest recorded in Wyoming here in 1982. Rock Wrens abound everywhere, along with Mountain Bluebirds. At 36.4 miles there is a track to the left. Take this, and 0.4 mile down this road one meets a cross track taking you to nice camping spots and birding areas on the left. All camping here is dry.

From here you can backtrack the way you came, or read the original directions to Powder Rim in reverse and leave via the road by the Powder Wash Oil Camp.

Every time I go to Powder Rim it seems more remote and wild. The last time I met a group of Elk. Powder Rim is all public land (BLM).

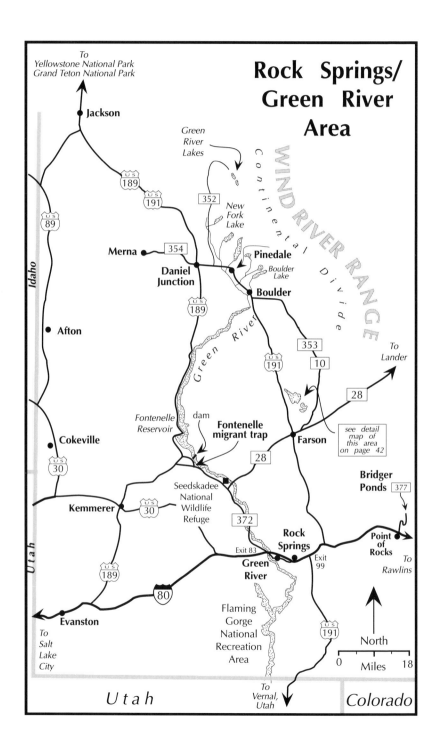

Rock Springs/ Green River Area

To
Yellowstone National Park
Grand Teton National Park

Jackson

Green River Lakes

WIND RIVER RANGE

Continental Divide

US 189

US 191

352

New Fork Lake

US 89

Merna

354

Pinedale

Boulder Lake

Daniel Junction

Boulder

US 189

Afton

Green River

353

10

US 191

To Lander

28

Cokeville

Fontenelle Reservoir

dam

Fontenelle migrant trap

Farson

US 30

see detail map of this area on page 42

Seedskadee National Wildlife Refuge

28

Bridger Ponds 377

Kemmerer

US 30

372

Rock Springs

Point of Rocks

To Rawlins

Idaho

Exit 83

Green River

Exit 99

US 189

Evanston

To Salt Lake City

80

Flaming Gorge National Recreation Area

US 191

North

0   Miles   18

Utah

To Vernal, Utah

Colorado

5. ROCK SPRINGS/ GREEN RIVER AREA

In the center of this region lie the towns of Rock Springs and Green River. Both serve as departure points for investigating the area's birds. Over the years I have visited this general area more than anywhere else outside of the Casper region. It offers fascinating birding with the Fontenelle Trap, Seedskadee National Wildlife Refuge, and Farson not far away. South of Rock Springs/Green River there is a sizable region of juniper, the largest in the state, stretching to the Utah border 50 to 60 miles away. The juniper forests are made up of mostly Utah Juniper and some Rocky Mountain Juniper at higher elevations. Green River is, not surprisingly, on the Green River. It is called the "Trona Capital of the World." Above it to the north the river flows about 50 miles from Fontenelle Dam, forming a remarkable valley which is in many ways like the Snake River Birds of Prey Area in southwestern Idaho. Ornithologically, it is the major migration route for birds in western Wyoming, but there is no Morley Nelson to publicize it. It remains an unknown, primitive backwater. North of Rock Springs 39 miles lies Farson, the site of an irrigation project called the Eden Valley. There is no valley to be seen, but there are vast sagebrush flats that stretch miles on all sides with a spectacular mountain range to the northeast, the Wind River Range, Wyoming's highest—snow-covered until well into summer. This land is full of monuments to the pioneers of the Oregon Trail and the Mormon Trail, which split here, one route going north of the Great Salt Lake through what is now Nevada to California, and the other following the Snake River down to Oregon. The most interesting places for birds in the region are as follows:

1. **Bridger Ponds**. Take Interstate 80 west of Rawlins for 82 miles to Point of Rocks. Take the only paved road from that point, Route 377, north to the huge (1,400 megawatts) Jim Bridger mine-mouth power-plant. The plant is operated by Pacific Power and Idaho Power. Coming off Interstate 80 you make virtually a U-turn. The first deep freshwater pond that you come to usually isn't worth looking at, so continue around the plant to the north side, 9 miles from Point of Rocks (avoid the fork going to the plant), and drive to the top of the dike on your left. This overlooks a shallow-water evaporation pan, which is very worthwhile for ducks and geese (usually in October and November) and other birds. Rare ducks like scoters and Oldsquaw have been

35

seen here; look for shorebirds in April, May, August, and September. Look for Horned Grebes in spring. American Avocet and Black-necked Stilt should also be present. The next impoundment used to be excellent for shorebirds, but it has deteriorated in the last few years because the plans of Pacific Power and Light call for leaving this impoundment dry. I hope that these plans change. All the water here has been pumped up from the Green River.

Almost anywhere in the surrounding greasewood and sage areas you may also look for Sage Thrasher, Sage Sparrow, and Brewer's Sparrow. Burrowing Owls are sporadic north of the ponds in prairie-dog towns.

2. **The Juniper Country.** Some 3.6 miles west of the Rock Springs Elk Street Interchange on Interstate 80 there is a large Conoco Truck Stop. This is exit 99. Turn south at this point onto US Highway 191 and drive 4.2 miles to Little Firehole Road on the right. This is a fair-quality dirt-and-gravel road which is well-marked. In the rare event that the weather and ground are wet, avoid this road.

Go 3.3 miles to the approach of a pipeline crossing. (When a pipeline crosses a road in Wyoming, the only indication is a small triangular sign and a strip of obviously disturbed vegetation on each side of the road. Pipelines in Wyoming are not necessarily obvious to visitors.) Turn south on the track just before the pipeline and drive to the bottom of a juniper-covered hill. From there walk along the pipeline right-of-way and seek your birds. This is the summer home of Bewick's Wren (very common), Plain Titmouse, Gray Flycatcher, Ash-throated Flycatcher, Scrub Jay, Black-throated Gray Warbler, and Sage Sparrow. Sage Sparrow won't be found in the juniper but rather in the sage between the hills. Sage Sparrow is found all over southwestern

Along Little Firehole Road   Oliver K. Scott

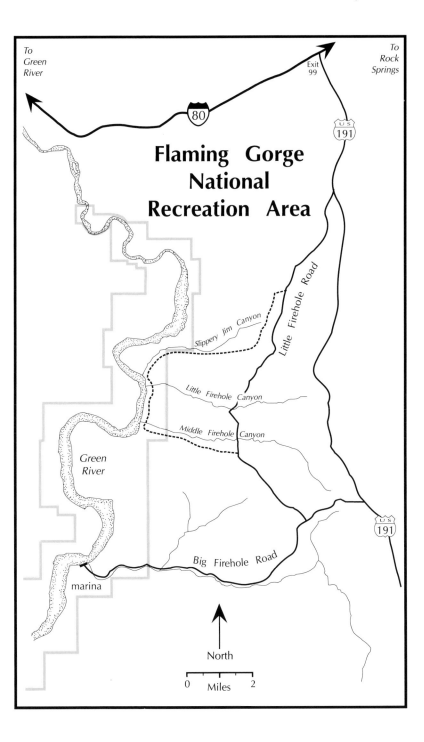

To
Green
River

To
Rock
Springs

Exit
99

80

US
191

**Flaming Gorge
National
Recreation Area**

Little Firehole Road

Slippery Jim Canyon

Little Firehole Canyon

Middle Firehole Canyon

Green
River

US
191

Big Firehole Road

marina

North

0   Miles   2

Wyoming along with Sage Thrasher and very rarely with Black-throated Sparrow. Bushtit is a rarity here but nested once on the first hill. Solitary (Plumbeous) Vireos are fairly common.

If you go back to Little Firehole Road, you should drive 2.1 miles farther. Here you will come to a spot where there is a deep gully on the left with cottonwoods peeking out on top. This is probably the best area of the juniper country because, in addition to all the birds mentioned above, Scott's Oriole has nested in this area (under the cliffs on the right) for the past few years. Solitary Vireos nest a little farther down the canyon where it widens out; they can be found mostly on the hillside to the west. Bushtits have been seen more frequently here. Several pairs of Virginia's Warblers nest in this area. Rock Wrens and Blue-gray Gnatcatchers are also here. Common Poorwills are common in the summer—drive the roads at night looking for one in your headlights. They are easy to hear.

The best time to visit the juniper country is during June and July when the birds are singing and are not so elusive. (However, Plain Titmouse is more noisy in March and April, and by June, when they have young in the tree-hole nests, they are very hard to find.) The last time I visited this spot I had Chukar here. There are some Chukars in this country, but it is impossible to predict just where they will be. Sometimes they can be found on Big Firehole Road, which is paved and goes down to the marina at the head of the Flaming Gorge Reservoir. Little Firehole Road runs into Big Firehole Road.

Flaming Gorge Reservoir itself is usually not worth much of a look for waterbirds. However, it can have thousands of loons in migration, along with Canada Geese and an assortment of ducks. Western and Clark's Grebes nest north of Firehole, though without a boat finding waterbirds can be difficult. Most gulls will be California and Ring-billed; the terns are normally Forster's, occasionally Common.

If you are still missing some of the landbirds on this route, go back up to Highway 191 and turn right (south). Drive 5.5 miles to where the highway is about to climb to much higher ground. On the right side here there are a number of side tracks in the juniper. The birds you will see here are the same as on Little Firehole Road. Actually, these birds are all over this juniper country and you might see them anywhere, but the above spots are the best.

3. **FMC Park.** Go back to Interstate 80 and continue west 7.3 miles to the first entrance to the town of Green River (exit 91). Take this turn for 1.5 miles and turn right onto State Route 530. This swings around over the viaduct, so in the end you really have made a left turn. Go 1.5 miles to the fourth stop-light and turn left onto Monroe Street. After 0.9 mile Monroe Street runs into East Teton Boulevard. At this point the Green River sewer-beds are right in front of you. Go past the enclosed ponds, and follow the dirt road to the ponds that are closer to the Green River. Look for Virginia Rails and American Avocets. All expected "peeps" can be found here in

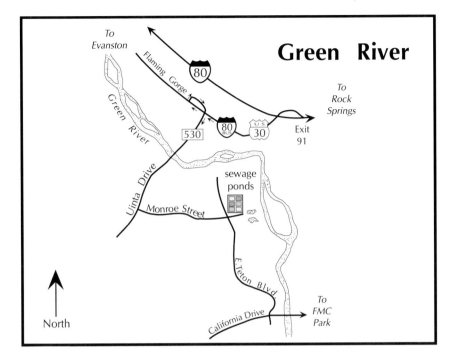

migration—Semipalmated, Least, Western, and especially Baird's. Sometimes there are some particularly good birds here, a recent one being a Lesser Golden-Plover in the fall.

Go back to East Teton Boulevard, turn left, and drive 1.5 miles south to a left onto a dirt road that goes down the hill for 0.5 mile, over the Green River on a one-lane bridge, and into FMC Park. (The FMC corporation was going to build a big plant here, but they decided against it and gave the land to the City of Green River for a park. There are plans to "improve" the park, which may actually make it less attractive to birds.) The road skirts FMC Park for another 0.5 miles before coming to the official entrance. The park is an excellent oasis of trees for passerines and hawks migrating up and down the Green River Valley. Many vagrant eastern warblers have been seen here, particularly in the fall (mid-August to mid-September). In summer look for Western Kingbird, Black-billed Magpie, Solitary Vireo, and Blue Grosbeak, among other birds. While it isn't as impressive as the Fontenelle trap, FMC Park is certainly second-best.

4. **The Fontenelle Trap.** Just below Fontenelle Dam is a landbird trap, probably the best in the state. To get to it take Interstate 80 west of Green River 5.9 miles to State Route 372 (exit 83). Turn right (north) and drive 27 miles through sagebrush to the junction with Route 28. The common birds along this route include Horned Lark, Sage Thrasher, Brewer's, Vesper, and

Sage Sparrows, and Brewer's Blackbird. Then continue 13.7 miles more on Route 372 to a crossroad with a gas-station on the corner. The Fontenelle Store is the only building on this road. You will be interested in knowing, however, that you have driven through the major trona fields of this nation. There are a number of big plants in the area that purify this hydrous sodium carbonate ore. The refined trona is loaded onto rail hopper cars and distributed throughout the nation and to some foreign countries to make sodium carbonate, a basic chemical used in the production of glass and numerous chemicals.

Go straight ahead 3.7 miles to Fontenelle Dam, which has a causeway across the top. Drive to the middle of the dam and take a road to the right that goes down the rear face of the dam to the flats below. Drive over to the trees on the river where there is a small campground. This is it—the Fontenelle Trap. From here north there is nothing but sagebrush and reservoir for some 20 miles; hence, migrants stop here. There is a fence just south of the campground and a stile over it near the river. The campground and the strip of trees just below it are great for migrants. It is particularly good in late May and early June for passerines, especially eastern warblers such as the rare ones like Northern Parula, Chestnut-sided, Magnolia, Blackburnian, Worm-eating, Hooded, and the only state records for Connecticut, Mourning, and Hermit, as well as the common ones like MacGillivray's and Wilson's. Large numbers of Western Tanagers can be held here for a while, along with Northern (Bullock's) Orioles. There are usually great numbers of swallows, of which the Violet-green will be the most common. Red-naped Sapsucker is common, and occasionally Lewis's Woodpeckers appear, as well as lots of other birds such as *Empidonax* flycatchers.

5. **Seedskadee National Wildlife Refuge**. This refuge (PO Box 700, Green River, WY 82935; phone: 307/875-2187) is easy to get to. Backtrack from Fontenelle 13.2 miles south from the crossroad with the Fontenelle Store on Route 372. Just before the junction with Route 28 you will see the sign to Seedskadee Headquarters on the left. There is a visitors center here with information on the 11,000-acre refuge. Seedskadee National Wildlife Refuge has an unusually interesting history. When the Bureau of Reclamation made Flaming Gorge Reservoir downriver, they took over a lot of land from the Fish and Wildlife Service. To compensate, they set up Seedskadee National Wildlife Refuge, which was to stretch from the present refuge downriver almost to the town of Green River. Due to inertia, no political push, and the Rock Springs Grazing Association, the plan has never been completed. There should be no conflict with the Grazing Association since cows are no threat to the birds and other animals. All the cows want from the Green River is some water. If you go down the river in a canoe, you won't even be able to discern where the Grazing Association waterholes are. In fact, going down the Green in a canoe is a real fun thing to do. I have done it with the Game

and Fish personnel in early June. There are Beaver everywhere. Golden Eagles nest along the river, as well as Prairie Falcons, Merlins, and now probably Peregrine Falcons since the restoration program got going. There were formerly aeries in this area. You can put your canoe in just below Fontenelle Dam and take out at the Firehole Marina at the head of Flaming Gorge Reservoir after two days of leisurely paddling. There are a fair number of islands on the way down. Some have goose nests which you wouldn't disturb; by June the geese have long since left.

The headquarters and visitor center at Seedskadee National Wildlife Refuge is on top of a flood plain with impoundments of water below on the flat which stretches out to the river. The river has stands of cottonwoods which have warblers at migration times. In the fall there are often lots of Townsend's Warblers in these cottonwoods. It is easy walking-distance from the refuge headquarters to the river. Lewis's Woodpeckers may be encountered here in migration, particularly in fall. Short-eared Owls can be seen and at times may nest. The impoundments themselves have many waterbirds during migration, including some Barrow's Goldeneyes in April and early May. The usual common waterfowl nest here, such as Canada Goose, all three species of teal, Mallard, Northern Pintail, Northern Shoveler, Gadwall, American Wigeon, Redhead, and Ruddy Duck. Seedskadee has had its share of rarities over the years. The most famous, perhaps, was a Common Moorhen. There is a sizable colony of Great Blue Herons, also. From headquarters one can drive a couple of miles south to the south end of the impoundments, where there is a stile over the fence and an easy walk in. This is perhaps the best place to see the waterbirds, which include grebes, White-faced Ibises, Soras, Virginia Rails, and Forster's Terns. (Incidently, "Seeds-ke-dee-a" is either a Crow Indian word meaning "prairie hen", or "Seedskadee" is a Shoshone Indian word meaning "river of the prairie hen." In either case, there are some Sage Grouse on the western edge of the impoundments, or, more likely, just off the refuge. These birds are not easy to find.)

6. **Farson.** To travel to Farson, head north on US 191 from Rock Springs (measured from the exit 104 interchange for US 191 at Interstate 80).

On the way up US 191 you might want to check Fourteen Mile Reservoir, a well-marked rest-stop some 14 miles north of Rock Springs. It can be rather good during migration, and nesting birds include Sage Thrasher, Rock Wren, and Brewer's Sparrow. Some 21.6 miles beyond Fourteen Mile Reservoir on US 191 there are some ponds to the east which are good in migration with terns, White-faced Ibises, and other waterbirds, but they are on private land, and you have to have permission (from the trailer near the highway) to go in to see them. In spring migration there are irrigated fields near the highway that may have Long-billed Curlews.

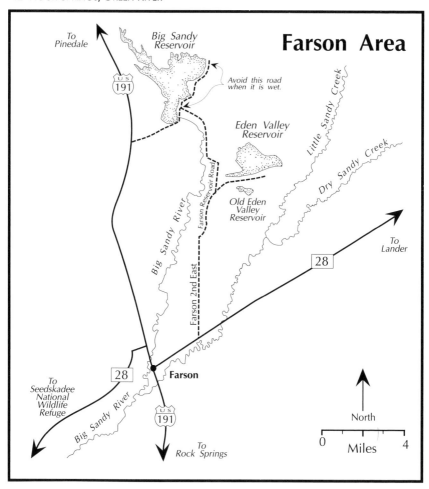

Farson Area

To Pinedale

Big Sandy Reservoir

Little Sandy Creek

Avoid this road when it is wet.

Eden Valley Reservoir

Dry Sandy Creek

Farson Reservoir Road

Old Eden Valley Reservoir

To Lander

28

Big Sandy River

Farson 2nd East

28

Farson

To Seedskadee National Wildlife Refuge

Big Sandy River

North

0 Miles 4

To Rock Springs

Some 2.6 miles after these ponds you will arrive at the crossing of State Route 28 and US 191. This is Farson, which has some facilities (including great ice cream at the Farson Merc). It is the site of the Eden Valley Irrigation project, which has had its problems with too little water and too much alkali. From the crossroads drive east on Route 28 for 2.3 miles. Turn north onto Farson 2nd East, where there is a sign that says *Farson Eden Reservoir 4.2 miles*. This is an improved road that goes through irrigated fields on which Sandhill Cranes (and sometimes Whooping Cranes from Grays Lake National Wildlife Refuge in Idaho) may congregate from late August into October. If you go 4.2 miles north on this improved road, you will come to a fork. Bear right for 1.5 miles and bear right again for another 1.7 miles. Here you will see Old Eden Valley Reservoir on the right, which often has a selection of ducks, shorebirds, Black-crowned Night-Herons, Snowy Egrets,

Yellow-headed Blackbirds, and other birds. There is a track down the bank, so you can get closer to Old Eden Valley Reservoir. On the left you will see a larger reservoir, Eden Valley Reservoir, which usually doesn't have too much on it.

Now turn around and go back on the road that you came in on. Drive 1.7 miles to the last place you had to bear right on the way in. Make a hard right and continue 4.2 miles to an intersection by the southeast corner of Big Sandy Reservoir. This reservoir is usually devoid of much birdlife, though some shorebirds may gather there from late August through mid-September. If it looks promising—*and if it has not rained recently*—a right turn at this intersection will take you on a two-mile-long road skirting the east side of Big Sandy Reservoir. During the experiment of trying to re-establish the Whooping Crane at Grays Lake National Wildlife Refuge, a Whooping Crane usually spent the summer here in the Farson area, often in the Big Sandy drainage.

In general, active reservoirs like Big Sandy and Eden Valley vary in level a great deal and so have little food for birds. Old Eden Valley Reservoir, although small, no longer varies and has lots of food, even though it is practically dried up. Hence, it has lots of birds.

The Farson area is one of the two spots in Wyoming where the Sage Grouse is plentiful. (The other is the headwaters of Bates Creek just north of Shirley Basin and south of Casper.) To see Sage Grouse on the lek, however, you should be on site before sun-up. Still, you have a good chance to see the bird on this drive in the Farson area at other times of day. If you missed Sage Grouse on the drive in, continue westward 2.6 miles to US 191 and turn left. Drive about 6 miles south and try any of the tracks and roads to the east and northeast (back toward Big Sandy Reservoir). Searching here may often produce a Sage Grouse.

7. **Pinedale.** Now return to US 191 and go north some 57 miles toward Pinedale. En route, before Boulder, you travel through vast sagelands inhabited by Horned Larks, Sage Thrashers, and Brewer's, Vesper, and Sage Sparrows. In Boulder, some 47.7 miles north of Farson, there is a well-known Osprey nest close to the road as you go over a creek. (The gravel roads from the Boulder area east toward Boulder Lake and Meadow Lake often have Sage Grouse along the roads in sagebrush areas.) There is another Osprey nest just 6.1 miles beyond the first one that even has a Game and Fish sign telling you all about Ospreys. In another 5.4 miles you will reach Pinedale. The City Park in Pinedale is wooded, so it is sometimes worth a stop to look for montane species. Beyond Pinedale there is a vast meadow on the right, starting at the bridge over the New Fork River 1.5 miles west of Pinedale and running for the next 3.5 miles, that harbors Sandhill Cranes and sometimes Long-billed Curlews. In early September I have seen Long-bills congregate here. Since

Wyoming is part of the breeding-grounds of these birds, they rarely occur in flocks in this state.

8. **New Fork Lake**. Some 6 miles west of Pinedale on US 191 take a right turn onto State Route 352 and go 14.4 miles to the turnoff to New Fork Lake. It is well marked. The lake is only 3.4 miles in. When you get there, bear left and go up the north side of the lake to a campground at the end. Western Screech-Owls have been heard here for several years, and at dusk you have a good chance of seeing the bird as well. The best place is just as you approach the campground. Most observations have been in July. Other birds in the area include Blue Grouse, Ruffed Grouse, Red-naped and Williamson's Sapsuckers, Dusky Flycatcher, Steller's Jay, Hermit Thrush, Black-headed Grosbeak, Lincoln's Sparrow, and Red Crossbill.

9. **Green River Lakes**. Return to the New Fork Lake Road junction, turn right (north), and continue 30 miles to the end of the road in a forest campground. A short walk to the shore of the lake (Lower Green River Lake) will provide what many people feel is the most beautiful and spectacular view in the state of Wyoming. When you are competing with the Tetons, this is a remarkably strong statement. Square Top is something else. If you have seen pictures of this scene, the reality is twice as impressive. Birdwise, this area is also interesting. There is a path along the right side of the lake at the end of the campground. There are Three-toed Woodpeckers in the woods along the path. Ospreys nest at the upper end of the lake. In the more open lands just short of the campground you may find Dusky and Olive-sided Flycatchers. It is a good area for birding. The campground has an adequate supply of Gray Jays which live up to their nickname of "Camp Robbers." Other birds here include Red-naped Sapsucker, Steller's Jay, Clark's Nutcracker, Fox Sparrow, and Cassin's Finch.

10. **Merna area**. Now return to US 191 and turn right (west) 5.3 miles to Daniel Junction. On the far side of the junction take the North Horse Creek Road, State Route 354, 12.4 miles to a crossroad which is in the middle of a huge meadow. About the first week of August this meadow is cut for hay and put up in big round bales. While the grass was growing, the mice were growing in numbers, too. When their hay is cut, they are exposed to the elements or more particularly, to the Swainson's Hawk. While there are a few Red-tails and Northern Harriers here, the Swainson's Hawks are the most common raptors. They perch on the hay bales and partake of the feast. I have seen up to a hundred hawks here at this time of year scattered over the meadow. Along the south side of this meadow is a creek. There is a fair-sized group of Sandhill Cranes in the area, and during the height of the Grays Lake experiment, young Whoopers were frequently found here and may still sometimes be found. In fact, if the experiment had not been conducted at Grays Lake, this might have been the best place to relocate the transplanted Whooping Cranes. There are vast wet meadows along the Green River and

its tributaries on all sides, except to the southwest where, over the hills, lies the fledgling Cokeville Meadows National Wildlife Refuge and the upper reaches of Hams Fork. This area has lush, broad, wet meadows which seem to be the preferred habitat of the Whooping Crane. All of these areas have very successful groups of Sandhill Cranes—so successful, in fact, that the Wyoming Game and Fish Department has started an open hunting season on them. By August, when the hay is cut, the young birds have long since fledged. The other inhabitant of interest in these meadows is the Long-billed Curlew.

I actually never have found Merna. (In Wyoming there have been lots of tiny hamlets which have virtually disappeared with the development of good highways and supermarkets in the larger towns. Merna is apparently one of them.)

Next, you will probably want to continue north on US 191 to the Tetons and skip to Chapter 14 of this book. But maybe your plans require you to go back to Interstate 80. If so, take US Highway 189 south, which takes you back through Kemmerer to Interstate 80 near Evanston.

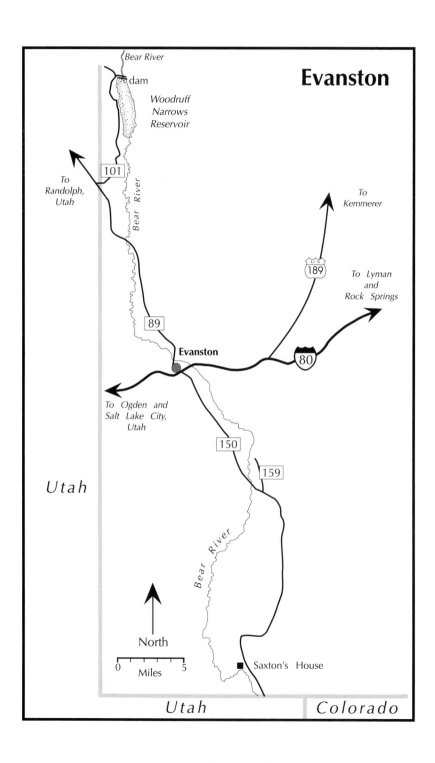

6. EVANSTON

Tucked into the southwestern corner of the state, Evanston, with its population of about 11,000, is the last town in Wyoming on westbound Interstate 80. It is only 5 miles from the Utah border. Birdwise it doesn't add much to what you have probably already seen. However, Black-chinned Hummingbirds occur on Wyoming's western border, and they can be found around Evanston.

1. **Black-chinned Hummingbirds**. Evanston has 3 exits on Interstate 80; take the middle one (Front Street) and turn left (south) under the Interstate. Go 21 miles south on Route 150 to just 1.8 miles short of the Utah border. The street number is 21444. This is Glen Saxton's place. He has a feeder in his yard just south of the house. The feeder may be alive with hummers in season. Mostly these are Broad-tails, but there are also Black-chinned. In recent years this has been the most reliable spot to see them. Black-chinned Hummingbirds are present from late May to mid-August. Mr. Saxton doesn't mind if you look at his hummers, if you have decent manners. You can park just off the highway.

Black-chinned Hummingbird
Gail Diane Luckner

2. **County Road 159.** Some 7.4 miles south of the interstate on Route 150 you cross the Bear River. Take the first left, a dirt road which is County Road 159. For a couple of miles you go through excellent passerine country, marshy on the left. This is a good place to see common Wyoming birds. Look for Broad-tailed Hummingbird, Western Wood-Pewee, Black-headed Grosbeak, Fox Sparrow, Lazuli Bunting, and Northern (Bullock's) Oriole. The road leads to Hight Profitt's place—the home of a well-known and established rancher—but the first two miles is the best of it.

3. **Woodruff Narrows Reservoir.** North of Evanston on the Bear River is Woodruff Narrows Reservoir. It has the common ducks and sometimes American White Pelicans. At the lower (north) end of the reservoir there is a dam. (The river flows north.) Just below the dam is Woodruff Narrows. Eagles, both Bald and Golden, congregate here, particularly in early winter. The difficulty for birders is access. The land is private, and there has been trouble in the past—mostly with fishermen—but that is now over.

To observe the early-winter eagles below the reservoir, take the middle (Front Street) exit off Interstate 80 at Evanston. Turn right for 0.5 mile and then right onto Route 89, which you will follow to the Utah border, a distance of 12.7 miles. Go a few feet into Utah, but then turn right and go back into Wyoming on Uinta County Road 101. In 0.5 mile bear left and continue another 6.8 miles to a left-hand track beside a north-running fence. Take this track for 2.0 miles. It is a terrible road—probably the worst one recommended in this book. The end of the track goes down a very steep bank to the Bear River. If you are reluctant to drive down this steep hill, you can look for the eagles from the top of the bank.

On the way in on Route 101 you paralleled Woodruff Narrows Reservoir for some miles. It is quite a walk down to the water, but there are a few waterbirds and a few shorebirds present in the appropriate seasons that you might want to check out. You have probably seen them more easily elsewhere.

Golden Eagle
Charles H. Gambill

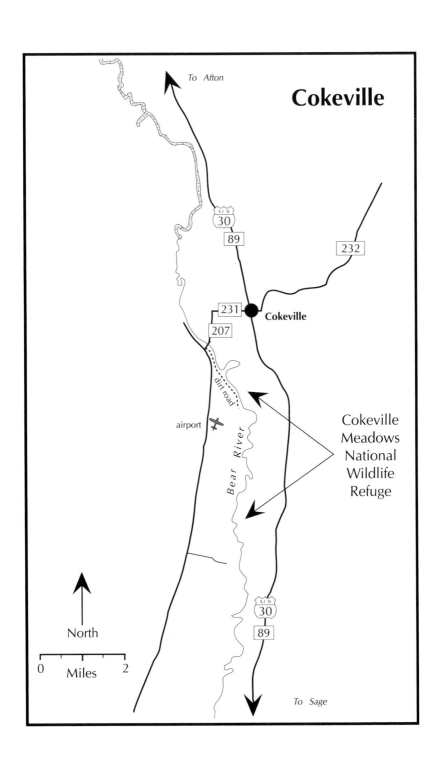

Cokeville

To Afton

30 / 89

232

231

207

Cokeville

dirt road

airport

Bear River

Cokeville
Meadows
National
Wildlife
Refuge

30 / 89

North

0　Miles　2

To Sage

7. COKEVILLE
AND AFTON

The sites in this chapter may seem to be a bit of a detour for you, but there are good reasons to sample the birds in this part of the state. To get to Cokeville from the Woodruff Narrows Reservoir stop in the last chapter, you follow Route 89 as it goes through Utah and re-enters Wyoming just west of Sage. Continue north to Cokeville on combined Route 89/US 30, a total of 67 miles from Evanston.

(There is another good way to get to Cokeville from Interstate 80 in the Evanston area. Take US 189 east of Evanston north to Kemmerer, which is 35 miles away. Then take US 30 west 25 miles to Sage—which has no buildings—and continue north 19 miles to Cokeville.)

The Great Marsh—or Cokeville Meadows National Wildlife Refuge, as it has been designated—will appear on the left as you traven north on Route 89/US 30 from Sage to Cokeville.

1. **Cokeville.** In 1989 the Wyoming Legislature finally approved a National Wildlife Refuge on the Bear River south of Cokeville. It was bitterly opposed by the people of the hamlet of Cokeville although the ranchers who owned the designated land were in favor of it. One year earlier the legislature had turned the idea down. I think that this refuge, when finished, will be one of the better ones in the United States. This is why this refuge-to-be—Cokeville Meadows National Wildlife Refuge—is being included in this book.

There is presently a great marsh which stretches almost 25 miles upriver (south) from Cokeville. Great numbers of ducks nest here as well as other marsh-birds such as White-faced Ibis, American Bittern, Sandhill Crane, Long-billed Curlew, and so on. Nesting ducks include Mallard, Northern Pintail, three species of teal, Northern Shoveler, Gadwall, American Wigeon, Canvasback, Redhead, and Lesser Scaup. The only unusual one here is the Canvasback.

When the refuge is completed—perhaps several years from now—it is expected that the duck and other bird populations will have increased ninefold. At present, access to the area is very difficult. In time there will be a visitor center and access roads. The present plan involves only about 26,000 acres. The original plan was for around 50,000 acres, extending the refuge north of Cokeville. If the refuge turns out to be as advantageous to the local ranchers as they think that it will be, there will be a move to extend the refuge. The agricultural occupation here is growing hay for winter feeding of livestock. There is only one crop of hay per year, and it isn't ready to be cut until August. By August most of the young wildfowl are on the move, so growing ducks, cranes, or curlews and harvesting hay are highly compatible activities. Furthermore, the techniques and changes in the land that the US Fish and Wildlife Service will make will increase the amount of good hay land. From an agricultural point of view, much of the land is at present virtually useless. On top of that, the local rancher who sells or gives an easement to the Service gets a preference for haying. Cokeville is over 6,700 feet in elevation, so hay is about all that one can grow.

To see something of the area, go west from the town of Cokeville on Route 231. Drive through town to the end of the road, where it connects with Route 207; turn left (south) onto Route 207 (Colette Street). This road shortly crosses to the west side of the Bear River. Around the bridge look for Willow Flycatchers. Just past the bridge, turn left (south) onto a dirt road that follows the river. Travel 1.5 miles to a small marsh, a good spot for Sora, Black Tern, and Yellow-headed and Red-winged Blackbirds. Go back to where you turned off Route 207 and continue south on that road. You will soon come to the airport. Some 2.7 miles beyond the airport there is a track that goes east toward the river. This road goes through sage, but at the end you will find a hay field between you and the river. Don't go onto the hay field without permission. Most ranchers in this area are friendly. This particular spot gives an idea of what the area is like. There are also good views of the marsh a few miles south of Cokeville on US 30. The rest of the highway is too far away from the marsh for you to see much, though you should watch for Sandhill Cranes feeding in the meadows. Large numbers of White-faced Ibis also nest, and in August, congregate here. One year over 900 were reported.

2. **Afton.** Our next stop, Afton, is the center of Star Valley, an interesting and beautiful place. The easy way to get to Afton, with its population of about 3,500, is to go north on Wyoming Route 89 (which changes to US 89 after 24 miles) from Cokeville for about 54 miles. Afton has been a rather isolated, largely Mormon community. (Many Star Valley settlers originally came here to escape prosecution for polygamy in Utah.) As far as agricultural interests go, it has become somewhat overpopulated, so the area's residents have tried to diversify and industrialize—with some success. The wide main street in Afton—Washington Street—is spanned by a large elkhorn arch.

Birdwise, the interest is mostly in Swift Creek. In Afton turn east (right) onto Second Avenue. This road takes you 6 miles up Swift Creek to a parking lot. This trip is mostly at 15 miles per hour through a canyon with extraordinarily thin rock walls on both sides. The parking lot at the end of the road is for Periodic Spring. This spring is billed as "North America's only

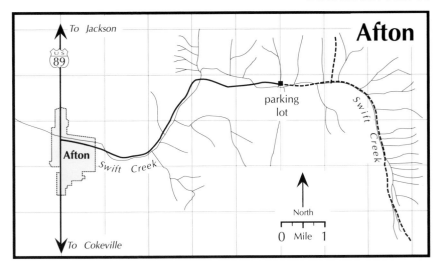

cold-water geyser," and it cycles about every 18 minutes in fall and winter. It is three-quarters of a mile from the parking lot.

For birds, however, don't go to the spring, but continue to walk up the canyon for at least three miles. The trail forks after about two-and-one-half miles, but don't take the left fork up the mountainside; go straight ahead up Swift Creek to an area of big boulders. There have been Winter Wrens here, but whether they are always here is not known. Elsewhere in Wyoming this species is rare and not regular in nesting. The walk up the canyon is fine with lots of common birds like Western Tanager, Townsend's Solitaire, and a host of others. This country has quite a few Elk, also. The most common owl in this terrain is the Saw-whet.

The routing in this book takes us back to eastern Wyoming, to Goshen Hole. However, you may want to skip to Chapter 14 and go directly to Jackson Hole from Afton. If you would like to do that, just continue up US 89 through Alpine and along Snake River Canyon to Hoback Junction, a total of about 56 miles. Then take US 191 for another 13 miles to Jackson. You will miss the most dramatic views of the Tetons on this route, but you will still reach the fine birding areas at Jackson Hole.

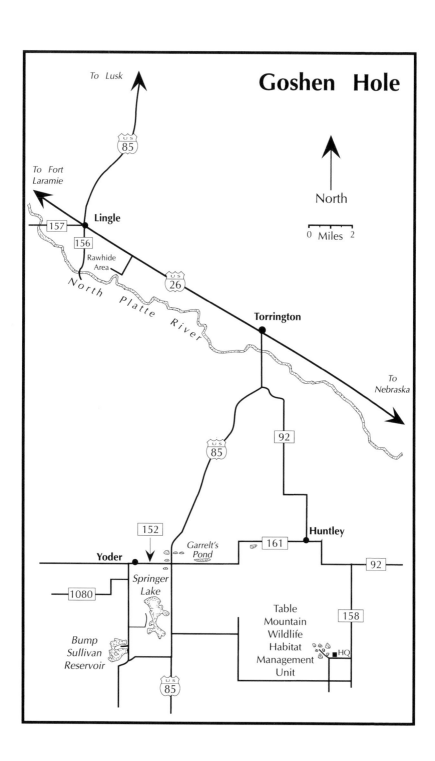

8. GOSHEN HOLE

Torrington and the area to the south and east comprise the Goshen Hole. In Western parlance a "hole" is a valley enclosed by hills or mountains. Goshen Hole is bounded by high escarpments to the south and west and high ground to the north. It is open toward Nebraska on the east. Its brightest star is the Game and Fish Department's Table Mountain Wildlife Habitat Management Unit. During March of each year, many thousands of Snow and Canada Geese passing through stop to rest and feed here.

Historically, the area marks the convergence of the Oregon, Mormon, and Texas Cattle Trails. Torrington served as the "Western doormat" for many pioneers.

Ordinarily, in rural, agricultural areas in Wyoming most roads are on section lines, so you have two choices—you can go north and south or east and west, and that's it. A section is one square mile. That is why many of the directions in this chapter will be at right angles. Be aware that roads often retain their route numbers in spite of numerous right-angle turns as they follow the section lines—but this is not always the case. (See Route 92 on the map on the previous page.)

1. **Yoder Ponds**. Starting from the railroad tracks in Torrington on US Highway 85, go south 11.0 miles and check the two ponds, one on each side of the road. These ponds can be good for American Avocet, Wilson's Phalarope, both Yellowlegs, "peeps" (Western, Semipalmated, Least, and Baird's Sandpipers), and Marbled Godwit, among other birds. In another 0.2 mile you will reach State Route 152. Turn right onto this route for only 0.3 mile. There are some small ponds on both sides of the road. In late May, White-rumped Sandpipers have been seen here several times. I once had 24 of them on the 25th of May. Now turn around and go east across US 85; the state route number changes to 161.

2. **Garrelt's Pond**. Go east on Route 161 for 1.3 miles to a pond on the left with most of the common ducks and a fine marsh on the right with Sora and sometimes Virginia Rail, as well as Marsh Wrens. If the water is high, there is good shorebird habitat on the eastern end. Birds along any of the roads in the area may include Swainson's Hawk, Ferruginous Hawk, Eastern, Western, and occasionally Cassin's Kingbirds, Lark Bunting, and Lark Sparrow.

3. **Huntley**. Zig-zag 3.0 miles farther east on Route 61 to a pond on your right. There are the common ducks and Wilson's Phalarope, often in numbers, here. A recent spring trip here produced Stilt Sandpiper, as well as the more expected Western and Baird's Sandpipers. (Later in the year, however, this pond can dry up.) Go farther east for 1.9 miles to Huntley, which consists of a school. At Huntley you join State Route 92.

4. **Table Mountain**. Go east on State Route 92 for 2.8 miles to State Route 158 and turn right onto it. Go 4.0 miles to a sign on the right to Table Mountain Wildlife Habitat Management Unit. Turn right here and proceed 1.0 mile to the entrance. Inside the entrance is a map showing the eight ponds that comprise the refuge.

At the first impoundment on the right (Pond #2) there is a fine marsh on the right with a colony of Marsh Wrens. American Bitterns, Black-crowned Night-Herons, and Forster's Terns nest here. After this first impoundment you can turn right to a sizable prairie-dog town with Burrowing Owls, or bear left for the best shorebird habitat at Table Mountain. Check the pond on your left and the west end of the pond on your right. In spring, from late April into May, there have always been a number of Stilt Sandpipers in breeding plumage in the left-hand impoundment. The right-hand pond has had Snowy Plovers at times as well as many other shorebirds. American Avocet and Wilson's Phalarope are all over the place. Some of the common ducks—such as Northern Pintail, the three teals, Northern Shoveler, American Wigeon, Redhead, Ruddy Duck, and Lesser Scaup—as well as Canada Goose—are found here. In the fall, during the waterfowl and upland game bird seasons, Table Mountain Wildlife Habitat Management Unit is out-of-bounds. Hunting is highly organized, and those without an assigned location in which to hunt are excluded from entry. In October, before hunting-season, Table Mountain has, at times, Greater White-fronted Geese. Ross's Goose has been seen here; Sora and Virginia Rails nest here. In migration there are usually some American White Pelicans in small numbers, and Snow Geese congregate by the thousands. Considering the birding opportunities, Table Mountain is the gem of Goshen Hole.

5. **Bump Sullivan**. This is the next-best spot for waterfowl after Table Mountain. To get there from Table Mountain Wildlife Habitat Management Unit, go south on the gravel road 1.0 mile from the Table Mountain entrance to another gravel road. Turn right, go 4.0 miles, and again turn right. Go 2.0 miles and turn left for 2.7 miles, and you should come out on US 85.

Turn left onto US 85 and travel 1.0 mile; turn right on an unmarked road with a group of farmers' names on it, as well as a sign for the Wyoming Game and Fish Department; go 1.8 miles to a fork in the road. Bear right. You have gone past the south end of Springer Lake (which usually isn't worthwhile). Go north 0.7 mile, then left and straight over the railroad tracks. Bump Sullivan Reservoir often isn't full. It is shaped like a U, and you are in the

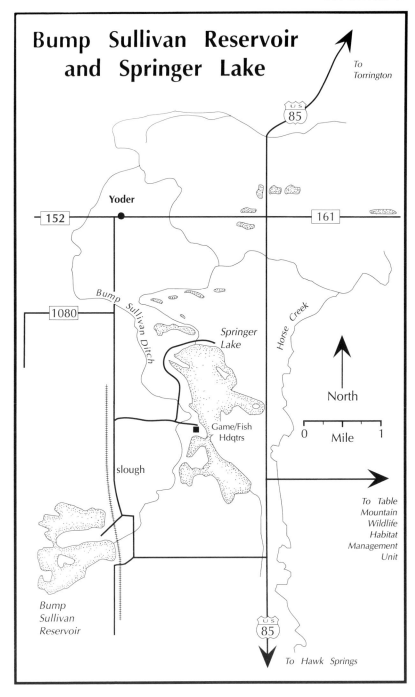

Bump Sullivan Reservoir and Springer Lake

middle of the top of the U. If it isn't full, there are often some shorebirds here, such as American Avocet and Lesser Yellowlegs. In spring one can find Horned Grebe here in breeding plumage. Otherwise, the waterfowl are much like those at Table Mountain except that there is no marsh here. (In the summer, both Bump Sullivan Reservoir and Springer Lake allow boating in the summer which greatly reduces the birding possibilities.)

6. **Springer Lake**. After scanning Bump Sullivan Reservoir, return to the gravel road over the railroad tracks and continue left. After 0.6 mile, the road crosses a slough that is very alkaline for the most part. It often is a good place for shorebirds in migration. In another 0.9 mile, there is another gravel road on the right that goes into the Game and Fish headquarters for the area. Go 0.5 mile and turn left to reach the north end of Springer Lake. This end of the lake can have a fair show of waterbirds such as geese, American White Pelicans, cormorants, and grebes. If the lake isn't full, which is usually the case, there can be a number of shorebirds, also. Should there be a barrier across this road, you will have to get permission to enter from headquarters.

Wilson's Phalaropes
Gail Diane Luckner

After you visit Springer Lake, go back to the main gravel road and continue north 2.0 miles, where you will turn right onto State Route 152 into Yoder—which is almost where you started. You can then follow Route 152 to US 85, where you can turn left and return to Torrington.

7. **Cassin's Sparrows**. In 1990, while doing a Breeding Bird Survey, William H. Howe found a colony of Cassin's Sparrows in this area. They have been found each year since, but may have a tenuous hold here. To find them, start at the railroad crossing on Main Street and drive north 0.9 mile to 30th Avenue East. Turn right and drive 1.8 miles. There will probably be a Burrowing Owl in a prairie-dog town on the left. You should also check the next small valley, where you might see Orchard and Northern (Bullock's) Orioles, as well as Blue Grosbeak. Continue until you have gone 2.4 miles beyond the prairie-dog town where you looked for the Burrowing Owl. You will have just gone under a power-line. This seems to be the center of the Cassin's Sparrow colony area. The birds have been seen both north and south of this area. They don't arrive until early June, and the flight songs seem to end after the territory is established. You may see them singing from fenceposts. This area also has plenty of Lark Sparrows, so beware. It can be a good place for Grasshopper and Clay-colored Sparrows in migration. Sage Thrashers nest in the vicinity, along with Vesper Sparrows. Retrace your route to Torrington.

8. **Rawhide**. In the center of Torrington, after crossing the railroad tracks, make a left turn onto US Highway 26 and head northwest toward Lingle, ten miles away. After 6.6 miles there is a dirt road on the left and a sign for the Rawhide Creek Wildlife Habitat Management Unit. Drive 0.5 mile across the first field; there is a road to the right that leads 0.7 mile to a parking lot for the eastern side of this Wyoming Game and Fish facility. As you drive this last stretch of road, check for Red-headed Woodpeckers and American Kestrels in the cottonwood trees. The path from the parking lot leads west, and the first one-half mile can be rewarding with passerine migrants and resident songbirds such as Eastern and Western Kingbirds, Blue Jays, and Lark Sparrows. You pass over Rawhide Creek and go along the river. The Wyoming Game and Fish Department has made considerable effort to attract Wood Ducks, with some success. Sometimes they nest in this area. Moreover, this area is the best place for landbirds near Torrington. In migration there are often warblers—Yellow-rumped, Yellow, Orange-crowned, and Yellow-breasted Chat—and, occasionally, rarer birds. There should be Orchard Orioles and Blue Grosbeaks here in spring and summer. During much of the year one can find Eastern Screech-Owls in the evening. (There can also be plenty of ticks at Rawhide, so take the proper precautions.)

Also try the west side of the Rawhide Area. To reach it, return to US 26 and go 3.0 miles to Lingle. As you enter town, turn left onto Route 156.

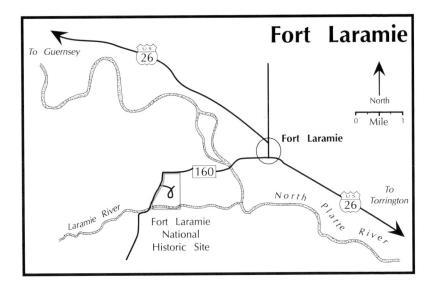

Proceed 2.0 miles to the North Platte River. The facility spans both sides of the river and both sides of the road. Just before you cross the river there is a turn-out on the right, a consistent spot for Eastern Screech-Owl.

9. **Fort Laramie**. Continuing west beyond Lingle on US 26, you will come to Fort Laramie after 10.0 miles. The town of Fort Laramie is maybe six blocks by six blocks. By driving the streets that have lots of trees, you should be able to find Orchard Orioles in spring and summer. White-throated Swifts are also found in the area. In migration Fort Laramie is sort of an oasis and can be good, but the best attraction is the area around the old fort itself.

Fort Laramie was a pivotal site in the on-again-off-again relations between settlers and Indians from the 1840s to 1890, and especially in the "Indian troubles" from the mid-1850s through the dangerous 1870s. The fort is now a National Historic Site. To reach Fort Laramie National Historic Site, turn left onto Route 160 from the west side of town. It should be well-marked; the fort is 2.5 miles down the road. (Twenty-two structures are at the fort, many of which have been restored and refurbished to recreate the feeling of life at the fort in its heyday. Artifacts at the museum help illustrate the civilian, military, and Indian history of the region. It is certainly worth a look if you have the time.)

In migration look for mixed flocks of Clay-colored and Chipping Sparrows along the road to the fort. Just 0.5 mile beyond the fort the road crosses the Laramie River. Along its brushy banks is a good place to find Blue Grosbeaks, which prefer this type of habitat. Many Blue Grosbeaks are found in the North Platte Valley from Torrington up to Gurnsey.

If you wish to pick up the route in the next chapter, return to Lingle, eastward on US 26 for 10.0 miles, and travel northward on US 85 for 47 miles to Lusk; then drive east on US 20 for 20 miles to the little hamlet of Van Tassel.

American Avocets
Shawneen Finnegan

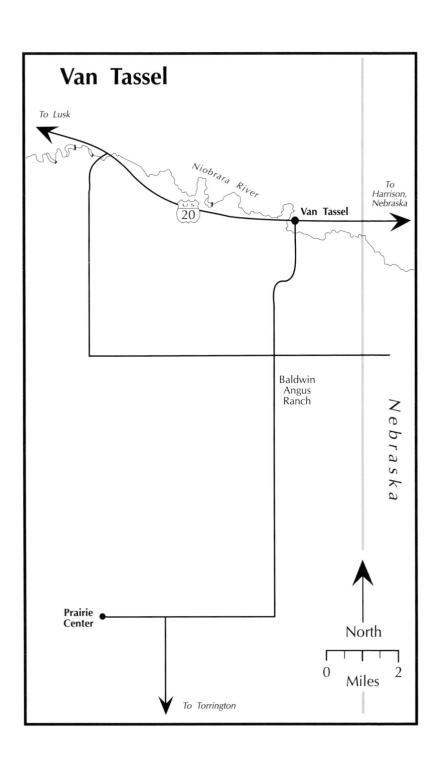

9. VAN TASSEL

If you come into Wyoming on US Highway 20 from Nebraska, after 2.0 miles you will go through Van Tassel. At the turn of the century Van Tassel, known locally as Homesteader's Landing, was a supply point for settlers living as far south as Torrington. Easily obtainable water—available at a convenient depth—was instrumental in fostering early settlement, but was not plentiful enough to support intensive agriculture. Today Van Tassel has a population of eight although it used to be much larger. There's a post office, but not much else.

Just west of the railroad-track crossing in Van Tassel, you will see a gravel road leading southward. By turning onto this road, you have a chance to sample about the best in eastern Wyoming grassland birds. After 1.0 mile on this gravel road, you come out of the valley of Van Tassel onto a rough plateau. Start looking for birds. From the middle of April through May, Baird's Sparrows are possible. In May there ought to be Grasshopper Sparrows as well as Chipping, Clay-colored, and Savannah. The predominant nesting sparrow here is the Vesper. Upland Sandpipers are seen often, and sometimes Burrowing Owls. In May, Cassin's Kingbird goes through along with the more common Western and Eastern. Western Kingbirds will nest around ranch-houses here. You should also see Ferruginous and Swainson's Hawks in this prairie country. Other birds in the area may include Long-billed Curlew, Short-eared Owl, Say's Phoebe, Western Meadowlark, Horned Lark, and Lark Bunting.

At 3.0 miles from Van Tassel there is a large field on your left that will have both McCown's and Chestnut-collared Longspurs nesting by May and June. Their flight songs are interesting to witness. In April there are sizable flocks of these birds. In fact, this strip of grassland seems to be sort of a migratory corridor, and large numbers of sparrows and longspurs are found here. The best of this country is in the first 5.0 miles to the Baldwin Angus Ranch. It is the first ranch close to the road. The ranch, which sells bulls, is well-labeled.

One can go beyond this area to where the road becomes paved after 15 miles near Prairie Center—which is practically a ghost town. Look for Long-billed Curlews, Upland Sandpipers, and Short-eared Owls along the way. This area used to be fairly heavily populated as rural areas go, but in the last 60 years the population has steadily declined. This is true of most of rural Wyoming unless there is irrigation or an extractive industry. Congress, in its wisdom, allowed a homesteader 640 acres, a square mile, but if it takes 25 acres to support a cow and a family needs 250 to 300 animals for a reasonable lifestyle, the average ranch has to be a lot bigger. As one goes west in Wyoming, the rainfall decreases and the acreage needed to support a cow increases.

By continuing on this paved road you end up in Torrington on Main Street, about 35 miles away. Going straight ahead at that point, you will be at the start of the tour of Goshen Hole (the previous chapter).

If you want to see more of the grassland and stay on US 20, you can backtrack 0.8 mile from the Baldwin Angus Ranch to the only crossroad that you passed and turn left (west). After 5.0 miles you will come to a road on the right (north) on which you can get back on US 20 in 5.1 miles. On this last stretch you might see some McCown's Longspurs and a few Chestnut-collared Longspurs along with other grassland species. Where the road rejoins US 20, there is also a nice pond and a small marsh that attracts Virginia Rail and Sora.

Once US 20 joins with US 26 and Interstate 25, it is only 14 miles to Douglas, the starting-point for our next chapter. Looking at a state map, you might be tempted to consider a side-trip to the Thunder Basin National Grassland, taking up so much space as it does to the north and northeast. The

Thunder Basin National Grassland is a product of federal government efforts in the 1930s to halt dust-bowl devastation. Distressed and abandoned homesteads were acquired, allowing the soil to begin to recover. But there were lots of private and state holdings left, resulting in a hodge-podge pattern. The US Forest Service, not the BLM, administers this property. Today, cattle and sheep graze much of the land under permit, and there is plenty of mineral extraction in the area (for example, coal, uranium, and bentonite). The area has a huge surface coal-mining operation. Birdwise, it is little different from surrounding semi-arid grasslands, so if you planned to make a special trip there, forget it. Inviting though it looks on a map, it is not what you think it might be, and it is nothing like the well-known Pawnee National Grassland in neighboring Colorado. The Ranger District Office in Douglas is more concerned with administering the northern half of the Medicine Bow National Forest than with Thunder Basin.

It is 35 miles north on Route 59 before you enter the Grassland. A curiosity, however, might be the large Buffalo ranch owned by the Durham Meat Company, located just north of Wright on Route 59. It's hard to miss.

From Douglas it is but a short drive westward on Interstate 25 to Ayres Natural Bridge.

Burrowing Owls
Shawneen Finnegan

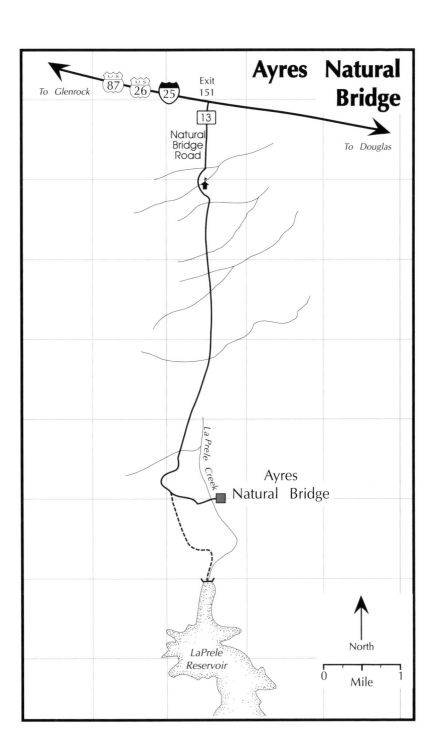

Ayres Natural Bridge

To Glenrock

US 87 US 26 25 Exit 151

To Douglas

13

Natural Bridge Road

La Prele Creek

Ayres Natural Bridge

LaPrele Reservoir

North

0 Mile 1

10. AYRES NATURAL BRIDGE

Ayres Natural Bridge is off Interstate 25 between Douglas and Glenrock. This beautiful little spot in a rather spectacular canyon is only 4.6 miles south of Interstate 25 on Natural Bridge Road (County Road 13). The well-marked turn (exit 151) is 14 miles west of Douglas. (If you are coming from the west, it is 9.3 miles east of the East Glenrock exit.) Interstate 25 is generally a north-south highway, but between Glenrock and Douglas it is an east-west highway.

Part of the interest in the Natural Bridge area is birding along the access road. Exactly 1.0 mile down Natural Bridge Road you come to an old schoolhouse on a little knoll at a bend in the road. This site has had Say's Phoebes nesting in one of the outhouses for years. (Say's Phoebe can also be found on the east side of the road just after you turn off Interstate 25.) Listen for its song from mid-April until July. Beyond the schoolhouse the road crosses several little water-courses. These are chock full of reeds and have Marsh Wrens in season. Common Snipe can be found winnowing up until July. Northern Harriers nest here. Don't be surprised if you see a green pheasant. Good numbers of this form of Ring-necked Pheasant have been released in this area.

The area of the natural bridge itself—3.6 miles south of the old schoolhouse—is a park run by the Converse County County Park and Recreation Commission (phone: 307/358-3532). The park has camping and picnic facilities. Don't go there on a summer holiday, though. There are so many humans that you can't turn around. The park is usually open (8am to 8pm) so that you can drive in, from April 1 to October 31. However, even if the park is closed you can walk in, and this method of access is not strenuous. It is at most a one-half-mile walk from the gate to the interesting part of the park.

The natural bridge is part of the Casper Sandstone Formation, laid down more than 280 million years ago. Water has eroded a hole in the rock, allowing a stream to flow through it. The bridge arch is 50 feet above the stream and 100 feet long. The stream that goes under the bridge is LaPrele Creek.

American Dippers are common and nest here. Their bulky nests can be found on ledges just above the water. The young fledge usually very early in May before the hoards of summer locals arrive. The last nest I saw was right under the arching bridge itself. Canyon Wrens often nest here and can be heard from February on. Much of the canyon is a great deal larger than it is in the park and runs above it a mile or more to a large dam on LaPrele Reservoir. The whole canyon is great for hawks and eagles, particularly in migration. In the area look for Sharp-shinned Hawk, Northern Goshawk, Merlin, Prairie Falcon, American Kestrel, Red-tailed Hawk, and Northern Harrier. Golden Eagles almost always nest in the canyon. White-throated Swifts can usually be seen in the park from late April onward. The park is a great catch-all for migrants; some of our rarer warblers have been seen here. For the out-of-staters, our warblers are not too exciting unless you come from the country west of Wyoming since our vagrants are from the East. Some of the local birds include Turkey Vulture, Great Horned Owl, Western Wood-Pewee, Rock Wren, Green-tailed Towhee, Black-headed Grosbeak, and Northern Oriole.

Ayres Natural Bridge   Paul J. Baicich

If you go up the canyon from the park, you will need to get permission from John Meyer (phone: 358-6465) since this is private land. He has been very kind to birders. Golden Eagles nest up the canyon from the park. (As is usual for this species, these Golden Eagles seem to have several nests but use only one per year.) Canyon Wrens are also found up the canyon from the park.

Northern Goshawk
Gail Diane Luckner

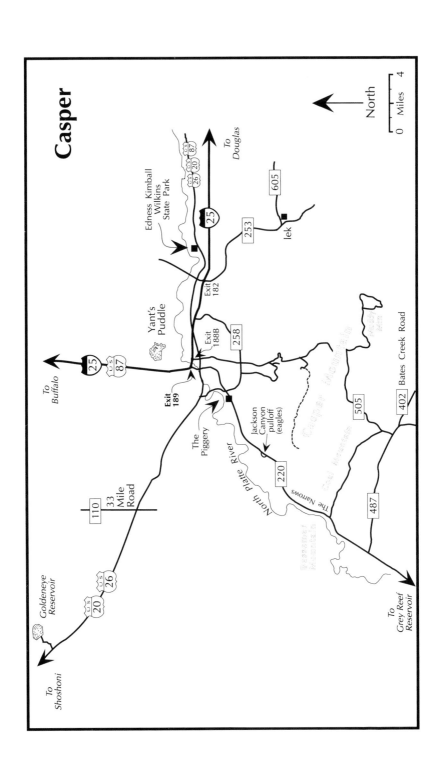

Casper

North

0 Miles 4

To Douglas

87
20
26

Edness Kimball
Wilkins
State Park

25

605

253

Iek

Exit 182

Yant's
Puddle

Exit 188B

258

25   US 87

To Buffalo

Exit 189

The Piggery

Jackson Canyon
pulloff
(eagles)

North Platte River

220

Casper Mountain

East Mountain

505

402 Bates Creek Road

487

The Narrows

Beartrap Meadow

110   33 Mile Road

US 20   US 26

Goldeneye
Reservoir

To Shoshoni

To Grey Reef Reservoir

11. CASPER AREA

Casper, the focal point for much of Wyoming, is primarily an oil-and-gas exploration town. It is busy, modern, and clean. The first oil well in the Salt Creek oilfield was tapped in 1889, and by the end of the new century's first decade the town was on the edge of a major oil boom. (Notoriety was also brought to the area by the nearby Teapot Dome oilfield and its attendant political scandal in the 1920s.) Casper has the state's only heavy industry and, in general, is the industrial and retail center of the state. This active city also has the best and most extensive medical facilities in the state. Casper has the largest group of active birders in the state and is the home town of the author of this book. The following sites around Casper should produce a variety of birds:

1. **Sage Grouse lek**. In Wyoming many towns have a place where you can see the Sage Grouse perform. Most of these places are inconvenient, but a few are not. While the Sage Grouse lek is fixed and always in exactly the same place from year to year, the Sharp-tailed Grouse are more flexible. You can see them performing individually from time to time, and their lek locations can change. In any case, both these birds put on a real show; if you are fortunate enough to be in Wyoming in the spring, don't miss it. Of the two, the Sage Grouse is the more spectacular. To see this performance you should be on site shortly before sun-up (5:30am) in late March, April (best), and early May. After the sun gets up and the light is good, the birds will leave the lek. Some people will tell you that you can see the performance in the evening, but that is a poor show compared with the morning one. The evening event lacks the females, the numbers are poor, and it just lacks the zip of the morning performance. Those who go in the evening have been sold a bill of goods.

If you wish to visit a Sage Grouse lek: coming from the east on Interstate 25 approaching Casper, take the Hat Six (exit 182) interchange and turn south onto Route 253. Drive 8.2 miles to Natrona County Road 605 and turn left. The lek is only 0.1 mile down this road on the right side. There may be a sign marking it. This place is probably the most accessible Sage Grouse lek in the state. Try to get to this spot before dawn between March and May for a fine display of strutting Sage Grouse. Unless you get out of the car, the strutting birds won't fly.

The number of leks waxes and wanes depending on the number of birds in the area. At this particular lek I once brought in 150 people in 75 cars to

Casper Sage Grouse lek—typical of surrounding areas   Paul J. Baicich

see the show. I tried without much success to get them to combine cars. I had them park in two rows with the second row placed in the gaps between cars in the first row. We had a great show, but after about 30 seconds a woman in a first-row car jumped out to take a picture—and off went the whole show of 75 birds. I thought we might have a lynching. However, I have seen photographers start from a distance and gradually come closer so that they eventually were virtually within the circle of birds.

2. **Edness Kimball Wilkins State Park**. Return north 8.2 miles on Hat Six Road, and go over Interstate 25. Drive an additional 0.4 mile over the railroad tracks and turn right onto US 20/26/87. This is the old highway from Casper to Glenrock. Go 2.3 miles, and the approximately 300-acre Edness Kimball Wilkins State Park is on your left. It is well marked. It is representative of the riparian zone on a major river—the North Platte—in Wyoming. After driving in as far as the river, take a one-way loop that goes around the eastern part of the park. From the one-way sign at the beginning of the loop, drive 0.7 mile to a small parking lot. Follow the paved walking-trail to the right. The best birding is beyond the fence; this route gets you away from many of the people but keeps you close to the river. There are Common Nighthawks, Red-headed Woodpeckers, Eastern and Western Kingbirds, Western Wood-Pewees, Black-headed Grosbeaks, Lark ˙Sparrows, and Northern Orioles, to mention only a few species. Look for ducks along the river. During migration most of our landbirds can be seen here with sometimes a

vagrant warbler, such as the Magnolia Warbler that was seen here during a recent spring migration. The real excitement, though, has been a nesting pair of Bald Eagles. In 1989 they fledged two young. Bald Eagles have nested elsewhere on the North Platte but not previously on this section of the river from Glendo to Saratoga, a stretch of some 170 miles, as far as we know. The history of this pair is interesting. The year before they started nesting we thought that they were going to nest, but one day in April they got into a fight with a pair of Golden Eagles that nested on some cliffs to the north about a mile away. The battle lasted all day, and we thought that the Balds had the better of it. Nevertheless, a few days later the Balds disappeared for the season.

The eagles' nest was actually on the north side of the river across from the park, but it could best be seen from the park side. The nest was on private land, and the owner was so fierce about protecting his eagles, bless him, that no one got closer to the nest. With this kind of protection these birds may continue nesting here. Activity at this site was from late March to mid-July. In the winter of 1989-90 the tree with the nest blew down. In 1990 the birds didn't nest here, but Bald Eagles hang around some, so we hope that they will return.

3. **Piggery**. After returning to Interstate 25, go west again through much of Casper for 6 miles to the turnoff to State Route 220 (exit 188B). As soon as you are off the interstate, turn left and go under the interstate. You are now on Poplar Street, which takes you across town 1.7 miles to the south. Watch for a right turn which is really well marked and thence southwest on Route 220. Although 220 is only a state route, it is one of the major arterial highways of the state and carries plenty of heavy truck traffic. It leads to Rawlins on Interstate 80. After 2 miles Route 220 crosses State Route 258. About 100 yards beyond this intersection there is a Quonset hut on the right with a paved loop to park on. In this area pigs were once raised. Today the land from here to the river is a small refuge of the Murie Audubon Society. Just behind the Quonset hut (to the north) is the top of a bank with two small reedy marshes below. The bank protecting against the prevailing southwest wind, the marshes, and the surrounding vegetation combine to make this an excellent place for migrants. Soras nest in the marshes. Further, Virginia Rails have successfully over-wintered here. These little marshes are fed by warm springs and remain open all year.

4. **Nancy English and Adams Parks**. Now return to Poplar Street, turn right, and go to 23rd Street and again turn right to the crossing of Garden Creek. Park beside a natural area along Garden Creek on the right called Nancy English Park. There is a grassy piece near the street, but the riparian vegetation along the creek is intact. This is a great place for migrants in May, August, and September and is much visited by local birders. From Nancy English Park continue 0.1 mile to the stop sign at Coffman Street and make a

left. The first open grassy area on the left (0.3 mile) is an unnamed park (often called Audubon Park by local birders) which is a continuation of the area along Garden Creek. The park stretches from 23rd Street to 25th Street. It is excellent for spring and fall migration. One can also go up Garden Creek, cross 25th Street along a path close to the creek, and be in Adams Park. Adams Park has a lot of brush close to the creek and is good in migration, also. Lazuli Buntings nest there. In the spring of 1988 vagrant warblers such as Blackburnian, Blackpoll, and Northern Parula were seen in these two parks.

5. **Base of the Mountain Loop.** Go back to Poplar Street on 25th Street and again go south 3.6 miles to where the road loops to the east across a meadow with considerable brush. Green-tailed Towhees will be on the right in the brush. They will be teed up and singing from mid-May until early July. After that time you will mostly hear their cat-like "mew". Continuing on the loop for 0.8 mile you shortly come to a series of houses on the right with big pine trees behind them. From about May 20 on noisy Broad-tailed Hummers are much in evidence. They leave by September 1. There are a number of bird feeders in this group of houses, so Clark's Nutcrackers and Steller's Jays are here year-round—along with Pine Siskins and goldfinches. Cassin's Finches usually are not here in the middle of the winter but at other times can be seen. They tend to be more irregular than the species already mentioned. You can also expect House Finches. Continuing farther on the loop for 0.5 mile to the east, cross the main stem of Garden Creek, and then turn right. Go to the end of the road where there is a little picnic spot below Garden Creek Falls called Rotary Park. (During winter and early spring the road is blocked by a gate, but it is only a short walk from the gate to the park.) Hillsides on both sides are steep and moist with brush. MacGillivray's Warblers nest here and sing from late May through the first week of July at least. They don't tee up and are hard to see. They tend to skulk in the lower part of the brush.

6. **Jackson Canyon Eagle Roost.** Return to the loop and you will join the Mountain Road (Route 251) in 0.3 mile. Now turn left (north) toward Casper (you can turn south up the Mountain Road and take a short-cut to stops 11-14). Run north toward Casper for 1.6 miles until you come to Route 258. Turn left. After 2.7 miles you will join Route 220 again. Turn left and continue on past the Piggery. At 7.1 miles past the Piggery there is a turnoff for a parking lot on the right. From here at Jackson Canyon you can view the largest winter eagle roost along the North Platte River—perhaps the largest concentration in the Rockies. Jackson Canyon is a spectacular gash in the west end of Casper Mountain. You can see only the edge of it from the highway. The canyon has a twist in it a mile or two above the entrance, and that is where the actual roost is located. From this observation site up to 40 Bald and Golden Eagles have been observed. On a winter afternoon between November 15 and March 10 you can see the birds wheeling about in the air in the usual

southwest wind before going in to roost. This road stop is the best place to see the birds, and the landowner takes a dim view of anybody disturbing the roost.

Since 1980 the canyon has been protected by an ACEC (Area of Critical Environmental Concern) of the Bureau of Land Management and a conservation easement given to The Nature Conservancy of 8,300 acres by the local landowner (the author). Unfortunately, the fate of the Jackson Canyon eagle roost is in doubt. This uncertainty is due to ignoring federal regulations. (The risks to birds involved in *strictly enforcing* some federal regulations will actually be described at the end of this chapter.) Locally the BLM has given its approval to protecting the Bald Eagle roost here. However, as of 1992, the BLM is planning to swap lands with the state of Wyoming so that the state would have a royalty-generating property to lease where a limestone quarry would be constructed. The quarry would be near enough to scare eagles and also allow access to winter snowmobiles. (This invasion would finish the job of destruction to the roost.) Those who live far away from agencies like the BLM may think that they are benign and work for conservation and for the good of the nation. Some of us who have to live and work with them think otherwise.

7. **The Narrows.** From the Jackson Canyon site to the Narrows is 3.8 miles on State Route 220. The Narrows are where the state highway and the river cut between Coal Mountain and Bessemer Mountain. Pinyon Jays come here for water, usually at sun-up, all year. However, they may come at any other time, too. There is a feeder which they visit at the bottom of the only side-road on the right (0.1 mile down the hill) in the Narrows. In the colder months Pinyon Jays stay much of the day near the feeder. In this juniper country there are sizable flocks of these jays, but where they are at a given moment is hard to say. The Narrows is the most consistent place to see them.

8. **Grey Reef Reservoir.** If you are interested in some ducks, you can try Grey Reef Reservoir. It is on the left some 14.7 miles beyond the Narrows. (If you want to skip this stop, you will want to stop at Coal Mountain Road, just 0.7 mile beyond the Narrows, and move to stop 9 below.) Grey Reef is a small reservoir just below Alcova on the North Platte River. Since Alcova has a hydroelectric plant that operates only on peak demand, Grey Reef merely converts the river-flow back to normal. This means that the Grey Reef Reservoir has daily fluctuations with much turbulent water, so that it is open in all but the coldest weather. As a result, many ducks congregate here during late winter when other locations are frozen over. When the ice goes out elsewhere, interest among the birds in Grey Reef diminishes, so the place has a somewhat limited status as a good spot for ducks.

To cover most of the reservoir you only have to go in about a half-mile from Route 220, but bring a scope. A paved road on the left that goes along the north side of the reservoir is high enough to provide excellent views.

Casper Area Detail

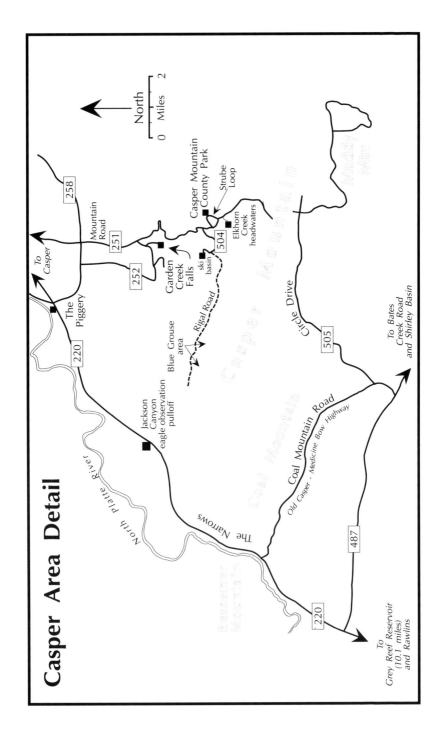

Barrow's Goldeneye
Gail Diane Luckner

Besides the common ducks and geese, we have had Barrow's Goldeneye and Hooded Merganser regularly, and Eurasian Wigeon several times.

9. **Coal Mountain Road.** Some 14.0 miles back from Grey Reef Reservoir (or 0.7 mile beyond the Narrows) there is a road labeled Coal Mountain Road. It is really the old Casper-Medicine Bow Highway, which has too many letters for one sign. Take this road. For about 2 miles you are on top of a ridge with a good chance of meeting up with Pinyon Jays. In summer there are Black-throated Gray Warblers, Chipping Sparrows, and sometimes Blue-gray Gnatcatchers here. (Should you happen to be here in wet weather, turn around and take Route 220 left for 3.9 miles to Route 487 and then turn onto it for 8.3 miles until you come to Circle Drive.) If the weather is dry, as it usually is, continue on the Coal Mountain Road.

You are in Golden Eagle country here. From the road you can often hear immature Golden Eagles hollering for food from mid-July, when they fledge, though October. Then you usually hear the adults answering. The principal sparrow in the sage is the Vesper, but along here are a number of Brewer's Sparrows. There are also Sage Thrashers. (These birds can be found almost anywhere in the sage country.) In this area look also for Virginia's Warbler, Black-throated Gray Warbler, and Blue-gray Gnatcatcher.

After 8.0 miles the road joins Circle Drive. Bear right and join State Highway 487 after 0.8 mile.

10. **Bates Creek Road**. Turn left onto Route 487 for 0.7 mile and bear left onto Bates Creek Road, Route 402. Incidentally, all this country is part of Bates Hole. Originally, this was part of the huge Swan Land & Livestock Company. The first land was taken up in 1886 here, the earliest in this part of the world. Sometimes it is hard to realize how recent many of the settlements of the west are. Swan was badly hurt by the terrible winter of 1886-87, when some of the silly myths of the West—such as "you never need to feed your cattle in the winter"—went down the tube. During Prohibition large amounts of liquor were produced in Bates Hole. Some was so good that it brought a premium price in Chicago. Go up Bates Creek Road for 3 miles to a narrow valley with a steep hill or mountainside—whichever you prefer to call it—on the left. This hillside, in the colder months of October to May, has Pinyon Jays, Townsend's Solitaires, and often Golden Eagles. This is part of a major flyway to the south for the eagles.

11. **Muddy Mountain**. Now return to State Highway 487, turn right, and go back to Circle Drive, Route 505, and go up it 8.2 miles to the junction with the road to Muddy Mountain. It is the first road you actually meet on the right, so it is easy to find. It may not be easy to drive on in wet weather, however, and it is closed in winter. Go to the right up the Muddy Mountain Road for 0.4 mile to where the road cuts through a thicket of trees. There are Orange-crowned Warblers nesting here as well as Dusky Flycatchers. They sing from late May to mid-July. Below the trees White-crowned Sparrows nest in the sage. Green-tailed Towhees are very common in the sage, also.

12. **Lions Camp**. Now turn around and go straight across the intersection (where Circle Drive makes a sharp left-hand turn) and up Casper Mountain. Drive 2.0 miles to the top of Casper Mountain to where the road becomes paved again. Continue another 1.8 miles from the beginning of the pavement to a little unmarked turn to the left which leads to the Lions Camp for the Blind. (There should be a picnic table at this turn.) This is the headwaters of Elkhorn Creek and always has a pair of Lincoln's Sparrows nesting. The male sings from late May well into July. Continue on this road 0.3 mile back to Circle Drive. After 0.1 mile there is a short loop, called Strube Loop, to the right for 0.9 mile that follows two branches of Elkhorn Creek and often has Cordilleran Flycatchers nesting. Cordilleran Flycatchers are often found along water-courses. There is a half-mile Braille trail on Strube Loop along Elkhorn Creek that is good for Lincoln's Sparrows and MacGillivray's Warblers, among other birds.

13. **Elkhorn Creek**. Continue on Circle Drive after the loop for 0.4 mile to another brushy, wet place on the right. Again Lincoln's Sparrows nest here as well as the common Swainson's Thrushes and sometimes Hermit Thrushes. You should also see Steller's Jays. Anywhere along the top of the mountain in this area there may be Townsend's Solitaires nesting.

14. **West End of Casper Mountain**. This stop is described here with some trepidation. To get there one has to follow a track—it can't classify as a road—for a fairly long distance. The average Detroit car can't make it, but many foreign cars with good clearance or a pick-up can. You have to be reasonably able to keep out of ruts. A number of times during the last 40 years Casper Mountain has recorded the highest number of Blue Grouse seen on any Christmas Count in the nation. This stop gives you the chance of seeing some.

Just beyond the previous Elkhorn Creek stop, turn almost a U on the blacktop onto County Road 504 and go 1.3 miles west. The blacktop stops at Hogadon Ski Basin; just before you get there, take a sharp left onto a well-used gravel road that is marked by several signs. One says "Archery Range." The road shortly passes through an area of houses and then aims at a telephone relay-station on the top of a rise. At the bottom of this rise, after 1.3 miles, turn left onto Rigal Road which goes through the woods and on to the west. There are various tracks running off to the left and right to cabins. Avoid these and stick to the top of the mountain. Finally, after 2.6 miles, there is a fence across the mountain with a gate on your track. Pass through this gate and drive for an additional half-mile or more; then walk cross-country to the woods on the south side of the mountain, a distance of only about one-quarter mile. This whole south side, mostly near the top, is great Blue Grouse country. Although Blue Grouse can be seen anywhere on the mountain, the chances on the south side are higher. Since the Blue is the only grouse on the mountain, identification is easy, but saying just where a gallinaceous bird of this kind is at a given moment is impossible. This stop is possible from mid-June until the snow flies again in late September or early October. Best of luck!

15. **33 Mile Road**. Now return to Mountain Road and go down it 8.2 miles to 12th Street in Casper. Turn left for one block to Center Street. Turn right onto Center Street (north), which leads to the interstate. Go west on the interstate less than a mile and bear right onto US 20/26 (exit 189), which promptly turns left under the interstate. From this point proceed west on US 20/26 beyond the Natrona County International Airport entrance at 7.0 miles. Then go 3.1 miles farther on US 20/26 to 33 Mile Road, Route 110. Turn right onto 33 Mile Road and go straight 3.9 miles to the first turn. This is a good spot. There are Burrowing Owls in the field ahead (as if you didn't go around the turn). There are usually McCown's Longspurs on the right in a relic piece of unplowed prairie. In winter and early spring (late February and early March) the next mile is a great place to find Lapland Longspurs and Snow Buntings among the numerous Horned Larks. By turning left onto the dirt road and going 1.3 miles to irrigated fields, one can often find Long-billed Curlew in June.

16. **Goldeneye Reservoir**. Now return to US 20/26 and go right 12.9 miles to the turnoff for Goldeneye Wildlife and Recreation Area. It is visible to the right of the highway. Take the gravel road 1.1 miles to the parking lot. This lake is under control of the Bureau of Land Management (BLM). Vehicle

traffic is not allowed, but you are permitted to walk around the lake. The lake has fish, so that means lots of fishermen. However, some birds like fish, too, so there are often terns (Forster's and Caspian), American White Pelicans, loons, Western and Clark's Grebes, White-faced Ibis, and lots more. Sometimes there are interesting shorebirds here, such Snowy Plover, Long-billed Curlew, Whimbrel, and Red Knot. Landbirds in the area may include Sage Thrasher, Loggerhead Shrike, Lark Bunting, and McCown's Longspur.

17. **Yant's Puddle.** This is an extraordinary place north of town. Back in 1957 the Standard Oil of Indiana refinery needed a place to dump their effluent. They had been dumping it into the North Platte River, which flows by the works. The river stank for fifty miles downstream and had few fish. Joe Yant was then chief engineer at the refinery as well as President of the local Audubon group. He was also placed on the advisory board of the State Department of Environmental Quality. The refinery found a sizable natural depression a short distance away with a little alkaline puddle at the bottom. In spring for a short time there would be some water in it. They acquired 2,200 acres, constructed a pipeline to the area, built some small settling ponds, and then a much larger one from which a tricky siphon taking water out of the middle layer of water led to the depression itself. They call it Soda Lake, but since every county in eastern and southern Wyoming has scores of Soda Lakes, the Audubonites dubbed it Yant's Puddle or just The Puddle. It has grown to about 2 square miles of lake with several islands in it. There are no fish in it yet, and it is somewhat alkaline—with the result that there is an enormous amount of food for birds. The water teems with little red dancing copepods, the lake is almost full of Pond-weeds, and there are repeated blooms of algae which die and are washed up on the shore, making a wonderful rotting mess which the shorebirds just love. It has become the finest place in Wyoming to see birds associated with water. There is a big colony of California Gulls there with over two thousand nests. For food, they are dependent on the nearby Casper City landfill dump. There are a few Ring-billed Gulls nesting with the Californias. This is the only place in Wyoming where the Ring-bills have been found to nest. There are also several hundred Double-crested Cormorant nests. The Puddle has a sizable colony of Black-necked Stilts; there is perhaps only one other colony in Wyoming. Black-crowned Night-Herons nest here, as do Snowy Egrets. Local nesting birds like American Avocet and Wilson's Phalarope are present in good numbers. All the prairie-breeding ducks nest here, and so do a lot of Canada Geese. During migration the estimates of ducks have run from 15,000 to 25,000. In other words, this place does better than many National Wildlife Refuges.

Large numbers of rarities show up here, such as Piping Plover, probably every year in the fall. Buff-breasted Sandpipers are almost regular. Late in the season Oldsquaws have been regular in recent years. Almost every year there is a jaeger. The only two records for Heermann's Gull in Wyoming are from here, and so the list goes on and on. The local Audubonites interested in birds spend half their birding time here. This is all great, but there is a catch. The whole place is well-fenced and the gates are under lock and key, so it is not open to the public. If it were, it would be promptly destroyed, because it is so close to the city of Casper. The refinery people have kindly allowed Audubon members access; to visit Yant's Puddle contact the Murie Audubon Society at Box 2112, Casper, WY 82602, by letter. Or call the Natrona County Information and Referral Service at 307/234-6715, and they will have the current number of someone to call. With a little advance notice, there is always someone available to take you there. Of course, the life of the puddle is dependent on the life of the refinery, which is now closed. Also, the Environmental Protection Agency tried to restrict the settling-pond because it has some unpleasant chemicals in it. The Puddle sits in an isolated basin with impervious rock under it, so water-tables can't be contaminated if noxious things get farther than the settling-pond. The settling-pond appears to deposit all the nasty things, so they don't get into the large lake. For the past 35 years the river water being pumped in has attracted the birds, and the chemicals have simply accumulated in the bottom of the pond. If the pond is now allowed to dry, the EPA would classify the area as a hazardous-waste site. *That's* sticking to regulations. However, we are told that The Puddle's existence is guaranteed for at least 10 years. The tremendous amount of food for birds, as well as the numbers of birds in the puddle itself, attest to a lack of pollutants in the main lake. Thus, strict adherence to regulations administered by bureaucrats who live by the words of the regulations destroys the things the organization was set up to protect. (Another example in another federal agency is the BLM, which is supposed to improve the range, but it has regulations which, if strictly adhered to, prevent such improvement.) Clearly, we need some flexibility here.

Casper birders at Yant's Puddle   Paul J. Baicich

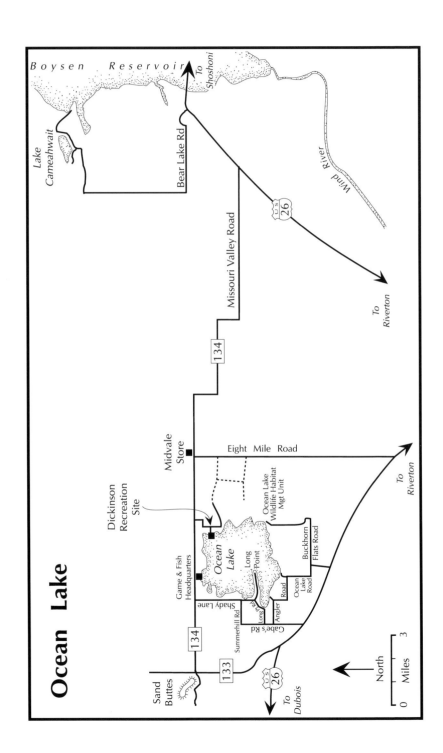

12. OCEAN LAKE

The Ocean Lake Wildlife Habitat Management Unit in central Wyoming is an excellent place for water and marsh birds. The Wyoming Game and Fish has bought up most of the land around Ocean Lake and controls the hunting. The entire property is over 12,000 acres, half of which is water. The best time to visit is during migration in spring and fall. Ocean Lake is an artificial lake made to control irrigation in the nearby Missouri Valley Project.

Approaching Ocean Lake from the east, take US 26 through Shoshoni and cross the upper end of Boysen Reservoir on the causeway. Occasionally from this causeway one can see shorebirds and a few gulls and terns. You can park on the east side of the causeway and walk out to scope the birds, but often the pickings are slim. You may, however, want to stop by Lake Cameahwait.

Go 1.0 mile west of Boysen Reservoir to a right turn onto Bear Lake Road which you will follow to Lake Cameahwait. The road to this lake is paved. After 8.6 miles turn right for 1.8 miles. The 250-acre lake is on your left. The lake is in the Game and Fish Department's Sand Mesa Wildlife Habitat Management Unit. Lake Cameahwait regularly has a lot of ducks and grebes. In the fall I once saw 20 Common Loons here, the largest concentration I have seen in the state. (However, Lake DeSmet has had lots more.) Beyond the lake, the road turns to gravel and leads down to an arm of Boysen Reservoir where more ducks can be observed.

Going back to US 26, turn right and continue on the road for 2.6 miles to State Route 134, Missouri Valley Road. Turn right here and drive for 17.9 miles to the well-marked road on the left for Ocean Lake at Dickerson Park. (You will know that you have only 2.5 miles to go when you pass the Midvale Store.) Go in here, bear right at 0.2 mile, and take the next right (at a sign) at 0.5 mile to Dickinson Recreation Site, which overlooks the northeast corner of the lake at another 0.3 mile. There is camping here. In spring migration there are lots of Red-breasted Mergansers and Horned Grebes in breeding plumage on the lake, particularly in April. Next, go back to where you turned into Dickinson Recreation Site and turn right. This leads southward after 0.7 mile to the irrigation canal out of Ocean Lake. This is another good overlook. Keep out of the next area if it the ground is wet; the road can be difficult. Cross the bridge over the canal, and turn left immediately. In about 0.8 mile the track leads to a place to park. Marie Adams says that if you leave your car here and follow the embankment off to the left, you will see a small pond

Marsh at Ocean Lake boat ramp   Paul J. Baicich

that is good in spring. She has had Oldsquaw and Barrow's Goldeneye here, as well as the common ducks. The meadow beyond the parking area usually has Sandhill Cranes and, on occasion, Whooping Cranes. Often there are Long-billed Curlews in season, also. The track continues around on the right-hand side of the meadow. On the flats to the right after you get by the meadow there have been Snowy Plovers. Then retrace your way back to Route 134. (Or you can wend your way on various tracks eastward for a mile or more and come out on Eight Mile Road, turn left, and end up at the Midvale Store.) After getting back to Route 134 turn west (left) to reach the headquarters of the Game and Fish on your left. This is 2.4 miles on Route 134 if you returned via the road to Dickinson Recreation Site. A short drive will take you down to the Game and Fish boat ramp. The big marsh on your right has both Sora and Virginia Rails. There is a big colony of Yellow-headed Blackbirds and Marsh Wrens here. Short-eared Owls have nested on the left and can be seen at dusk over the nearby meadows fairly often. You can never tell what you might see here. Sam Fitton had a Red Phalarope in November 1988 here. There was a Parasitic Jaeger out on the lake at that time, also.

Go back to Route 134, turn left again for 1.0 mile to the first road on your left, Shady Lane. This road goes straight south for 2.0 miles. If the ground is dry, and if you have good clearance and springs, you can continue straight ahead to the road to Long Point. If you don't go straight ahead, turn right for 1.0 mile on Summerhill Road, and then to the left for 1.0 mile on Gabe's Road, and then left again on Long Point Road. There is a sign here for Long Point. Take this road 0.7 mile, which brings you toward the shore of the lake. Bear left through the grove of trees and follow the road to Long Point. This point sticks out in the lake for one mile. From the point there are excellent views of the lake. On the left side one can usually find Common Loons in migration and in the fall sometimes Pacific Loons as well. On the right side in spring there are lots of noisy Western Grebes and often a few Clark's Grebes with their single-note calls. Directly across the lake from Long Point is a sizable colony of Western Grebes. Clark's also nest here.

You can get to the grebe colony by going two miles back to the sign for Long Point and then turn left on Gabe's Road for 0.5 mile and again turn left onto Angler Road. (What you are doing is going around the lake on the road closest to the shore. All turns are at right angles.) Follow Angler Road; it turns right and left to its end at 2.5 miles. Turn right onto Ocean Lake Road for 1.7 miles to a right turn. Don't make this turn; go straight ahead on Buckhorn Flats Road over a little rise for another 1.4 miles to a sign marked *Ocean Lake Wildlife Habitat Management Unit.* Drive down this road, bearing right after 0.9 mile, to a parking lot another 0.8 mile farther down. If there is a closed gate, open and close it on the way down. When wet, this road is bottomless gumbo. Stay away. However, it is rarely wet. You are now on the south side of Ocean Lake, and the reedy estuary on the left has the mixed Western and Clark's Grebes colony, but it is mostly Westerns. There are Forster's Terns nesting here as well as Double-crested Cormorants on offshore islets. American White Pelicans used to nest here and may well do so again in the future. The Game and Fish Department has found too much turbidity (suspended solids) in the lake for a good fishery. They also found that only two streams of irrigation run-off were providing the turbidity. By putting small dams in these streams they have cut down on this problem and the lake is improving. It should be a good fishery again. Some of the catch has been rough fish like carp, which fishermen don't like but pelicans love. There are some California Gulls and Sandhill Cranes nesting here at Ocean Lake. This is also a staging area in the fall and spring for cranes. In the past an occasional Whooping Crane was seen here. In 1985 I saw a Whooper in May and again in October here.

Now you can return to Route 134. A good way to get there is to go back to the turn that I warned you not to take. That's the Ocean Lake Road and Buckhorn Flats intersection. Turn left (south) on Ocean Lake Road for 0.6 mile to US 26. Turn right for 4.7 miles to Route 133, and right again for 4.0 miles to Route 134.

To the west will be the Sand Buttes, which is private land so you have to ask permission to be there. There is a covey of Chukar on these buttes. If you go 1.0 mile on the dirt road and skirt the Buttes, you will see a place on the right belonging to Rick Klein. He is a nice fellow and knows a lot of birds. He owns a big piece of the Buttes. November seems to be the best time to see the Chukars. From mid-June to mid-August it is very hard to find them. In any case, check in with Rick first.

You can then go back south on Route 133 and join US 26 again.

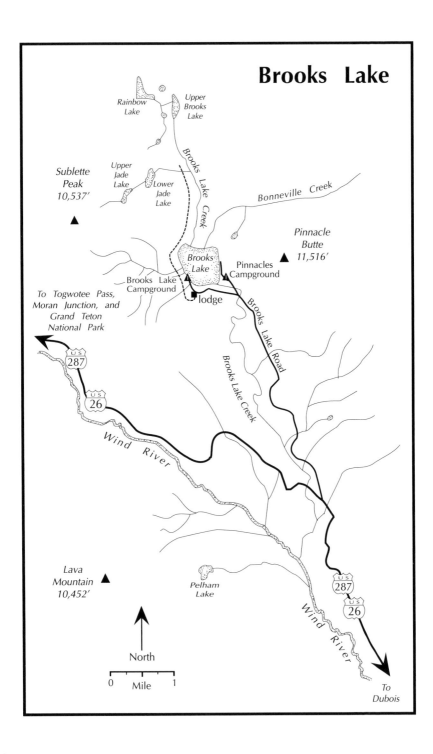

Brooks Lake

Rainbow
Lake

Upper
Brooks
Lake

Brooks Lake Creek

Bonneville Creek

Sublette
Peak
10,537'

Upper
Jade
Lake

Lower
Jade
Lake

Pinnacle
Butte
11,516'

Brooks
Lake

Pinnacles
Campground

Brooks Lake
Campground

lodge

Brooks Lake Road

To Togwotee Pass,
Moran Junction, and
Grand Teton
National Park

Brooks Lake Creek

US
287

US
26

Wind River

Lava
Mountain
10,452'

Pelham
Lake

US
287

US
26

Wind River

North

0   Mile   1

To
Dubois

13. BROOKS LAKE

Brooks Lake is located in the Shoshone National Forest. Shoshone was the first National Forest established in the country (created in 1891 by President Benjamin Harrison). It contains over 2.5 million acres; there are five designated Wilderness Areas within it. Shoshone National Forest is large enough so that we shall encounter it again in the last chapter of this book.

Brooks Lake Road is off US 26, 22.5 miles west from the center of Dubois. When you come to a curve to the left on US 26, Brooks Lake Road is off to the right and well-marked. It is a good Forest Service dirt road leading 4.3 miles up to the lake. At one time there was a famous dude ranch, the Diamond G, at this site.

Just as you arrive at Brooks Lake, Pinnacles Campground is on the right. Drive over the bridge into the campground area. It has a steep old-growth forested hillside on the side facing the lake. If you climb the hillside, you should find Three-toed Woodpeckers. You should look for mountain birds such as Williamson's Sapsucker, Hairy Woodpecker, Gray Jay, Clark's Nutcracker, Common Raven, Mountain Chickadee, nuthatches, White-crowned Sparrow, Pine Siskin, Pine Grosbeak, and Cassin's Finch.

At the far side of the lake, 0.6 mile beyond the Pinnacles Campground turn-off, there is a fine lodge which maintains a hummingbird feeder. We are virtually certain that they have had Magnificent Hummingbirds in August. Usually they will have Broad-tailed Hummingbirds; sometimes there are Rufous and Calliope Hummingbirds, too.

Some 0.3 mile after the lodge is the Brooks Lake Campground and a boat ramp. From here you can scope the lake. Around the lake you may find Osprey, California Gull, and Spotted Sandpiper, among other birds.

There are other places in Wyoming, easier places, to find these birds, but Brooks Lake is a fine place to stop nonetheless. Because Brooks Lake is high, the snow doesn't melt out until the last of June. Some 7.4 miles beyond the Brooks Lake turn-off on US 26 is Togwotee Pass, crossing the Continental Divide at an elevation of 9,658 feet. Near this area Boreal Owl has been reported, but you would need to be very lucky to find one.

From here on you can continue on US 26 to Grand Teton National Park. You will experience stupendous views of the Tetons. (You can reach the areas covered by the text in the next chapter from Moose Junction or from Jackson.)

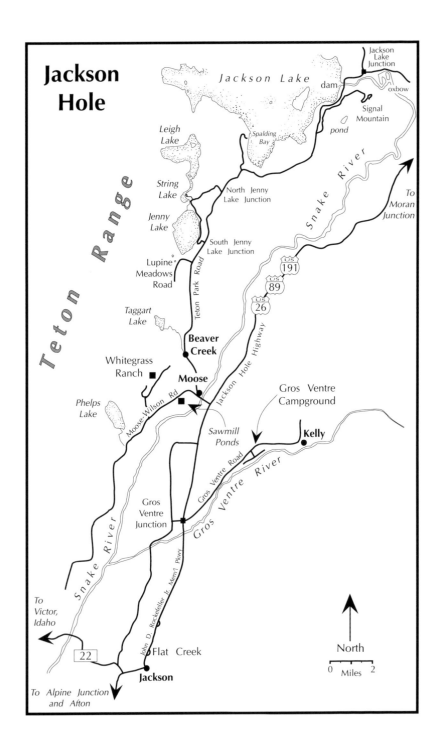

14. JACKSON HOLE

This is undoubtedly one of the most beautiful spots in America. Grand Teton National Park, established in 1929, used to be a small affair of just the Tetons themselves, excluding the valley floor. The Rockefeller family has made it into a great National Park. Many of the local people fought its establishment tooth and nail, but it has made them all millionaires. The floor of the valley was rescued from development by the purchase of private lands for their inclusion in a stunning national treasure. The average tourist doesn't realize how much he owes to the Rockefellers.

In 1926, Horace Albright, then superintendent of Yellowstone National Park, with the assistance of local preservationists, got John D. Rockefeller, Jr. interested in buying up the lands around Jackson Hole in order to turn them over to the Park Service. There was much fury and lengthy political fighting involved, with Grand Teton National Park finally securing the valley floor in 1950. In all, 52 square miles were given to the US by John D. Rockefeller, Jr. Although there are some inholdings left, most of Jackson Hole is now National Park or National Elk Refuge or National Forest. The small amount of private land remaining around and south of the town of Jackson has been spoiled by development, with the value of land going through the stratosphere. We have lost a few Bald Eagle aeries and Elk wintering-grounds, but almost everything to the north is preserved. Due to the beauty of the area and winter skiing, increasing numbers of people are retiring here, hence the population pressure.

You must remember that a "hole" is essentially a valley. This impressive valley varies in width from 6 to 12 miles for some 60 miles north to south. Jackson Hole is bounded on the west by the Teton Range, on the north by National Forest and the high ground of Yellowstone National Park, on the east by the Gros Ventre Range (scuttlebutt has it that there was a Gros Ventre ladies club in Jackson until somebody learned some French and found out what it meant), and on the south by the Snake River Canyon. When considering the Great Parks of Wyoming, Yellowstone has some interesting birds, but, birdwise, Jackson Hole is the place to be.

Here are some places to check out in Jackson Hole:

1. Starting from the center square of the town of Jackson, drive north on the combined US Highway 26/89/191, the only route north through the Hole. On the north edge of town you drive over Flat Creek, which drains the

National Elk Refuge (Box C, Jackson, WY 83001; phone: 307/733-9212). It is fed by warm springs, so it stays open all year. In winter huge numbers of Elk congregate here and are fed by the government. Just beyond the bridge there is a parking turn-out on the right. This is an excellent place to see Trumpeter Swan, Barrow's Goldeneye, and Ring-necked Duck. Trumpeters congregate here in the fall, starting in September, and usually nest here, so there are almost always at least a few in this location. Barrow's don't nest here. They like small ponds throughout the Hole and Yellowstone. The Ring-neck is probably the most common duck nesting in Jackson Hole. At this first stop there is also quite an assortment of more common ducks.

2. Next go up US 26/89/191 for 2.5 miles to a turn-out on the right just before you go up the hill and out of the Flat Creek drainage and the National Elk Refuge. Here one can usually find Sandhill Cranes raising young in summer; sometimes you will see Long-billed Curlews here.

3. Drive north on US 26/89/191 3.5 more miles to Gros Ventre (locally pronounced *Gro-vont*) Junction. As soon as you are out of the Elk Refuge you are in Grand Teton National Park. (Park Headquarters, Moose, WY, 83012-0170; phone: 307/733-2880.) Though you are officially in the Park, this routing will not take you through the entrance gate—and fee collection—until it takes you toward Taggart Lake (#6 in the text).

Take the paved road to the right toward Kelly for 4.5 miles to the Gros Ventre Campground. The campground is a good place for Cordilleran Flycatchers. The most common *Empidonax* in the Hole is the Dusky, found in aspen forests throughout the valley. Red-naped Sapsucker is particularly common here in the Gros Ventre Campground with its *ratatat-tat*, and it is

Trumpeter Swan
CHarles H. Gambill

common throughout the Hole. If you are camping, Gros Ventre Campground is attractive but has plenty of mosquitoes. Next go back to US 26/89/191.

4. Turn right and go north on US 26/89/191 for 5.3 miles to the left turn to Moose. You will go by the Jackson Hole airport, the only major airport in a National Park and very controversial. The sagebrush which you have been driving through is home for Sage Grouse, Sage Thrasher, Vesper Sparrow, and Brewer's Sparrow, among other birds. If it is early spring, you may be able to visit a Sage Grouse lek in the vicinity of the airport. (Ask about tours in April run by the Park Service at the Park headquarters ahead.)

After you turn left for Moose, go just beyond the bridge over the Snake River to the Grand Teton Park Headquarters. You can pick up a free bird checklist, a free backpacking permit if you wish, and other information on the Park, its potential hazards, and how to get around. *Birds of Grand Teton National Park* by Bert Raynes is available there. Sometimes the Park personnel will also have information on the location of Great Gray Owls. However, most of the people on duty have interests and training other than birds and are of little help. Beyond headquarters to the west immediately turn left onto Moose-Wilson Road. Go 0.9 mile to the Sawmill Ponds on the left. It is an overlook. It often has Trumpeter Swans and almost always Ring-necked Duck, American Wigeon, Green-winged Teal, Mallard, and Barrow's Goldeneye. Very often there are Olive-sided Flycatchers on the tops of the huge Douglas-firs beyond the ponds. One can walk south along the top of the bank and see all of the ponds. The hike is about one-quarter mile or more.

5. Continue on Moose-Wilson Road for two miles to the first road on the right. This is called Death Canyon Trailhead Road, and it is paved. It goes to Whitegrass Ranch, which has recently changed from a private inholding to Park property. It was a dude ranch on the edge of a large natural meadow with some cows on it. The ranch buildings and cows are gone and the Elk have taken over in a big way—not that there weren't plenty of Elk before. The number of cows was controlled, but the Elk are a different matter. They may well eat themselves out of house and home. In controlling Elk, the Park authorities have had their hands tied, with disastrous consequences to the vegetation.

Some inholdings have been sold to the Park Service with the former owners retaining life-time leases. This one was turned over to the Park on the death of the operator. The road skirts the left edge of the meadow and ends up at the Whitegrass Ranger Station. Just before you get to it, there is a parking area and trailhead. One can hear Ruffed Grouse drumming here through May and June and into July. Park your car and go up the trail less than one-quarter mile to where it meets another trail at right angles. If you turn left up Death Canyon, you can hike about 7 miles to Alaska Basin. During early August Alaska Basin has perhaps the most gorgeous display of wildflowers in the

Rocky Mountain region. The whole basin is almost solid in bright colors. There has been a marauding Black Bear in the lower reaches of Death Canyon, so don't plan to camp there.

For birds, turn right onto the Valley Trail. For the first mile this pathway skirts the face of the Tetons and the Whitegrass meadow. The trail runs through the forest, but the meadow is close by. In September and early October, before there is much snow, the Elks bugle in this area. Their numbers and volume sometime approach near-bedlam and deafening levels of sound. I never thought this was possible. You may also meet Moose on the trail.

The trail goes through a mixed growth with lots of Ruffed Grouse. They act very differently from the eastern Ruffed Grouse, which gets up with a bang and puts a tree between you and itself instantly. These birds walk away growling and grousing, resenting your intrusion into their domain. This is good Great Gray Owl country, and at dusk I have found a Northern Pygmy-Owl here. Western Tanagers are very common. Look here also for Three-toed and Hairy Woodpeckers. The Valley Trail has another advantage: it is little used. Perhaps the first couple of miles are the best, but you can walk through to Lupine Meadows, viewing Dark-eyed (Oregon) Juncos, Chipping Sparrows, Yellow-rumped Warblers, Ruby-crowned Kinglets, and other songbirds. Watch for Williamson's Sapsucker, too. You pass Bradley Lake and parts of the Beaver Creek Fire of 1985, but a better approach to this fire-site is just ahead in the text.

Great Gray Owls have nested for at least 50 years in an area bounded by the Moose-Wilson Road on the southeast, the Taggart Lake Trail on the north, the Valley Trail on the west, the Whitegrass Ranger Station on the south, and the Teton Park Road on the east for at least 50 years, but they are still hard to find.

A fine wilderness walk that goes right through this area starts at the old entrance to the Whitegrass Ranch. There is a trail on the right (now blocked off) that skirts the Whitegrass meadow on the south side, crosses a bog, and continues east for perhaps four miles to the old headquarters on Beaver Creek where most of the Park personnel now live. I have seen Great Gray Owls a number of times in this region. Sometimes in the day they give out low hoots, enabling one to locate them. It is best to start from the Whitegrass end because the Beaver Creek end is not well marked. If you wear a red hat, beware of hummingbirds. They will come up to within an inch or so of your face to investigate. These are mostly Broad-tails. You will encounter most of the common birds of the Park on this walk.

6. Return to Moose and enter the Park in the proper way, passing through the entrance gate 0.3 mile north of Moose on the Teton Park Road. (The $10 vehicle admission that you pay for Grand Teton is good for both Grand Teton and Yellowstone for seven days. An annual permit—the Golden Eagle, which

is good for all National Parks and many National Wildlife Refuges—is only $25. The entrance fee is charged from May 1 to October 1.) Some 2.7 miles from the entrance, just after you pass the Beaver Creek Service area, stop at the Taggart Lake parking area for the Beaver Creek fire-site of 1985. The trail enters the burn on the right. A walk of one mile or so up this trail has yielded Three-toed Woodpeckers and usually Black-backed as well. As you may know, a recent fire almost guarantees both Three-toed and Black-backed Woodpeckers in the Jackson Hole and Yellowstone areas, but Three-toed is usually more common. The trail works to the right from the parking lot. You will find the emergent forest well-started. Even if you miss Black-backed and Three-toed Woodpeckers, there are usually Red-naped Sapsuckers and Dusky Flycatchers near the approach to the fire-site. Olive-sided Flycatchers, Western Wood-Pewees, Mountain Bluebirds, and Yellow-rumped Warblers are in the area, too. Check the willows for Calliope Hummingbirds.

7. Now continue up Teton Park Road 1.6 miles to Lupine Meadows Road, just short of the South Jenny Lake Junction. Lupine Meadows Road is a left turn down and across Cottonwood Creek, the outlet for Jenny Lake. The road is unpaved. Follow along the signs and end up at the parking area at the south end of the meadow. There will be a lot of cars here and perhaps some rugged climbers. This is the Lupine Meadows Trailhead. It is the principal trail to Garnet Canyon, the approach for climbing the Grand Teton. The first 100 yards of the trail are excellent for both Three-toed Woodpeckers and Williamson's Sapsuckers. This is another place where I have seen Northern Pygmy-Owl during the day. Olive-sided Flycatchers and Western Tanagers abound here. The first mile or so of the trail is worthwhile; it starts to get steep after that but still follows good bird habitat. Pine Grosbeaks, Red Crossbills, and Dusky Flycatchers are common.

Early one morning in early August before the climbers got on this trail, I was walking along and met a family of Blue Grouse. I froze. The hen sat preening on a rock about five yards away while six chicks rummaged around on the forest floor and found some berries, which they quickly ate. One chick became intrigued with my shoelaces, but after a very close and careful look it made the right choice. The shoelaces were not edible, and the chick wandered off. In the meantime a Mule Deer came down the trail, halting about 15 yards away. I guess it had never seen a human that stayed still before. Finally, the hen marched her crew off, and the deer made a detour.

After visiting the south end of Lupine Meadows, go to the north end where there is a little parking place and a trail that leads north a short way to the trail around Jenny Lake. Bear left onto the Jenny Lake trail. You are now in MacGillivray's Warbler country. This species is very common on the south and east sides of Jenny Lake from June 1 to the middle of September. Most of the birds mentioned for the Valley Trail are here, too, but particularly Williamson's Sapsucker. A nice walk is along this trail around Jenny Lake to

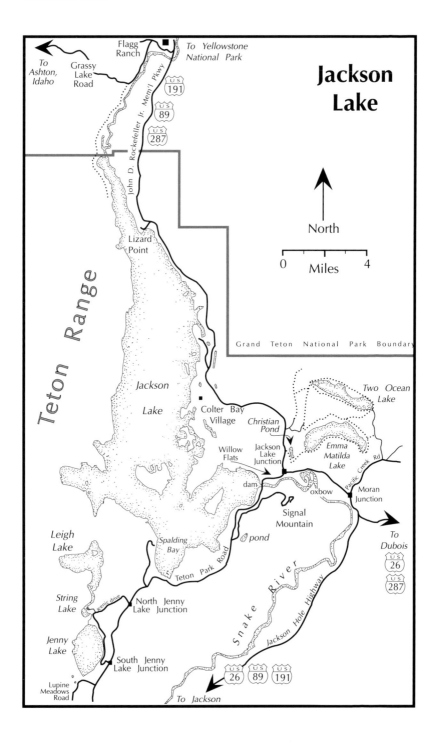

Hidden Falls, a beautiful cascade on the west side of Jenny Lake. There are usually Golden-crowned Kinglets in the tops of huge Douglas-firs just before you get to Hidden Falls. Look for American Dippers near the falls. The only drawback to this trail is that horses use it for part of the way. One can take a much longer walk up Cascade Canyon beyond Hidden Falls. Lots of tourists take this walk. At the west end of the canyon the trail and Cascade Creek split. The left fork goes to Alaska Basin while the right fork leads to Lake Solitude. Above the roar of Cascade Creek at the split, I have heard the beautiful voice of a Winter Wren a number of times, but not consistently. They have nested just up the Alaska Basin fork. The tourists mostly head for Lake Solitude, so much so that the locals call it Lake Multitude.

8. Backtrack out of Lupine Meadows and turn left onto Teton Park Road, which goes north 0.5 mile past the South Jenny Lake turn. If you want to see tourists *en masse,* turn in. Jenny Lake headquarters is the most popular place in Grand Teton National Park. It has a ranger station and a tents-only campground that is difficult to get into because of the competition for it. The scenery is magnificent. It used to be in a grove of superb trees, but a violent windstorm in 1977 blew many of them down. They are slowly growing back.

Keep north on the Teton Park Road 4.4 miles and turn left onto Jenny Lake Scenic Drive, a one-way road south to String Lake. The views from this road are breathtaking. In 1.5 miles you will reach the String Lake parking and picnic area; turn right to the nice picnic ground. There are often Gray Jays here, and they may help themselves to your food. Continue on Jenny Lake Road. Again there are spectacular views, but also good places for Williamson's Sapsuckers. Hermit Thrushes can be heard, as well as the more common Swainson's. There are MacGillivray's Warblers along the shore of Jenny Lake. The road eventually takes you back to the Teton Park Road.

Turn left (north) and go about 1.3 miles beyond the Jenny Lake loop to a gravel road on the left that goes to Spalding Bay and the area of the Mystic Isle fire of 1981. One can still find Three-toed Woodpeckers here although it is getting more difficult to do so. The young forest is well started. Williamson's Sapsuckers can be found here, also. In fact, Williamson's are common from the Valley Trail through the Mystic Isle fire area and can be expected anywhere in the area. The Three-toeds are most common in the first year after a burn and then slowly diminish. If the bark is burned off a tree, they are not interested, but in a fire many trees retain their bark although they have been killed by the heat. I thought that after the fires of 1988 in Yellowstone National Park the Three-toeds would be sucked north into Yellowstone, but this has not been the case. However, with the National Park Service rescinding the excellent "let it burn" policy, from now on finding a fresh burn is going to be hard. We will be back to the old days of handling artificial forests. Of course, one can find Three-toeds in a non-burned forest, but there they are much fewer and farther between. The upper echelon people of the National Park Service management seems to concern themselves with catering to the tourists and forgets that their organic act requires them to preserve the wildlife and its habitat. If you meet any Park personnel, remind them to support the "let it burn" policy.

9. Return to the Teton Park Road, turn left (north), and go 5.6 miles to the Signal Mountain turn to the right. The top of Signal Mountain offers the most superb view of the Teton Range. About 0.5 mile from the turn-off there is a pond on the right where Great Gray Owl has been seen sometimes and where Barrow's Goldeneyes usually nest. From the pond, it is an additional 3.5 miles to the top of Signal Mountain (El. 7,593 ft.). From early July to the middle of August there are often Rufous Hummingbirds in the open area near the top, as well as the local Broad-tails.

10. Return to Teton Park Road and continue north to Jackson Lake Dam. There is a turn-out on the right, and with a scope you might just see Trumpeter Swans and American White Pelicans on the north shore. Beyond the dam you cross Willow Flats for a mile. Here there are extensive willow thickets and marshy grass meadows. Sandhill Cranes, American Bitterns, and Soras all nest here. Between late May and mid-July, Willow Flycatchers can almost always be heard morning and evening, as well as Fox Sparrows. Sometimes there are Northern Waterthrushes and Calliope Hummingbirds. For many years the Calliopes were here regularly, but for the last few years they have been missing. It is such an excellent place for them that they ought to be back before long. These feisty mites sit on the topmost dead twigs and harass *all* the bigger birds that come by. That means *everything*. Wilson's Warblers are common here. The problem with birding this spot is the heavy traffic that can pass by here.

11. Just beyond Willow Flats is Jackson Lake Junction. To visit a similar marsh without the continual roar of heavy traffic turn right for 2.8 miles and then turn left onto Pacific Creek Road. You will pass on the way the well-known Oxbow Bend, which usually has a few American White Pelicans and Trumpeter Swans. Also, look for Moose browsing on the willows across the lake. When you turn left onto Pacific Creek Road, drive up this road 2.1 miles to a marked left turn for Two Ocean Lake. As you go up to Two Ocean Lake, there is a big marsh on your right. This marsh has Sandhill Cranes, Calliope Hummingbirds, Willow Flycatchers, Fox Sparrows, and Lincoln's Sparrows. The Wyoming-nesting Sandhills are all the Greater subspecies. In going up to Two Ocean Lake, a distance of 3 miles, at first one goes through a wood which has a Moose and Elk wallow-and-lick at the far end. Next you reach a meadow; in late July or early August when the larkspurs are in bloom, it can be alive with hummingbirds—Calliope, Rufous, and Broad-tailed.

Two Ocean Lake is a great place. The far end of the lake almost always has Trumpeter Swans. Great Gray Owls have often been seen in the vicinity. Ruffed Grouse are common. Western Tanagers, Pine Grosbeaks, and Cassin's

Finches should be seen in the trees surrounding the lake. From the parking lot a three-quarter-mile well-marked trail to the south takes you to Emma Matilda Lake, which also has Trumpeter Swans. The trail along Emma Matilda can be rewarding. Three-toed Woodpeckers can be seen often, and Red-naped Sapsuckers are common. This trail is not often traveled by hikers, but it is used by Moose, and even bears, so take care. To the north of the parking lot you will find a trail that goes around Two Ocean Lake. About a mile or more down the north side Sam Fitton found Hammond's Flycatcher singing and probably nesting in June in the first grove of conifers encountered.

12. Go back to Jackson Lake Junction and drive north on the John D. Rockefeller, Jr., Memorial Parkway. Within a mile you go by Christian Pond on the right, opposite Jackson Lake Lodge. Christian Pond has had a nesting pair of Trumpeter Swans for many years. *Because of the potential disturbance, please remain on the trail on the west side of the pond at least 300 feet from its edge, and obey all posted warnings.* About 0.5 mile north of Christian Pond on the right there is a little road that goes to a parking area and trailhead. A short distance up the steep trail Bert Raynes of Jackson showed me a Great Gray Owl's nest on a snag. These snags (and there are dozens in this vicinity) are big trees that have been broken off about 20 to 30 feet above the ground and are favorite places for Great Grays to nest although by no means the only sites they choose. This trail is a fine wilderness walk and connects with the Two Ocean Lake trail as well as the one around Emma Matilda Lake. These are longer walks. It is about a 10-mile walk around Emma Matilda.

Next on the Parkway, going north about 5 miles one comes to the Colter Bay Village on the left. This is a Park installation that has just about everything. At times the Park staff here knows where to find Great Gray Owls. Traveling north again on the Parkway for about an additional 20 miles you will come to Flagg Ranch, administered by the Park Service. There is a road here—first paved, then dirt—the Grassy Lake Road, that goes west to Ashton, Idaho. This is sometimes called the Ashton Road. About 4.4 miles on this road you come to a trailhead. This is a fine wilderness trail that leads south to Jackson Lake and connects with the Webb Canyon trail in the northern Tetons where there has been a hacking-station for the release of Peregrine Falcons. This trail is less used and can be depended on for Three-toed Woodpeckers particularly since there was a fire on it in 1987. Getting onto the Grassy Lake Road may be tricky, though. The best way is to go north on the Parkway 0.5 mile past the Flagg Ranch and turn left onto a paved road to a campground. This route circles around the Flagg Ranch and ends up as the Grassy Lake Road.

If you follow the Parkway north just a few miles, you will find the South Entrance to Yellowstone Park.

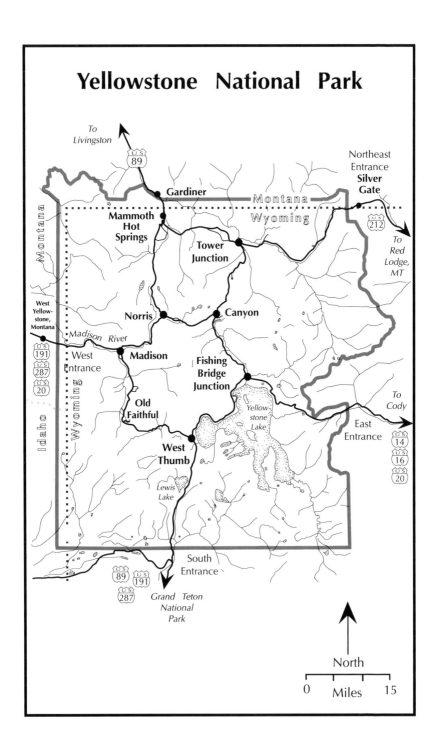

Yellowstone National Park

To
Livingston

US 89

Gardiner

Montana

Wyoming

Northeast
Entrance
Silver
Gate

US 212

To
Red
Lodge,
MT

Montana

Mammoth
Hot
Springs

Tower
Junction

West
Yellow-
stone,
Montana

Norris

Canyon

Madison River

US 191
US 287
US 20

West
Entrance

Madison

Fishing
Bridge
Junction

To
Cody

Old
Faithful

Yellow-
stone
Lake

East
Entrance

US 14
US 16
US 20

West
Thumb

Idaho

Wyoming

Lewis
Lake

89 US 191

US 287

South
Entrance

Grand Teton
National
Park

North

0   Miles   15

15. YELLOWSTONE NATIONAL PARK

by W. Edward Harper

One of the world's greatest natural wonders, Yellowstone became the world's first national park on March 1, 1872. Fur-trapper and explorer John Colter is credited with being the first white man to visit and describe the Yellowstone region. The description made of his 1807 visit included vast mountains with steaming geysers, bubbling mud-pots, boiling pools, and abundant wildlife. Since then, and especially with the establishment of the Park, millions have come to experience the 2.2-million-acre Yellowstone National Park. (Park Headquarters, PO Box 168, Yellowstone, WY 82190; phone: 307/344-7381.) But in spite of Yellowstone's long history and renowned status, its avian community has been overlooked until recent times. When compared to most other national parks in the United States, relatively little is known about the seasonal distribution and abundance of bird life in Yellowstone or how it has changed in over a century. Indeed, it is a surprise to many that more is known about the avian community of Big Bend National Park, established only in 1944 in Texas and visited by far fewer people, than is known about Yellowstone.

Clearly, it has been the thermal features, geological phenomena, and dramatic scenery together with the dazzling presence of large mammals that have long been the primary pursuits of park visitors. Responding to these interests, park administration, rangers, and interpreters, whose work often involves considerable "people management," have almost neglected Yellowstone's interesting bird life. Until recently, the few earnest attempts to list and to quantify the general distribution and abundance of bird life were hampered by a paucity of firm information.

Interest in the avian community is now awakening, however, and a number of bird species are being seriously monitored. Much of this increased interest is a result of the widespread wildfires of 1988 that seriously changed the face of Yellowstone. Undoubtedly, the avian community of Yellowstone will undergo a change as well. This alteration will most likely be one of enhancement, however, due to the renewed diversity and vigorous growth resulting from the burn. (For another view, see Oliver Scott's comments on page 102.) Birders visiting Yellowstone have a very real opportunity to document these changes and to add significantly to the understanding of the park's avifauna. Birders are encouraged to take field notes on significant numbers, behavior, and distribution of birds in and around Yellowstone, while being careful to document unusual sightings with written descriptions and/or photographs. Completed notes should be sent to: Research Office, PO Box 168, Yellowstone National Park, WY 82190.

HELPFUL PUBLICATIONS

As one begins to explore the avifauna of Yellowstone, a very useful book for birdfinding in the Park is *Birds of Yellowstone* by Terry McEneaney, published in 1988. This excellent publication features an informative habitat-guide to the birds of Yellowstone National Park and contains many maps for prime birding areas throughout the Park. The book's checklist of birds uses bar-graphs to depict relative abundance throughout the year and also lists the chances of observing each species.

A useful Yellowstone National Park bird checklist can be obtained at all Visitor Centers. A helpful booklet, though somewhat outdated, is the *Birds of Yellowstone and Grand Teton Parks* by Dick Follett.

WHERE TO GO FOR BIRDS IN YELLOWSTONE

Although exploration of Yellowstone's avifauna might invite one to bird all major regions of the Park, time is a limiting factor for most visitors. Therefore, the following information is written with the typical visitor in mind who simply wishes to see as many birds as possible during an all-too-brief visit to Yellowstone, while also trying to take in all the majesty and awe of this great park.

Given a map of Yellowstone, imagine a line drawn diagonally across the map from the northwest corner down across to the southeast corner. Generally speaking, the best birding in Yellowstone is found northeast this diagonal. Included within this choice region are notable areas consisting of the Lamar Valley, Mount Washburn, the Mammoth Hot Springs vicinity, the famous Hayden Valley, and portions of Yellowstone Lake. The vast excluded area below the drawn diagonal does indeed also have some fine birding, and, since the 1988 fires, it also offers a splendid opportunity for exploration. Although much of this area experienced some degree of burn, from slight to severe, that which was untouched forms extensive stands of climax forest dominated by Douglas-fir and Lodgepole Pine. Here there is less diversity of both plant and animal life. Therefore, one's limited time is best spent in the rejuvenating areas associated with the burn. It will be interesting to see how many Black-backed Woodpeckers and Three-toed Woodpeckers invade these areas. Be advised that it is southwest of the drawn diagonal where one encounters the majority of Yellowstone's active thermal basins and their associated geysers and boiling cauldrons. Here, too, is the most famous of all geysers, Old Faithful. Thronging to see it are the vast crowds of visitors, particular in summer. Everyone, of course, wants to see and should see Old Faithful, but if it is the fascination of birds that highlights your interests, you will soon leave the congested parking lots of Old Faithful to scamper back across the drawn diagonal to explore the best birding spots. Here is where one also finds the best viewing of mammals within Yellowstone. (First-time Yellowstone visitors should also realize that each side of our drawn diagonal encompasses an area larger than the state of Rhode Island.)

TIME OF YEAR AND WEATHER

For the best diversity of species at the peak of activity, early June to early July is the prime time to bird Yellowstone. Also, migration from mid-August to late October can be a productive time. From mid-July to mid-August, when the greatest numbers of visitors descend upon Yellowstone, birding is actually rather slow since the birds have stopped singing and many species are in molt. The weather is very erratic in this high plateau country, and cold snaps frequently occur. Adequate, **warm** clothing is a must along with appropriate footwear such as boots. It is prudent to bring along raingear. Hats, gloves, and a jacket are most welcome items of clothing for any time of year when the weather turns cold. June is often wet with either rain or snow, and August, although drier, often has freezing nights. The weather is almost certain to change radically from day to day.

In winter most roads in Yellowstone are closed to wheeled vehicles, the Mammoth Hot Springs to Cooke City, Montana, route being the major exception. This route is good for winter viewing of Elk, Buffalo, and other big game along with scavengers such as Coyotes, Common Ravens, and Black-billed Magpies. Bald Eagle is the most likely bird of prey to be encountered in winter, but occasionally Northern Goshawk, Rough-legged Hawk, and Golden Eagle are reported.

Many people visiting Yellowstone in winter delight in traveling by snowmobile from West Yellowstone, Montana, to Old Faithful. Reservations can be made for the trip, which takes visitors over the buried route of the highway. Although it can be bitter cold at this time of year, it is a fascinating way to see Yellowstone. Trumpeter Swans, Canada Geese, and a few species of ducks can be found along the open water-courses between icy stretches of river. Seeing Elk, Moose, and Buffalo in a glistening winter setting of steaming geysers affords a unique experience.

Looking at the Yellowstone Fires of 1988

The spring of 1988 was very dry and June more so with the high winds which come with droughts. The fire danger was probably higher than it had ever been within memory. From tree-ring evidence and historical record we know that there had been major fires in the Park area in the 1690s, the 1740s, the 1790s, and the 1860s. In 1988 there were to be multiple forest fires in Yellowstone National Park.

These fires of 1988 received worldwide attention and "touched" at least 44 percent of the Park's 2.2 million acres. (The figure of 44 percent means a percentage of all of the Park, including lakes, rivers, and mountain-tops. If you consider only forested areas, about 65 percent was burned. One of the fires—the Clover-Mist Fire—started from lightning in June, burned out the central part of the Park, and extended on a huge front over the Absaroka Mountains on the east border of the Park onto National Forest lands. The Forest Service put it out in early September. Another fire—the North Fork-Wolf Lake Fire—that swept from the southwestern to the northern parts of the Park, started as a man-made fire outside the Park in Idaho. Firefighters saved the Old Faithful Inn, but lost some of its smaller buildings. We should recall that the wonderful "let it burn" policy of the National Park Service said that the policy should not apply to man-made fires or to those that threatened installations. This one did both. After the fires, the "let it burn" policy was cancelled.

There are at least two different approaches to interpreting the fires. The Park Service tries to put a happy face on these events, minimizing the impact on the Park, and puts a positive spin on the issue of developing tree-and-habitat diversity in the Park.

However, many people have been critical of the National Park authorities. Many have regarded Yellowstone National Park as starting to differentiate from a "Lodgepole Pine desert" into fir and spruce in a normal forest succession. These great fires of 1988 turned the process back, giving us more Lodgepole Pine desert for the next 75 to 100 years. It has already started; the new forest is virtually all Lodgepole Pine.

Further, the Park authorities should have appreciated the situation and jumped on these fires before they got completely out of control. The authorities never did allow all the modern fire-fighting techniques to be used—like bulldozers. (Incidentally, the Forest Service did have big fires nearby, but put them out relatively soon.)

The "let it burn" policy is a wonderful one, but it does require some common sense. In early June if the forest is drier than ever before, accompanied with high winds, it is time to modify the rules (which were made to be modified). I feel that the Great Yellowstone Fires of 1988 were an unnecessary tragedy.

Oliver K. Scott

DESCRIPTIONS OF BIRDING AREAS

An excellent base centrally located for visiting prime birding areas is Tower Junction. Situated near the confluence of the Lamar and the Yellowstone Rivers, the location is also convenient for birding the Mount Washburn, the Mammoth Hot Springs, and the Lamar Valley areas. Visitors can find lodging at Roosevelt Lodge at Tower Junction, or camping-facilities are available only two miles up the road at Tower Falls Campground. Reservations are strongly recommended. Meals can be obtained at Roosevelt Lodge where visitors can still reminisce over the historical reminders of Theodore Roosevelt's stay in Yellowstone. Rough Rider cabins are available here which, although rustic, are modestly priced and will satisfy a limited budget.

Some of the interesting birds to be found around Roosevelt Lodge, include Williamson's Sapsucker and Hammond's Flycatcher. If you do decide to headquarter here, you may also find the area's past history of some interest.

On the way to Tower Junction from Grand Teton. *Since this description of birding Yellowstone National Park is based on stationing yourself at Tower Junction, you should review the birding possibilities on the way to Tower. (The seven points that follow should take you northward to Tower with a number of interesting stops. But farther on in this chapter you will come across a section entitled "Tower to Mount Washburn and the Hayden Valley" which will bring you **back** southward on the road between Tower and Canyon to cover some alternate stops on some of the overlapped route.) Assuming that you are approaching Yellowstone from Jackson Hole (the previous chapter in this book), you might consider the following:*

1. The $10 vehicle admission which you paid for at Grand Teton is good for both Grand Teton and Yellowstone for seven days. (An annual permit is only $25.)

2. It is 22 miles from the South Entrance to West Thumb. Just before you get to West Thumb, you can go into the Visitor Center at Grant Village. You can orient yourself here and, if you want, ask about Three-toed Woodpeckers that occur in the dead woods to the left before you get to West Thumb. Gail Allison, the head custodian there, is very knowledgeable about the woodpeckers.

3. From West Thumb on, be on the lookout for Williamson's Sapsuckers. Turn right at West Thumb and go east toward Fishing Bridge Junction (sometimes referred to as Lake Junction). After 7 miles you come to a large bay on the right which is part of Yellowstone Lake. Barrow's Goldeneye can be found here all summer, along with more common ducks, but usually not until July.

4. From West Thumb to Fishing Bridge Junction you frequently drive close to Yellowstone Lake. It often has interesting birds on it. In fact, you might see almost anything—little is known about the lake except in summer. In late fall, winter, and spring it has been inaccessible with closed roads and deep snow, though snowmobile access has been changing things. Red-necked Grebes have been reported on the lake, as well as many of our rarer ducks such as Oldsquaw and scoters.

5. After viewing the big bay, continue on to Fishing Bridge Junction, about 14 miles from the bay. At the junction you meet the road leading to the East Entrance to the park (which in turn becomes the combined US Highways 14/16/20) over Fishing Bridge. From here on you are in particularly good Great Gray Owl country.

6. Some 2.9 miles north on the road to Canyon Village you come to LeHardy Rapids, a location for Harlequin Ducks. There is parking space and a boardwalk down to the rapids. A byproduct of the boardwalk construction has been that many tourists use it expecting something spectacular. As a consequence, you should count yourself as being very lucky if you find Harlequin Ducks at this tourist stop. This shy species used to haul out on the rocks of the rapids and feed a little way downstream. Until the last week of June it was drakes and females mixed. Then the males left for the Pacific Ocean, and the females left to tend to their eggs. About the last week of July the females with young reappeared here and stayed until the first week of September. Occasionally Harlequins can still be seen here. If you give it a try, look carefully at an island just below the rapids and scan the far shore of the river particularly. You may have to settle for seeing California Gulls, which are frequently found loafing on the small islands in the river at the foot of the rapids. (The Park Service is currently studying the effects of the boardwalk on Harlequin Ducks.)

7. The road from Canyon westward toward Norris Junction is the best area in Yellowstone National Park to see Great Gray Owls in Yellowstone National Park. Early morning and particularly late in the day near dusk afford the best opportunities for finding this elusive "gray ghost." Drive west of Canyon Village on the road toward Norris Junction. Any of the large meadows ringed by trees like the one just west of Canyon Village should be carefully checked. Pull completely off the road at safe locations and scan the large dead snags or other good perches on which an owl might sit to watch and listen for Meadow Voles, a favorite prey item. Lots of patience is required along with a fair measure of luck. According to McEneaney's *Birds of Yellowstone*, fewer than 100 pairs of Great Gray Owls are believed to inhabit the Park. If you are lucky and find an owl, please take special care not to disturb this secretive species. When not disturbed or harassed, these spectacular birds will return to the same territory year after year, as long as the prey base is sufficient.

Blacktail Plateau Scenic Drive   Terry McEneaney

Tower Junction to Mammoth Hot Springs. Driving northwest toward Mammoth Hot Springs from Tower Junction, note your odometer reading and drive for a distance of 3 miles to Floating Island Lake. This small lake is located to the left (south) side of the road and should be checked for waterfowl. Lesser Scaup and Cinnamon Teal can be found here, as well as Yellow-headed Blackbirds. Moose frequently graze in this lake. At 3.7 miles from Tower Junction note the gravel road on the right (north) leading to the Hellroaring Creek Trailhead. The trail leads to a suspension bridge over the Yellowstone River. The strenuous 600-foot descent to the river is very steep, but the area can produce Blue Grouse for the hardy hiker. Although the area doesn't usually have many birds, the trail can lead one to excellent fishing. Osprey can often be seen flying along the river as it rushes through a steep canyon. Back along the main road once again, continue on through an area with much dead timber, which can attract woodpeckers. Keep alert for Three-toed Woodpeckers along this stretch. At 8.7 miles from your starting point at Tower Junction, note a one-way gravel road to the left (south). This is called the Blacktail Plateau Scenic Drive and is an excellent birding road. The road is often closed, however, when wet weather conditions prevail. If open, the road is one of the best birding roads in the park. When the road is closed, one can still walk in; the birding is excellent. Aspen groves may yield

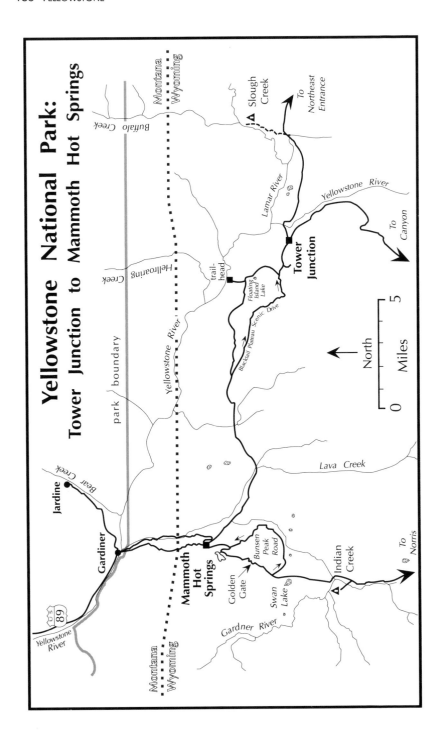

Yellowstone National Park:
Tower Junction to Mammoth Hot Springs

Blue and Ruffed Grouse, Red-naped Sapsucker, and MacGillivray's Warbler. Check the areas of sagebrush for Brewer's Sparrow and Sage Thrasher. The patches of burned timber with dead trees are good locations for finding either Williamson's Sapsucker or Three-toed Woodpecker. In mature stands of conifers look for nesting Red-breasted Nuthatches. Brown Creepers and Golden-crowned Kinglets are difficult to find in Yellowstone, but this area is one of the better locations for finding these birds. Although rare, Northern Pygmy-Owl has been recorded on this stretch of road. The road rejoins the main highway near Petrified Tree in an area that was extensively burned during the Big Fire. From here one can return to Tower Junction if time is short. Otherwise, take the main road west toward Mammoth Hot Springs. Four miles before reaching the Mammoth Hot Springs area, the road crosses Lava Creek. A picnic area here is also a good place to find American Dipper. This bird will nest under bridges and can be seen flying up and down the lively waters of Lava Creek.

The Albright Visitors Center at Mammoth Hot Springs is well worth a visit. A number of mounted specimens of birds found in Yellowstone are on display. Naturalists on duty here can also give you helpful hints about the park's birdlife. (From here, one may wish to drive to the North Entrance at Gardiner for supplies or a meal outside the park in addition to visiting Montana, an area beyond the scope of this book.)

Mammoth Hot Springs Toward Norris. From the Visitor Center at Mammoth Hot Springs drive 3.4 miles on the main road heading south for Norris Junction. This road leads one past impressive travertine formations to an area that features good birding. After negotiating the several switchbacks along the way, look for a safe area to park that gives you good access to the aspen groves south and below the road. A pond (called Africa Lake because, from above, it resembles the shape of that continent) should be visible, where Barrow's Goldeneye and other ducks are sometimes present. Walking down to the aspen groves and to Africa Lake, be alert for Green-tailed Towhees. This is one of the best areas in the park for the species. The bird often gives a kitten-like "mew" that helps you to locate it in low shrubs. Both in the sagebrush and around the aspen groves, one sometimes stumbles upon Blue Grouse. Early morning and late afternoon are good times during June and early July when the males may still be giving their very-low-frequency hoots. In the aspen groves, listen for Orange-crowned Warblers. This area is one of the few locations in Yellowstone where this ground-nesting species can be found.

Having explored this area, hike back up the hill to your car. Continue on your route, driving through the narrow rocky gorge called Golden Gate in the next mile. The stream cascading below you is called Glen Creek, and a look at its Rustic Falls is worth the brief stop. Leaving the gorge, the road enters an expansive area of open grassland dotted with wet areas. One mile beyond

Golden Gate and Rustic Falls is Swan Lake. There is a turn-out on the right (west) side of the road, and a short trail affords a good view of the lake. True to its name, the lake may have a pair of Trumpeter Swans. Other waterfowl, including Lesser Scaup, Green-winged Teal, and Bufflehead, may be present. Remember not to press the Trumpeter Swans too closely for viewing or photographs. Undue disturbance to the park's wildlife by the many visitors can stress wildlife to the point at which they do not reproduce.

If one continues down the road, Indian Creek campground is reached in a distance of three miles, where one can have a picnic lunch and search for Wilson's Warblers in the willow thickets. Otherwise, if optimal birding is your choice, return toward Mammoth Hot Springs. Just before leaving the open flats, turn right (south) at Glen Creek onto the Bunsen Peak Road. This narrow, one-way gravel road, if open, can be a very good birding route. Although passenger cars can readily negotiate the road, cars with trailers or large camper units are prohibited, due to one section's having a steep downgrade with sharp curves. If the road is wet from rain or snow, do not enter! (The road may be closed during poor weather conditions.) If, however, the weather conditions are good and the road is dry, this road loops through six miles of fine birding-habitat before joining up with the main road once again by the Mammoth Hot Springs terraces.

While driving this one-way road, stop often by pulling off to a side to listen and watch for birds. The aspen groves can be particularly productive. Violet-green Swallow, Dusky Flycatcher, and MacGillivray's Warbler are some of the many species that can be observed. Part of the route passes through fire-burn areas, and the dead trees may harbor nests of Mountain Bluebird and Red-breasted Nuthatch. Hairy Woodpecker and both Red-naped and Williamson's Sapsuckers are often observed along this loop road. The area is also productive for Three-toed Woodpeckers. Check overhead for White-throated Swifts. During June and early July this loop road is also one of the best locations in Yellowstone to find Blue Grouse. Where wildflowers blanket the areas between aspen groves and stands of sagebrush, look for Calliope Hummingbird, North America's smallest bird. Continuing on, one takes a steep downgrade through very thick stands of timber containing Hammond's Flycatcher, Red-breasted Nuthatch, Golden-crowned Kinglet, and Brown Creeper. Joining up with the main road once again outside of Mammoth Hot Springs, you may wish to return to Tower Junction to prepare for exploring the Tower to Silver Gate route.

Tower Junction to Silver Gate Entrance. Beginning at Tower Junction and driving east on the Northeast Entrance Road, one crosses the Yellowstone River in the first mile. Stop on either side of the bridge, walk back to the center, and look for Harlequin Ducks upstream and, especially, downstream. This general area is a good place for Harlequin Ducks, which are on the same seasonal schedule here as the birds at LeHardy Rapids.

By the second mile of travel, the first of a series of small ponds is encountered. Dug out by glaciers of a past era, the pot-holes now provide a haven for waterfowl. Both Green-winged and Cinnamon Teal are common. Blue-winged Teal are scarce, but one should have no difficulty in finding Ring-necked Duck and Lesser Scaup. Amid the tules along the edges of the pot-holes one should find Common Yellowthroat and Yellow-headed Blackbird. At a distance of 2.5 miles from our starting-point, a particularly good pond to check is near the geological interpretive display. Located on the left (north) side of road, this display has a parking area from which a short walk will afford a good view of a large pond below. Gadwall, American Wigeon, and Barrow's Goldeneye are species often occurring here. The large boulders that dot the landscape are glacial erratics; a check of these may produce an occasional Prairie Falcon. In late summer, the shrinking ponds expose a muddy shoreline that may attract shorebirds. Spotted Sandpipers and occasionally Least, Western, or Solitary Sandpipers may occur.

Continuing the drive east, the road passes through rolling sagebrush-covered terrain to the bridge crossing the Lamar River. The next quarter-mile brings you to the entrance to Slough Creek (north) via a gravel road that leads to a campground. There is not a large mix of birds in this area, but it is one of the best locations in the park for finding Prairie Falcon. Continuing past the entrance to Slough Creek, the main road passes through a broad valley where many years ago the National Park Service raised hay in irrigated fields for feeding the Elk and Buffalo in winter. This practice has been discontinued, but the area still holds large numbers of animals during winter months. Scanning the distant meadows and hillsides to the south in summer should still reveal scattered herds of Elk. Buffalo are often next to the road. In winter heavy browsing by Elk has eliminated most vegetation along the ridges with a southern exposure, and many aspen groves now contain only older trees that have been highlined by grazing. Most trees show extensive black blotches on the white trunks where Elk have eaten the bark. Of interest along this stretch of road is an exclosure where an aspen grove has been fenced to keep out grazing animals. The contrast with the other aspen groves is conspicuous.

The birds which one encounters along this stretch are Brewer's Sparrows in the sagebrush, Savannah Sparrows in the moist meadows, and the scavenging Black-billed Magpies everywhere. Due to lack of an understory growth, the aspen groves do not shelter many birds other than some cavity-nesters such as American Kestrel and a few perching-birds. One might speculate what the heavy grazing of the aspen groves has done to ground-nesting birds such as Ruffed Grouse or Orange-crowned Warbler and understory species such as MacGillivray's Warblers and Lincoln's Sparrow.

Having traversed the broad expanse of the Lamar Valley, the road and river converge once again just before the juncture of Soda Butte Creek and

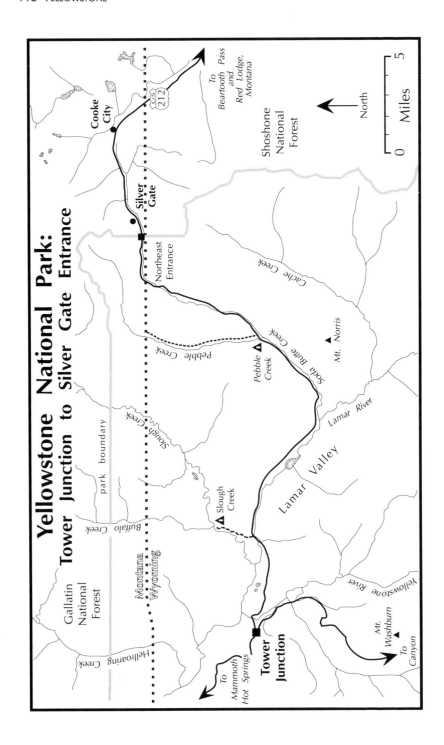

Yellowstone National Park:
Tower Junction to Silver Gate Entrance

the Lamar River. This stretch of road affords a good view of the river, where one should be able to pick up a Barrow's Goldeneye or a Spotted Sandpiper. Continuing up the road several miles, one is greeted by the prominent geological feature known as Soda Butte. Besides its geological interest, a very short walk around and behind this travertine dome will reveal an active colony of Cliff Swallows. There one can obtain close views of the gourd-shaped mud nests plastered onto the sides of this odd structure. Be sure to keep your disturbance of the swallows to a minimum, and stay off the fragile Soda Butte formation.

As the road continues along Soda Butte Creek, the landscape continues to change and the mountain peaks draw nearer. On the tops of tall snags one might catch sight of an Olive-sided Flycatcher, never a common bird in Yellowstone. It is easy to locate by its loud and distinctive call that some describe as *quick, three beers!* and others hear as *what peeves you?* Upon reaching Pebble Creek, one can leave the main highway, turning left (north) to drive up the side road to the campground-area just off the main road. Since campgrounds often attract birds, both Steller's and Gray Jays often occur here. The quick waters of Pebble Creek can produce American Dipper. Those wanting some exercise can take the trail leading out from the Pebble Creek Campground. The trail immediately climbs 500 feet on a series of switchbacks to a small meadow where normal people have to rest while drinking in the spectacular view of the surrounding countryside. After this the trail becomes more manageable and is worth exploring for the next two miles. Northern Goshawk has been seen along the trail, as well as Three-toed Woodpecker. Both Blue and Ruffed Grouse are possible although characteristically difficult to see, whereas Western Tanager, Swainson's Thrush, and Red Crossbill are often found. Until the middle of July one hears Ruby-crowned Kinglets belting out their songs. After this time they become much less detectable—as do many other species. August can be downright quiet; then birding forested areas can be very slow.

Continuing up the main road from Pebble Creek to Silver Gate, the visitor passes through forested areas where, besides the ubiquitous Pine Siskins and Mountain Chickadees, it is possible with extensive searching to pick up a Three-toed Woodpecker. Since it is rather a quiet species and a hard one to detect, one may have to settle for a more vocal Hairy Woodpecker instead.

Although one can turn back at the Northeast Entrance, the short drive on to Cooke City may be worthwhile. Besides the food and lodging afforded by this high-mountain-country town in Montana, the short drive passes through a good area for Ruffed Grouse, particularly toward dusk, when they are often found foraging along the road.

Because the only link which Cooke City has with the outside world in winter is this road, it is kept plowed throughout the year, unlike most of Yellowstone's roads.

Before returning to Yellowstone and Tower Junction from Cooke City, a side-trip possibility of great merit is to continue east from Cooke City to visit the Beartooth Plateau. (You will want to set aside the better part of a day for this trip even though the distance traveled is not very great. *To pick up that route, check Chapter 19.*)

Tower Junction to Mount Washburn and the Hayden Valley. By driving south from Tower Junction, one can enjoy both some of the best scenery and the best birding which Yellowstone has to offer. Driving toward Tower Falls, your first stop will be 2 miles up the road at a turn-out which affords a view of The Narrows, a steep gorge cut by the Yellowstone River. The high, steep, rocky outcroppings of basalt columns along here are not only great for their fascinating geological interest, but are also probably the best location in Yellowstone for finding White-throated Swifts. Violet-green Swallows are also common here. Continuing up the road, the next half-mile brings you to Tower Falls. The short walk of several hundred feet to the falls is well worth the time because of the splendid scene provided by the falls. If not too crowded, the trail may also provide an opportunity to see Western Tanager, Chipping Sparrow, and Green-tailed Towhee. Clark's Nutcrackers are common throughout Yellowstone; if you miss these noisy birds, you will be asked to turn in your binoculars!

From Tower Falls the road soon begins its climb up to the slopes of Mount Washburn (El. 10,243 ft.). Here the surrounding country opens up, giving one grand vistas of large sections of Yellowstone. A number of turn-outs are provided for travelers, and these can be used to scan for wildlife. Using a scope just might reveal a Grizzly in a distant meadow. Occasionally, Blue Grouse are encountered in the grassy-sagebrush slopes and are most readily detected by the hooting of male birds. This is a busy road, however, and traffic noises make listening difficult.

As the road climbs upward towards Dunraven Pass, look for a well-marked gravel road on your left (east), reached 8.3 miles from our starting point at Tower Junction. Called the Chittenden Road, it offers an easy drive up its moderate grade to a parking area. A three-mile hike from there will lead the hardy to the summit. Bighorn Sheep are the big attraction here. Birds to look for include Blue Grouse, American Pipit, (Black) Rosy Finch, and Pine Grosbeak, but they can be easily missed here.

Once the bird-finder is back on the main road again, upon reaching Dunraven Pass (El. 8,850 ft.) the picnic areas at the summit can be checked for birds. Here one might encounter Steller's Jays which are not easy to come by in Yellowstone. Gray Jays are much easier to find—in fact, they usually find you, in the campground and picnic areas. The descent from Dunraven Pass is rapid and soon takes one to a major intersection, Canyon Village. The normal amenities of the Park are available here. Continuing south 2.3 miles toward Yellowstone Lake, look for the left-hand (east) turn for Chittenden

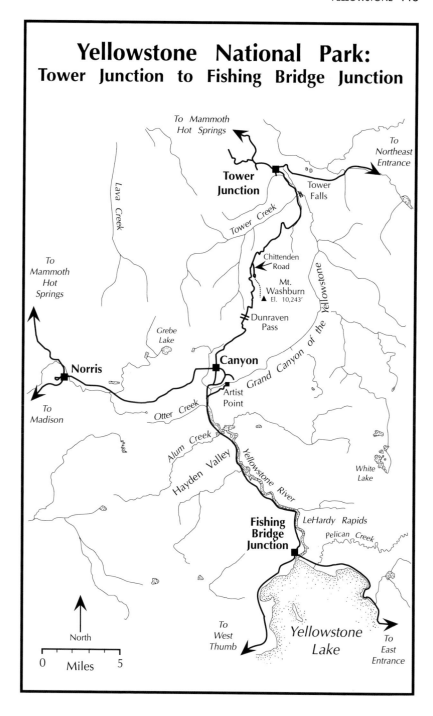

Yellowstone National Park:
Tower Junction to Fishing Bridge Junction

To Mammoth
Hot Springs

To Northeast
Entrance

**Tower
Junction**

Tower
Falls

Tower Creek

Lava Creek

To
Mammoth
Hot
Springs

Chittenden
Road

Mt.
Washburn
▲ El. 10,243'

Dunraven
Pass

Grebe
Lake

Norris

Canyon

Grand Canyon of the Yellowstone

Yellowstone

Artist
Point

To
Madison

Otter Creek

Alum Creek

Hayden Valley

Yellowstone River

White
Lake

**Fishing
Bridge
Junction**

LeHardy Rapids

Pelican Creek

To
West
Thumb

North

Yellowstone
Lake

To
East
Entrance

0   Miles   5

Bridge (the road may be more clearly marked as the way to Artist Point) and drive the road to its terminus at Artist Point. This location affords a spectacular look at the Lower Falls and the Grand Canyon of the Yellowstone. When not taking pictures, check the rocky spires of the canyon walls for Osprey nests. There are two or three that are fairly easy to locate on each side of the canyon. A spotting scope here can give you decent views of birds at the nest. You will also be mobbed by tourists who will be thrilled at the sight of an Osprey in your scope. The Ospreys are active here. With great luck, even a Peregrine Falcon may make an appearance.

Returning to the main road and continuing south, start checking the majestically flowing Yellowstone River for the next two miles. This stretch of river produces good counts of Common Mergansers and Barrow's Goldeneyes. A good birding area along this stretch is the picnic area on your left 0.3 mile beyond the turn-off to Otter Creek or 0.8 mile past the Chittenden Bridge/Artist Point road. This is a particularly good vantage-point in late June or early July to see large rafts of Barrow's Goldeneye. Sometimes a raft will contain over a hundred drakes that have left the family-rearing chores to the hens.

After the next mile one enters the famed Hayden Valley. This wide panorama is Yellowstone at its best. The next five miles provide a number of wide pull-outs for viewing wildlife. Besides Elk, Moose, and Buffalo, the birdlife is abundant. Hundreds of Canada Geese grace the sinuous course of the Yellowstone River, as do large numbers of ducks and all three species of teal. With so many waterfowl, the area is also attractive to Peregrine Falcons. Look also for Bald Eagles, which are found in Yellowstone year round and are often seen patrolling the river or commanding a prominent snag. Besides the ubiquitous Red-tailed Hawk, one often sees Swainson's Hawks and, occasionally, Northern Harriers during migration.

In your first mile of travel up the open valley, look for a sign marking Alum Creek. In late summer when water-levels have fallen, the muddy shoreline is one of the best places in Yellowstone to find shorebirds. Although never numerous here, some of the smaller "peep" such as Western, Least, and Semipalmated Sandpipers can usually be found. American Avocet, both yellowlegs, Willet, Baird's Sandpiper, and other shorebirds can also occur. One just might turn up an interesting shorebird species here during fall migration that would be new to the list for Yellowstone National Park.

As the birder continues the drive up the Hayden Valley, each pull-out along the highway can turn up something new. A spotting scope is very useful here. Most of the large white birds that you see from afar in the Yellowstone River will turn out to be American White Pelicans rather than Trumpeter Swans. A substantial colony of over 500 American White Pelicans exists far off on Yellowstone Lake. Fortunately, they seem to be holding their own now despite misguided attempts by park officials in the 1920s to eradicate both pelicans and otters because they preyed upon fish!

Buffalo grazing in Hayden Valley   Terry McEneaney

Sandhill Cranes can be found in the wet meadows. Sometimes one can be alerted to their presence by their resonant calls that can carry more than a mile. Also, in spring and early summer, listen for the winnowing of Common Snipe as they perform their courtship flights. Other sounds to listen for along here include the descending whinny of Sora and the wonderful vocalizations of Lincoln's Sparrow. Savannah Sparrows are common here, but their thin, scratchy songs can hardly be compared to the rich, exquisite songs of Lincoln's Sparrows.

The best times to view this valley are early morning and late afternoon. By scoping the distant slopes and meadows one can sometimes spot a Grizzly. (The bears tend to stay well away from the roads and should never be approached. Likewise, Moose and Buffalo can be very unpredictable and should not be "pushed" or approached, either.) As the road exits the Hayden Valley, the visitor driving south is soon greeted by the smell of sulfur and of hydrogen sulfide. The odors identify the approach on the west side of the road to The Dragon's Mouth, The Black Dragon's Cauldron, and other thermal features. These interesting phenomena are well worth the visit. Drive 2.7 miles farther up river from these thermal areas, look for parking on the left (east) for LeHardy Rapids. As mentioned previously, the location has become a popular tourist stop, so don't count on finding Harlequin Ducks here.

The last several miles of this route parallel the serenely flowing Yellowstone River just below its outflow from Yellowstone Lake. Sometimes an Osprey can be seen flying overhead, and both American White Pelicans and California Gulls work the river, but the birding along this stretch is not as

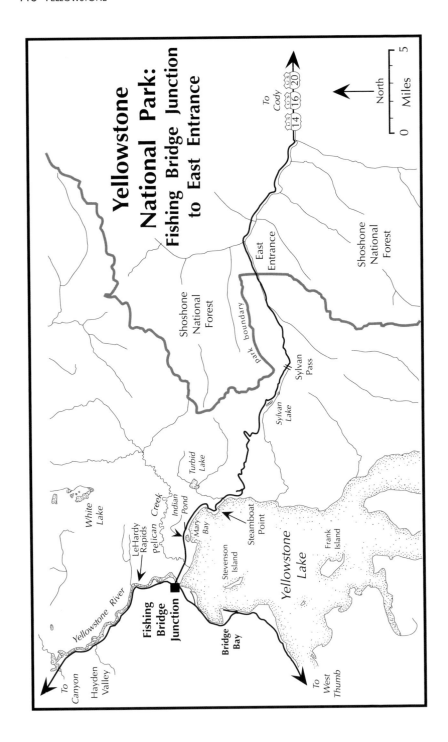

Yellowstone
National Park:
**Fishing Bridge Junction
to East Entrance**

interesting as that found in the Hayden Valley. The road junction at Fishing Bridge forms the starting-point for another segment of travel.

Yellowstone Lake to East Entrance. The Yellowstone River leaves Yellowstone Lake in the area called Fishing Bridge. Now closed to fishing, the bridge itself is a great viewing-area for watching native Cut-throat Trout swimming in the crystal-clear water. There is abundant birdlife in this general area. From this location, the East Entrance Road extends 27 miles to the eastern border of Yellowstone National Park and from there another 52 miles to Cody. The most productive birding along this road is the first 10 miles, which traverses the northeastern shores of Yellowstone Lake. From Fishing Bridge and its normal complement of American White Pelicans, Common Mergansers, Ospreys, and California Gulls, drive east 1.5 miles to the bridge over Pelican Creek. The extensive marsh area here is home to a broad array of wildlife. Moose are sometimes observed here, and the area is a prime foraging-area of Grizzly. Bald Eagles find this area to be a rich food source. The marsh between the road and lake can produce Virginia Rail, a rare species in Yellowstone. Sometimes a Caspian Tern puts in an appearance. The next mile of travel is to an overlook on the right (south) of Indian Pond, where a number of ducks can be observed. Bufflehead and Ring-necked Duck should be among the species present. Continuing another half-mile, the road now closely follows the shoreline of Yellowstone Lake. Here the road also passes close to some hot springs, and a large opening appears on your left. Be alert for a large pond (called Beach Springs Lagoon) which is just visible over a slight rise. This body of water is a very reliable place for finding Trumpeter Swan. (These swans are sensitive to undue disturbance, so make your presence as unobtrusive as possible and stay on the road. The pond area is closed and posted during nesting season. In most years, the resident pair here does not manage to nest successfully.) For the next three to four miles the road skirts the edge of Yellowstone Lake along Mary Bay. A stop at Steamboat Point may produce Common Loon. The best times for seeing a loon are in May and again in September and October when migrating birds stop over. Fewer than 15 pairs of loons nest in Yellowstone National Park, so summertime observations are infrequent. From Steamboat Point the road leaves the lake and begins its long climb to Sylvan Pass before descending again to the East Entrance. This stretch of road offers promising birding although it doesn't receive much coverage by active birders. Blue Grouse are sometimes recorded here, and meadows bordering forest edges may produce Great Gray Owl, a difficult species to find. The higher elevations may possibly harbor Boreal Owls. The latter species is very difficult to detect because it usually stops calling shortly after the road opens in early May. Moreover, these owls are not found in the same territories year after year.

Birding Elsewhere in Yellowstone. By having explored some of the major birding areas in Yellowstone described up to this point, the visiting birder should have a reasonable feel for birding in this vast region. With limitations in time, the described areas will have given the visitor much to see. Some general remarks about the remainder of Yellowstone are in order, however, if only to generate more ideas of what to visit.

Those who arrive in Yellowstone via the entrance at West Yellowstone have a good opportunity to see Trumpeter Swans on the Madison River. About seven miles into the park from the West Entrance, park just after crossing the only bridge over the Madison River. Look upstream—the swans often nest in an oxbow of the river. These swans seem fairly well accustomed to people. Still, the area in the nest vicinity is closed to the public, so please give the birds room.

From Madison Junction 14 miles inside the park from West Yellowstone, one can go either left (north) up the Gibbon River toward Norris, or right (south) up the Firehole River toward Old Faithful. Either route is good for finding American Dipper along these streams. Check areas around rapids and near bridges, where the birds like to nest.

Remember, Yellowstone National Park is larger than the states of Delaware and Rhode Island combined and has nearly 300 miles of public roads and over 1,000 miles of trails. There is much for the birder to explore and much to contribute. Enjoy as much of it as you can.

Great Gray Owl
Gail Diane Luckner

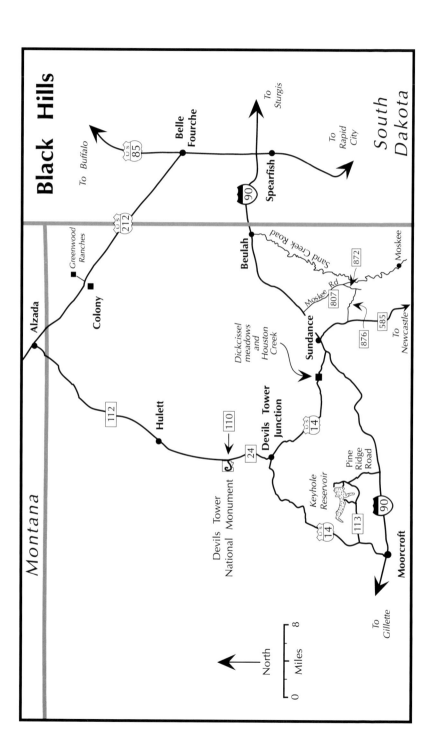

16. BLACK HILLS

The well-known Black Hills, or *Paha Sapa*, were named by the Indians for the darkness of their timbered slopes. Today, most people think of the Black Hills as part of South Dakota, but a significant portion of the Hills is actually in northeastern Wyoming. One of the most interesting spots in South Dakota's Black Hills is Spearfish Canyon, with its broad canyon, well-developed riparian deciduous forest, and pines along the canyon slopes. In Wyoming a rather similar area, Sand Creek at Beulah, is less well-known.

1. **Sand Creek**. Turn right off westbound Interstate 90 at Beulah (exit 205), the first exit in Wyoming if you are leaving South Dakota. Turn left (south) over the interstate and drive 2.0 miles south (bear right at the fork once you reach 1.2 miles) to Sand Creek, a beautiful little valley hemmed in by perpendicular rock walls in many areas. American Redstarts may nest in the first deciduous thickets. MacGillivray's Warblers skulk in the brush along the creek. Lazuli Buntings are common. Hybrids between Lazuli and Indigo Buntings can be found, and sometimes a pure Indigo is seen.

About 0.5 mile farther, the forest grows close to the road, good habitat for Solitary Vireos. In such places there will also be a few "White-winged" Juncos, the only breeding junco in the Black Hills. This form is now considered a subspecies of the Dark-eyed. Western Wood-Pewees occur, also, but these are very common throughout Wyoming and can be found wherever trees occur. The exception may be in communities which spray for mosquitoes.

Between 3.2 miles and 4.9 miles from the north end of the road, the property is owned by the Sand Creek Country Club. In this section one should bird only from the road. Since the valley is quite narrow, this should pose no problem. (Permission to bird off the road may be granted if you ask property-owners.) The land north and south of the country club is owned by the Wyoming Game and Fish Department, and there you may go where you wish.

Wyoming Game and Fish Headquarters is located 5.5 miles from the start in a particularly beautiful spot. It is the former home of Nels Smith, years ago governor of the state. Just beyond the headquarters, White-throated Swifts may be found at a huge expanse of rock wall of the canyon. Occasionally, Canyon Wrens have been found here. If they are here, their remarkable song is easily heard. In fact, I have heard them on most of the canyon walls in this

Townsend's Solitare
Shawneen Finnegan

valley, but they can't be counted on—which is true of this bird over most of Wyoming. Beyond headquarters 0.6 mile, look for Cordilleran Flycatchers. Past this area, the canyon is dry with fewer birds of note.

2. **Moskee Road and Bluebird Trail.** At this point, you can go ahead to the Moskee Road through Black Hills National Forest and then turn right to go back to Interstate 90. That is a long way. The best use of time is to retrace your route through the valley to Interstate 90, go west 14.0 miles to Moskee Road (exit 191), and turn south. It is Forest Service Road 807. At 7.5 miles, make a right turn onto a road unmarked except for a small post with #872 on it. This gravel road leads west with only one right-angle turn at 1.8 miles. Here the road changes number, to Forest Service Road 876. For the length of Road 872 and the first 3.1 miles of Road 876 you will see a series of bird-boxes on the fence posts, put up first in 1984 by Jean Adams, who lives not far away. Almost every year one or more of these boxes has been occupied by Eastern Bluebirds, a thundering-rare breeding bird in Wyoming. In fact, this is the only presently known nesting-site in the state. Many of the boxes are occupied by our more common Mountain Bluebird.

At 5.0 miles along Road 876 you reach paved Route 585. In the last 1.5 miles before Route 585, the road traverses meadows that have Grasshopper Sparrows, almost guaranteed, and Vesper, Savannah, and Lark Sparrows, too. Turn right (north) onto Route 585, which takes you 4.9 miles back to Interstate 90 (exit 187) at Sundance.

3. **Keyhole State Park and Reservoir**. Drive west on Interstate 90 for 20.5 miles beyond the last interchange in Sundance (exit 185). At Pine Ridge Road (exit 165), take a right (north) to Keyhole State Park and Reservoir. Keyhole Reservoir is interesting since it is the largest body of water in northeast Wyoming and attracts Great Plains migrants that are scarce in Wyoming. A map of the area shows many dirt and gravel roads, but some of these have been paved recently. From Interstate 90, go 6.9 miles to the end of the pavement. Turn left immediately; the road splits after a little entrance station. (Fee area: $2.00 for residents, $3.00 for non-residents, plus $4.00 for camping.) The right-hand road, Asher Road, goes 1.2 miles to the area just below the dam, where you should see Yellow-breasted Chats and Cliff Swallows. Eastern Phoebes have tried to nest in the rock wall along the way. Here, too, Great Egrets have been seen. One is never quite sure what will be encountered at this pleasant spot.

Return 0.7 mile and turn right to reach Rocky Point and the dam itself on the right. Hudsonian Godwits have been reported here, and rare loons, such as Pacific Loon, are possible in October and early November. Go back to

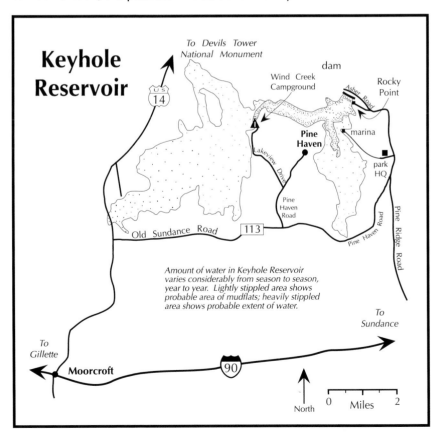

Keyhole Reservoir

To Devils Tower National Monument

U.S. 14

dam

Wind Creek Campground

Rocky Point

Asher Road

Pine Haven

marina

Lakeview Drive

park HQ

Pine Haven Road

Old Sundance Road   113

Pine Haven Road

Pine Ridge Road

Amount of water in Keyhole Reservoir varies considerably from season to season, year to year. Lightly stippled area shows probable area of mudflats; heavily stippled area shows probable extent of water.

To Sundance

To Gillette

Moorcroft

90

North   0   Miles   2

the pavement, drive 1.3 miles on the paved road, and then turn right past the headquarters of Keyhole State Park. Continue on the road 1.7 miles to the marina area to get good looks at the reservoir. Again, Pacific Loons would be most likely in the fall along with numbers of Common Loons. There is even a tantalizing report of a possible Yellow-billed Loon from the reservoir.

Return to the road beyond the headquarters and turn right for 0.5 mile, then bear right onto a dirt road, and continue right when the road forks in 1.5 miles. Drive for another 4.4 miles to the road into Pine Haven. Turn right and follow this road 1.5 miles to Lakeview Drive. Turn left onto Lakeview Drive and go 3.2 miles to the Wind Creek Campground. In summer you'll see Say's Phoebes and American White Pelicans. This road affords good views of the upper part of the reservoir. With a good scope I have seen Pacific Loons from here.

Return on Lakeview Drive and Pine Haven Road for 3.2 miles to Route 113, which leads west from the entrance to Pine Haven. Turn right and continue 5.0 miles to US 14, and turn right again. Drive 4.1 miles to an entrance on the right which is an old road across the flats on the northwest side of the reservoir. The following directions are for experienced birders with plenty of common sense and road-handling experience. The road is full of ruts and may be impassable when muddy. The object is to get close to the water without getting into soft ground where you might remain stuck for a long time. Go south on this old road as far as you can, following in the tracks of other vehicles. The full distance is about 2.5 miles. Turn left and proceed cautiously across the flats toward the water. The reservoir's height depends on how much moisture the area has received, as well as on how much water

Old burn area on the way to Devils Tower   Paul J. Baicich

the irrigators in South Dakota have taken. One never knows how far it is safe to go until one makes a judgment on the spot. I have had no trouble by being conservative and then doing some walking. During shorebird migration these flats can be worthwhile. In late May there can be a far greater concentration of Lesser Golden-Plovers here than anywhere else in the state, along with plenty of Black-bellied Plovers. Hudsonian Godwits and White-rumped Sandpipers have been reported, also.

4. **Devils Tower.** After exploring the flats, return to US 14 and go northeast 16.2 miles to Devils Tower Junction. Turn left on to Highway 24; drive 5.9 miles to the turnoff onto Highway 110 (west), looking for Grasshopper Sparrows and Sharp-tailed Grouse along the way. Devils Tower, the country's first National Monument, rises 1,260 feet over the Belle Fourche River (Monument Headquarters, PO Box 8, Devils Tower, WY 82714; phone: 307/467-5283). The imposing tower is composed of massive rock columns, 1,000 feet across at the bottom and 275 feet at the top. The columns were formed by the cooling and crystallization of molten rock in the neck of a volcano. The total area of the National Monument is about 8 square miles,

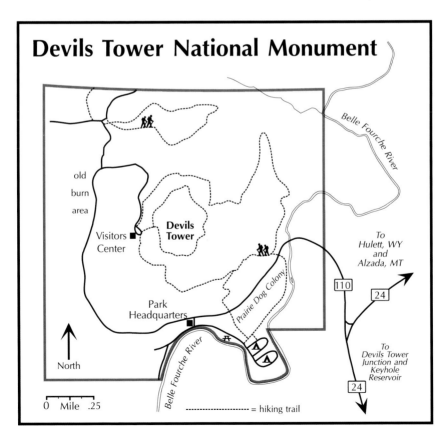

Devils Tower National Monument

old burn area

Visitors Center

Devils Tower

Park Headquarters

Prairie Dog Colony

Belle Fourche River

North

0 Mile .25

To Hulett, WY and Alzada, MT

110

24

To Devils Tower Junction and Keyhole Reservoir

24

•••••••• = hiking trail

with the tower itself in the center. Ponderosa Pine forests surround the tower, and deciduous forests (cottonwood, Western Box Elder, Bur Oak) line the Belle Fourche River. It is a fee area ($3.00 per car).

The imposing rock formation played an important role in the legends and folklore of Indian tribes. (Less anthropologically-minded folks may remember it as the alien spaceship rendezvous-site in the Spielberg movie *Close Encounters of the Third Kind*.) Dead trees here are left standing, which makes for excellent birding. Nearby National Forest land has few dead trees and few woodpeckers. There is a nice campground situated near the river on Tower land, but it is very popular and fills early during the summer season.

A fascinating Black-tailed Prairie-Dog town is on the left after you cross the Belle Fourche River bridge. The Black-tailed Prairie-Dogs produce concentrated towns with holes close together while the White-tailed Prairie-Dogs, also plentiful in Wyoming, excavate their burrows in a more widely-scattered pattern. This colony abuts the Belle Fourche River, where a family of Minks set up housekeeping in 1988. The Minks have diminished the number of Black-tails considerably, but since their colony has been established here since 1906, it will doubtless survive.

Common Poorwills can often be heard calling from the open slopes at the base of the Tower. The Common Poorwill wants it good and dark before he tunes up. For instance, if you are doing a Breeding Bird Survey route properly, the bird will stop calling either 5 or 10 minutes before you begin. Wild Turkeys, which nest here, are common in the Black Hills and can be seen and heard frequently. A walk around a burned area on the left side of the road up to the Tower may produce Black-backed Woodpeckers, which nest here. (Three-toed Woodpeckers do not occur in northeast Wyoming.)

A Black Hills specialty is the Solitary Vireo, which sings from early May to early July. This is virtually a guaranteed bird at the Tower in season. There are lots of Ovenbirds, perhaps not very exciting for most visitors from the East, but uncommon elsewhere in eastern Wyoming. Contrariwise, the Eastern visitor may have a first experience with Gray Jay, Townsend's Solitaire, and Pinyon Jay at the Tower, but these species are not guaranteed.

The Tower itself was formerly the aerie of Peregrine Falcons. At times Prairie Falcons may have nested here but are now only frequent visitors. Because so many rock-climbers scale the Tower, considered of only moderate difficulty as rock climbing goes, it is unlikely that either of these falcons will again nest on the tower. White-throated Swifts should be conspicuous, though. There are also lots of Rock Doves on the Tower. Brown Creepers are often seen and can be heard singing early in the season. Red Crossbills are usually common.

5. **Houston Creek**. After visiting Devils Tower, return to US 14 and drive east toward Sundance for 10.9 miles. On the right, at the bottom of the valley, is Houston Creek. This is private land, so if you want to bird off the highway

you will have to get permission at the ranch here. Birding can be good from the highway, however. Watch and listen for Veery. Lazuli Buntings are common and occasionally you might find Indigo Buntings. A little Beaver pond is located here, and in the vicinity you may find both Black-billed and Yellow-billed Cuckoos. Black-billed would be the more common species.

If Dickcissels are in the area, you will find them 3 miles beyond this stop in the open meadows to the left of the road. We have frequent incursions of Dickcissels in the Black Hills from the east, but they are not regular residents. At this point you can continue toward Interstate 90 at Sundance or retrace your route along US 14 to join Interstate 90 at Moorcroft.

6. **Colony**. This town, known for its bentonite mines, is located in extreme northeast Wyoming. Bentonite, a fine volcanic ash, is a component of the drilling mud used in oil and gas well-drilling operations. Colony is best approached from Belle Fourche, South Dakota. From there follow US 212 about 14 miles northwest to the Wyoming state line. From there drive 10.1 miles, turn right (north), and go 2.0 miles farther to the Greenwood Ranches. (For anyone approaching from Montana, the turn-off for the Greenwood Ranch is 10.0 miles southeast of the state line, or 12.3 miles from Alzada, Montana.) In the valley beyond is a sizable reservoir fed by a small stream. Trumpeter Swans have nested here each of the last ten summers. This swan colony is believed to be an offshoot of the colony at South Dakota's Lacreek National Wildlife Refuge 150 miles to the east. To get good views of the swans from the road, turn right at the Greenwood Ranches. When the birds are on eggs from mid-April to early May, they can be hard to see. If you have trouble getting good looks, the Greenwood Ranches staff can be helpful. Sometimes the Trumpeters are farther up this creek and can be found by turning left at Greenwood Ranches and going about one mile. Other birds on the water should be Mallards, Gadwalls, and Blue-winged Teals. In this area you may also see Great Blue Herons, Western Tanagers, Lark Sparrows, Red-winged Blackbirds, and American Goldfinches.

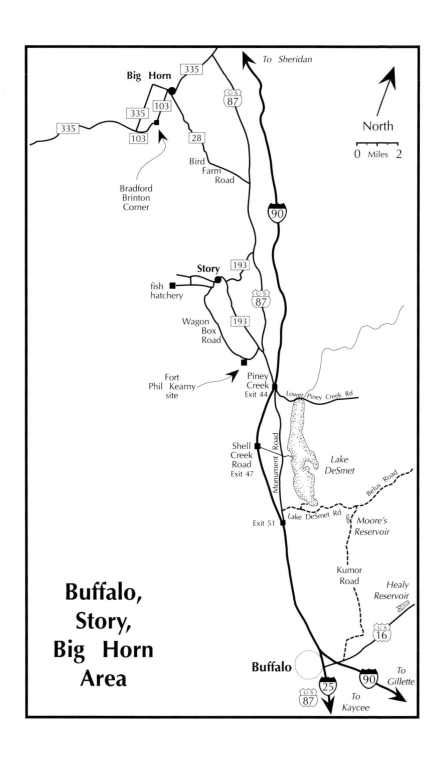

Buffalo, Story, Big Horn Area

17. SHERIDAN/STORY AREA

This is the east face of the Bighorn Mountains which has some interesting places to see birds. Besides, a more beautiful, lush ranching country can hardly be imagined. It is far greener than most of the rest of Wyoming.

1. **Healy Reservoir**. At the junction of Interstate 90 and US 16 outside of Buffalo, when you are going west turn right onto US 16 for 3.6 miles to Healy Reservoir—which is on your left. There is a road down the north side of the reservoir which is very bumpy but gives good views of the water. You will have to contend with fishermen here, but this is probably the best place for ducks in this region. It has the usual western surface-ducks including three species of teal, Northern Shoveler, Northern Pintail, Mallard, Gadwall, and American Wigeon plus common diving ducks such as Redhead, Lesser Scaup, Ruddy Duck, and Bufflehead. Late in the migration in October some real rarities have been seen here such as Eurasian Wigeon in 1985 and Red-throated Loon in 1986, both almost casual birds in Wyoming. Both White-winged and Surf Scoters have been seen here almost every year although they are rare in the state.

Sometimes there are ducks and other water-related birds at the Clear Creek Diversion Dam located just across the road from the entrance to Healy Reservoir. It is usually worth a look. As you leave the Healy Reservoir to reenter US 16, turn left and proceed to the dam structure across the highway where there is parking space. When the water-level is lowered, mudflats are exposed, giving good views of migrating shorebirds. This is currently the only good place in the area for shorebirding.

2. **Moore's Reservoir**. Locally this reservoir is called "Moore's Slough." On returning toward Interstate 90, take a right onto a gravel road 3.2 miles west of Healy Reservoir, just before you get to the junction of US 16 and Interstate 90. This gravel road, labeled "Kumor Road" by a sign, leads up through excellent hawk country (for Red-tailed Hawk, Ferruginous Hawk, and Golden Eagle as well as falcons) to Moore's Reservoir, some 7.5 miles, where Canada Geese nest along with ducks, American Coots, and Pied-billed Grebes. Migrant Hooded Mergansers are often seen here; rarely, Great Egret, Snowy Egret, Tundra Swan, and Oldsquaw have been present.

3. **Lake DeSmet**. After birding Moore's Reservoir continue northward to a T-junction; turn left here onto Lake DeSmet Road for 1.7 miles to the South Dam at Lake DeSmet. Lake DeSmet is an interesting place. It was discovered by the first Catholic missionary in this part of the Rockies, Fr. Pierre Jean DeSmet. It is also the source of many foolish legends about water monsters and Indian maidens.

For our purposes it is important for a number of reasons. There are few lakes in the region. This lake has no visible outlet, yet the water is fresh, not alkaline, so the outlet is subterranean. The lake is deep, which means that it freezes late, perhaps December, and doesn't open up until April. All these facts contribute to the lake's being a good birding-site.

The area is presently owned by Texaco, which has been rather mysterious with the local people about its purposes here. However, Texaco has bought water-rights on Clear Creek (which runs through Buffalo to the south) and has built an expensive aqueduct from there to Lake DeSmet. They also have water rights on Piney Creek to the north and have raised the level of Lake DeSmet some forty feet.

Prior to 1976 local observers had access all around the lake and excellent opportunities to find shorebirds, gulls, and terns here in migration. Mudflats, sandbars, and grassy areas made birdfinding a delight here. All sorts of rarities were found. The best areas were covered with water by 1977; the water was raised further until the level was forty feet above the early-1970s level. Presently, shorebirds are seldom seen at Lake DeSmet because the shoreline is at shale level, where there are no mudflats or sandbars. Now observers have access only at the county road over the South Dam, at the Johnson County Recreation Area on the southwest, at the Father DeSmet Monument, and on the county road across the North Dam.

Texaco has sizable coal deposits close by (unfortunately, the deepest coal deposit is reported to be under the lake), so you are looking at one of the first sites where a big coal-gasification plant may be built when the price of gasoline goes up enough for gasification to be profitable to Texaco. However, things have not developed as fast as Texaco had anticipated.

Common Loons are at Lake DeSmet in migration in greater numbers than anywhere else in the state, and every now and then a Pacific Loon will drop in. This is great country for hawks. Even Gyrfalcons have been seen here in winter. This portion of Wyoming is the only area where Gyrfalcons have been reported at all, except for one report from Shell Canyon on the other side of the Bighorns. Western Grebes also congregate at Lake DeSmet in migration, mostly during April in the spring and October and November in the fall. Rafts of diving-ducks occur but are hard to see since they are way out and require a powerful scope. Puddle-ducks can be seen along the edges of the lake. The Johnson County Recreation Area is on the west side of the south end of the lake and provides excellent viewing. Our black-headed gulls occur here in migration, both Franklin's from August on and Bonaparte's usually in October. Sabine's Gull is rare here, as it is in much of Wyoming; it is seen somewhere almost every fall season, though. First-year Herring Gulls should be looked for late in the season, mostly November. Otherwise, the common gulls are Ring-billed and California. The California Gulls clear out by mid-September usually, but the Ring-bills will be present almost until freeze-up. Later in the season, usually November, Snow Buntings can sometimes be found around the south end of Lake DeSmet.

After looking at the south end of Lake DeSmet, leave the Johnson County Recreation Area the way you came in and return to Lake DeSmet Road, but go west 0.8 mile to a stop-sign near the commercial "Lake Stop". Turn right onto Monument Road (check the grove of trees from a small bridge just north of the turn). Continue on Monument Road northward 2.4 miles to where the road is blocked off by a gate near a memorial to Father DeSmet. There is a rough road (sometimes blocked off by a gate, too) on the right, which leads down a steep hill to a small point (called "Lakeview" by locals) where you can get a good look at the mid-portion of Lake DeSmet.

After looking at the mid-section of Lake DeSmet, come back up the hill and go due west on the gravel Shell Creek Road, across a meadow to the Interstate 90 Shell Creek interchange; turn right (north) to enter the Interstate, and go 2.1 miles to the Piney Creek (exit 44); leave Interstate 90, and at the end of the exit ramp turn right. Travel on this road (Lower Piney Creek Road) for 0.8 mile to the North Dam of Lake DeSmet. It often is the least productive of the views of DeSmet, but if the light is right it can be worthwhile. The birds are about the same here as elsewhere on the lake, but good views of loon species have been had from here. Then backtrack to the interchange on Interstate 90, but rather than getting onto the interstate, turn right and take the underpass to US 87 straight through toward the Story turn at 1.2 miles. On the right just beyond the interchange, at the Piney Diversion Dam, there is a well-known Osprey nest on a special pole set up for them. Make a left turn onto County Road 193 as though you were going to Story. As soon as you cross the bridge over Piney Creek, turn left onto Kearny Lane and drive 0.4 mile to where the road turns right. You will be following the signs to Fort Phil Kearny. If you are a buff of the "Indian troubles", you will find this one of the more interesting spots. In December 1866, Lt.Col. W.J. Fetterman went out from here and got himself massacred and immortalized as a fool along with his 78 soldiers, followed immediately by Portugee Phillips' famous ride for help from Fort Phil Kearny to Fort Laramie 120 miles away in a sub-zero blizzard. Soldiers involved in the Wagon Box Fight also were stationed here.

4. **Wagon Box Road**. You are now on Wagon Box Road, known locally as Little Piney Creek Road. From the site of Fort Phil Kearny go west on Wagon Box Road across a meadow which harbors a colony of Bobolinks. About 0.7 mile from the Fort Kearny site on the west side of the meadow there

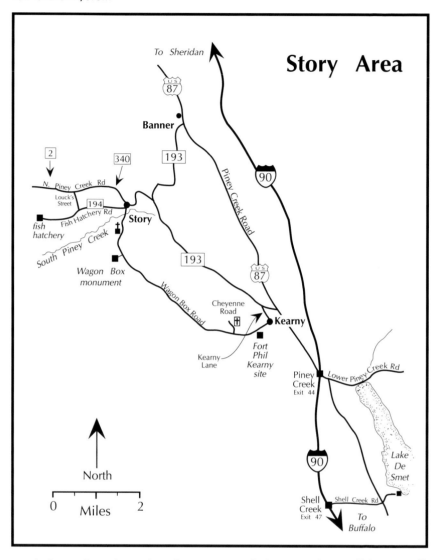

is a little road on the right, Cheyenne Road, that goes by an ill-kept small cemetery, Piney Cemetery, a short distance up the road. Sharp-tailed Grouse are often seen here. The last time I saw them was one October when the grouse were eating the berries on the conifers in the cemetery. I have also seen the grouse putting on a courtship performance on top of haystacks nearby. From here on along Wagon Box Road you are in excellent Sharp-tail country; they should be looked for everywhere. Continue on Wagon Box Road 1.5 miles to the beginning of a very good birding area. On a brushy hillside on the left Sharp-tails can often be seen eating berries on the top of the brush in late fall and winter. Just beyond in a wooded area in the warmer months, look for Veery. Lazuli Buntings are on the edges of the woods and brushy ravines for the next 0.6 mile. Lazulis sound like Indigo Buntings. American Redstarts nest in this area as well as MacGillivray's Warblers; listen for Ovenbirds and Least Flycatchers. Lewis's Woodpeckers are seen uncommonly on Wagon Box Road.

5. **Calliope Hummingbirds**. Some 1.2 productive miles beyond and over a few little bridges, one comes to the turn-off for the Wagon Box Fight. In August 1867, a group of 32 soldiers with their wagons on a wood-collecting detail were surprised by a force of 1,500 Sioux warriors, including Red Cloud and Crazy Horse. The soldiers quickly formed a circle, and the Indians attacked. Armed with new breech-loading rifles, the soldiers stayed behind their wagon boxes, methodically picking off the Indians. In all, the Sioux attacked four times and were turned back each time. The retreating Sioux had substantial losses among their force, and the wagon-box soldiers were relieved by additional troops. Red Cloud was humiliated.

It is just a short distance to the monument marking the historic spot, which has a fence around it where Calliope Hummingbirds often perch. In seasons with enough moisture the wildflowers in this area are spectacular and will attract the hummingbirds. The Wagon Box Fight site is sagebrush-grassland open country and supports grassland sparrows, mostly Savannahs; Mountain Bluebirds and Bobolinks are here, also.

However, in recent years the best place by far to see Calliopes is 0.8 mile up the road at a little Catholic church on the left with hawthorns grown up behind and beside it. Look at the top of the hawthorns, particularly on the dead twigs. This hummer is very small and can be overlooked easily. The male sits there and chases off anything that comes along. These are feisty little birds. This is a typical Calliope site, and other sites will usually look like this. The Calliope can be looked for from the third week of May to mid-July.

6. **Story Fish Hatchery**. Past the Catholic church the road crosses South Piney Creek and then leads through a wood that harbors Western Wood-Pewees and Dusky Flycatchers, to a paved road, Route 194, which is the main artery of Story. This is also called Fish Hatchery Road. Turn left at this corner. Most of the hummers in Story are Broad-tailed and Calliope; Rufous Hummingbirds arrive in late July. After turning the corner, go 1.8 miles to the fish hatchery at the end of the road. This hatchery, built in 1907-1908, is the oldest operating fish hatchery in Wyoming. There is a parking area there with a little stream going through the area. You will also see picnic tables. There is a path to South Piney Canyon that goes up the left side of the fish hatchery and then into a heavy wood. In spring and early summer there are Dusky Flycatchers here. On the right of the path in low, wet brush MacGillivray's Warblers can be found. The hillside often has Wild Turkeys; Mountain Chickadees are found along the path. In fact, this is a

good birding area much of the year. In October Golden-crowned Kinglets occur here; this may not be very exciting for many birders, but in Wyoming they are often hard to find. The path continues over some stiles to South Piney Canyon, a worthy trail for hiking and more birding.

If for some reason you have not seen Broad-tailed Hummingbird yet, look for them after visiting the hatchery. Leave the Story Fish Hatchery and turn left after 0.9 mile onto Louck's Street, a gravel road. Proceed another 0.3 mile to the pavement. This is North Piney Creek Road; turn left. The pavement ends abruptly, but proceed on gravel County Road 2. At 0.8 mile from the pavement look for Broad-tails on utility wires and tops of dead shrubs. A nice drive on to North Piney Creek is ahead. Some 0.6 mile past the stop for Broad-tails, County Road 2 ends. There is a turn-around at a gate across the road.

7. **Bird Farm Road**. Now go back to the pavement and drive to the center of Story, 1.0 mile, marked by a filling-station on one corner and a church across the street. Turn left (north) and proceed 0.3 mile to the end of this street and turn left again; proceed 0.5 mile to State Route 193; turn left (north). This road leads downhill 2.4 miles to US 87, and is another good place to see Sharp-tailed Grouse, particularly in the fall.

At US 87 turn left, and after 3.2 miles turn left again onto Bird Farm Road, County Road 28. There are Grasshopper Sparrows in suitable habitat from 0.6 to 1.2 miles on the left side of the road. About halfway along this road is the Wyoming Game and Fish Department Bird Farm where pheasants are raised. This activity attracts other gallinaceous birds, making this a good place to look for Sharp-tails, particularly in the fields on the west side of this farm. At 4.8 miles turn left (there is an ambiguous sign here) as County Road 28 continues left to State Highway 335 at 6.6 miles and a stop-sign; a landmark here is a transformer station across the road.

8. **Big Horn**. The little town of Big Horn is surrounded by State Highway 335 on the north and west (known locally as the "Upper Road") and County Road 103 on the south and east (known locally as the "Lower Road"). Turn left off Bird Farm Road and continue on Highway 335, which curves to the left at 1.2 miles (another ambiguous sign here); stay on paved County Road 335. On this route you will pass the village of Big Horn. It is a very nice little village, but don't blink or you will miss it. Continue south and look for Sharp-tailed Grouse in the windbreaks on both sides of the road starting at 2.0 to 3.0 miles. Route 335 makes a right curve to the west. Approaching the end of 335 is a great place for Sharp-tailed Grouse in the fall. It will seldom fail you, but grouse are hard to pinpoint. Sharp-tails can be common around this region and can be seen at all times of the year, but are hardest to find between June and late August when they are nesting or are with young.

9. **Little Goose Creek**. Turn around at the parking area where the pavement ends. Drive 3.1 miles back the way you came, leave Route 335,

and take County Road 103 straight ahead (eastward) to Little Goose Creek. This spot is known to locals as the "Bradford Brinton Corner." Look for American Dippers here. The entrance to the Bradford Brinton Memorial Museum is along the gravel road to the right. (The museum re-creates the atmosphere of old western ranch life and is open during the summer months. There is currently no charge to view the artwork on display, and the guided tour of the 1800s upperclass ranch building and a walking-tour of the grounds incudes part of Little Goose Creek.) The riparian habitat provides good birding along Little Goose Creek, and it is worth driving through the grounds to the museum building. This provides more birding opportunities, with chances for Great Blue Heron, Wild Turkey, Red-naped Sapsucker, Ruby-crowned Kinglet, House Wren, Mountain Bluebird, Swainson's Thrush, Yellow Warbler, Black-headed Grosbeak, Lazuli Bunting, Rufous-sided Towhee, Chipping, Vesper, and Savannah Sparrows, and the possibility of rare vagrants. From the Bradford Brinton parking lot, drive back to County Road 103 and follow the paved road northerly through riparian habitat along Little Goose Creek that provides good year-round birding. Western Wood-Pewees, Least Flycatchers, American Redstarts, and Lincoln's Sparrows can be found here in summer. The town of Big Horn is ahead.

At Big Horn, County Road 103 makes a right turn; watch for a sign on the right stating "Women's Club" at the end of the first block. Park at the parking lot. The Bozeman Trail Museum is located here (open summer weekends). Walk around to the back of the building, where a park is located down the hill at the edge of Little Goose Creek. There is good birding here. Both Sharp-shinned and Cooper's Hawks have been found here along with an occasional Merlin in addition to Black-crowned Night-Heron, nesting Common Merganser, Great Horned Owl, Least Flycatcher, Gray Catbird, Red-eyed Vireo, and Black-headed Grosbeak. A number of rare strays have been found here, such as Broad-winged Hawk and eastern warblers in migration. From the parking lot, return to the pavement and follow Route 335 for 3.1 miles to US 87. Turn left onto US 87 and proceed north 4.0 miles to Sheridan.

Sheridan began as a post for trappers in the 1870s and soon became a center for ranching, mining, and railroad activity. Today Sheridan has a population of about 16,000.

When approaching the first traffic signal in Sheridan, choose the right lane. To go through Sheridan continue northward on Coffeen Avenue. After four traffic-lights, Coffeen Avenue curves left, and there is another traffic-light at Main Street. Turn right onto Main Street, headed north; there are seven more traffic-lights; continue northward 4.0 miles after entering Main Street to the approach to Interstate 90; the sign reads "To Billings."

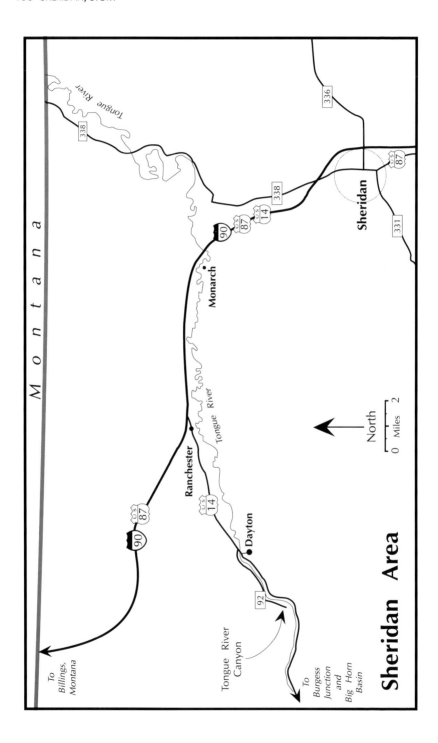

Sheridan Area

Incidentally, finding Bohemian Waxwings in Sheridan in winter (late November through February) is almost a sure thing. A half-hour drive through any residential area should produce them in flocks of 50 to 200.

Continue north on Interstate 90 for 12 miles and get off for Ranchester/US 14 (exit 9); at the end of the off-ramp turn left; go through the small town of Ranchester and on toward Dayton for 6.0 miles.

10. **Tongue River Canyon.** Just before you cross the Tongue River on the outskirts of Dayton turn right onto County Road 92 and go 5.0 miles, keeping close to the river; Lewis's Woodpeckers have been seen here occasionally. You end up in the Tongue River Canyon, a very spectacular spot. Conifers come down into the canyon on the north exposure, so Clark's Nutcrackers occur here often. On the south exposure there are the usual Rock Wrens and occasionally Canyon Wrens. White-throated Swifts are common, but the local birders find that this spot is a catch-all for rarer migrants such as Tennessee and Chestnut-sided Warblers. It is also a good stream for American Dippers. At any rate you will be glad you came.

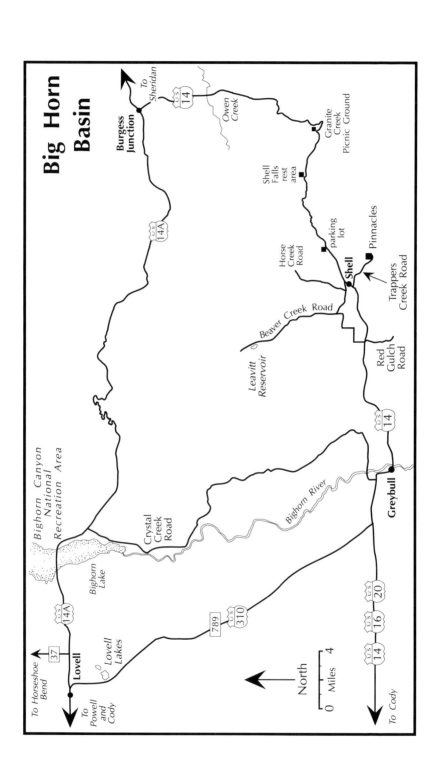

Big Horn Basin

To Sheridan
US 14
Burgess Junction
Owen Creek
Granite Creek Picnic Ground
Shell Falls rest area
Pinnacles
parking lot
Horse Creek Road
Shell
Trappers Creek Road
Beaver Creek Road
Red Gulch Road
Leavitt Reservoir
US 14A
US 14
Greybull
Crystal Creek Road
Bighorn River
Bighorn Canyon National Recreation Area
Bighorn Lake
US 14A
37
Lovell
Lovell Lakes
789
US 310
US 20
US 16
US 14
To Cody
To Horseshoe Bend
To Powell and Cody

North
0   Miles   4

18. BIG HORN BASIN

The Big Horn Basin is very dry, much of it having less than 10 inches of rainfall a year but variable. This natural valley covers more than 13,000 square miles in four counties—Big Horn, Park, Washakie, and Hot Springs. Surrounded by high mountain ranges on three sides and rough foothills in Montana to the north, the Basin resembles an enormous bowl with a center roughly 70 to 90 miles in size. The basin lies between the Bighorn Mountains on the east and the Absaroka Mountains on the west. The south is bordered by the Bighorns and the Owl Creek Mountains.

For birders, the most notable bird of the Big Horn Basin is the Chukar. But first one will travel from Dayton (at the end of the last chapter) through the scenic Bighorn Mountains in the Bighorn National Forest.

On the west side of Dayton note the dome-shaped high-school building on the right where you will start your mileage check for this part of the chapter—from the Dayton High School to Burgess Junction. At 9.9 miles there is a scenic overlook known as Sand Turn, a favorite place for hang-gliding. Violet-green Swallows nest in the road-cuts above the road here and for the next few miles. At 12.8 miles is an old state campground and corrals. Birding is good here for Red Crossbills, Pine Siskins, and Yellow-rumped Warblers. Continuing up the mountain, at 19.1 miles is Sibley Lake; there is a public picnic-area here where Gray Jays and Cassin's Finches are found. Follow signs to the boat dock and inspect the willow area for White-crowned and Lincoln's Sparrows; also look for Wilson's Warblers. At Arrowhead Lodge, 22.6 miles, there is usually an active bird-feeder in fall and winter and hummingbird feeders in summer. Gray Jays, Mountain Chickadees, White-breasted Nuthatches, "Pink-sided" Dark-eyed Juncos, and Pine Siskins are attracted to the feeder. In the coniferous woods near this area the elusive Williamson's Sapsucker is found; the more common Olive-sided Flycatcher and Clark's Nutcrackers are here, also. At 25.4 miles the remnant of an aspen grove is on both sides of the road. You will have to walk a way to reach the section on the left. Nesting Lincoln's Sparrows are numerous in this area, and in the larger part of the aspen grove on the left Red-naped Sapsuckers, Tree Swallows, Mountain Chickadees, and Red-breasted Nuthatches will nest in the cavities. The area from here through the intersection coming up is known locally as "Burgess Flats"; look for Mountain Bluebirds. Just ahead is Burgess Junction at 25.9 miles.

At Burgess Junction, where US 14 and US 14A split, take US 14 to the left. Start your mileage check again for the route between here and Shell. Just ahead at 1.4 miles is Blue Spruce Lodge; from here to the Owen Creek pull-out at 4.3 miles look for Sandhill Cranes, mostly on the right side of the road. The cranes are still uncommon but have been slowly increasing since about 1970.

Red-breasted Nuthatch
Cliff Scott

At 17.2 miles is Granite Creek Picnic Ground, where Western Tanagers and Mountain Bluebirds are seen; Shell Falls at 21.0 miles now has a Tourist Information Center. If you are there in spring, before the crowds come, walk around the center to the Shell Falls viewpoint and listen for singing Townsend's Solitaires. At 25.8 miles there is a large parking area above Shell Creek; look for Dusky Flycatchers, Red-eyed Vireos, Western Tanagers, and Lazuli Buntings. Harlequin Ducks were found in the rapidly falling waters of Shell Creek in 1978 and 1979. At 31.9 miles is the town of Shell. Now you are in Chukar country.

The habitat for Chukar in Wyoming is probably very similar to the kind of country these partridges came from in Asia. The state used to plant large numbers of these birds but no longer. They used to be everywhere, but a hard winter with lots of snow in about 1979 wiped out most of them. They also have been under heavy hunting pressure. With poor hunting success, the hunting pressure has eased up in the last few years. However, if you know where to look, there are still plenty of Chukars, and some people think that they are increasing in these areas. The Big Horn Basin itself is full of grassy ridges with lots of rocks and in some areas not much grass. Only the center of the Basin is really flat. Many of these ridges have had Chukars, and a fair number still do. What follows are some of the most likely spots.

Shell is the tiniest of hamlets, just a wide spot in the road with buildings on each side, but since it is the first such spot you have seen for miles, you will have no trouble finding it. Just to the west of Shell turn left onto Trappers Creek Road. Go 2.5 miles and you will see the Pinnacles on your left. Along this road you can look for Lazuli Bunting and the occasional Sage Grouse. Turn left onto the road that goes down across the creek and right under the Pinnacles. Look for Canyon Wren here, too. There is often a covey of Chukars very close—just under the Pinnacles. If you meet any locals, tell them what you are doing and you will find them cordial and helpful. Just remember that the usual people they meet who are looking for Chukars are hunters and poachers.

Retrace your route back to Shell and take Horse Creek Road, which leads off to the right just east of Shell. Go out on this road about 4 miles. There will be a steep grassy bank on the right for some distance. This is a good place for Chukars. Then turn back, but instead of going back to Shell take the only right-hand turn, which will take you to Beaver Creek Road in about 2 miles. Turn right onto this road and go 3.5 miles beyond the end of the pavement to Leavitt Reservoir, keeping left all the time on the Beaver Creek Road. This will be over 6 miles on Beaver Creek Road. There is a grassy ridge behind to the west (left) of the reservoir. This is a fine place for Chukars, but as you can see that ridge is quite a walk. The ridge, of course, is BLM land. In returning stay on Beaver Creek Road back to US 14, keeping right. The distance will be about 11 miles. Right across from you on US 14 is Red

Gulch Road. This is 4.5 miles west of Shell on US 14. The first mile-and-one-quarter on the Red Gulch is excellent for Chukars. Then return and continue on west on US 14.

A real expert where Chukars are concerned is Jack Lindsey, who lives near Greybull. His home phone number is 307/765-2835, or write to him at PO Box 192, Greybull, WY 82426. Jack is the Jack of a lot of trades. He is a biologist, part-time outfitter, oil-field expert, small farm operator, nice guy, etc. Currently he is helping out Terry Peters, the biologist at the Bighorn Canyon National Recreation Area.

Bighorn Canyon National Recreation Area is a unit of the US National Park Service and represents part of the area around the 47-mile-long Bighorn Lake created by the Yellowtail Dam in Montana. (Headquarters and visitor center, 20 Highway, 14A East, Lovell, WY 82431; phone: 307/548-2251) To get to this area go west on US 14 for 5.0 miles from the center of Greybull to the point where Route 789 turns off. Take Route 789 for 26.7 miles to Lovell. Just before Lovell you pass on your right the Lovell Lakes, where Clark's Grebe has recently nested. Just as you get into Lovell you join US 14A. Turn right onto US 14A and you will see the attractive, solar-heated visitor center for the Bighorn Canyon National Recreation Area. You can pick up some maps and perhaps inquire about local birds, including Chukar.

You can check out the south end of Bighorn Lake now. Some 8.5 miles on Route 14A beyond the visitor center, you will approach the causeway across the lake. Just after you cross the railroad tracks, there is an unmarked gravel road leading off to the right. You might want to take this road 1.9 miles to where you can walk to a set of reedy ponds to the left. (This is Wyoming Game and Fish property.) If you are willing to drive another 0.1 mile on the gravel road, you can overlook one of the ponds from the road. Check for water and marsh birds here.

Drive back to the causeway road on US 14A and turn right. The causeway extends 1.5 miles across the end of Bighorn Lake. Scope out grebes, ducks, and shorebirds on both sides. You will probably see American White Pelican and Sandhill Crane; there is a Great Blue Heron rookery nearby, and Bald Eagles have nested north of the causeway.

Go back toward the Visitor Center; in 6.2 miles you will encounter Route 37 heading northward. You can head toward the Horseshoe Bend area of Bighorn Canyon National Recreation Area, where Chukar have been seen. The general area has some good ridges for Chukars, along with Rock Wrens, and Brewer's Sparrows among other birds in lands between ridges. The Crooked Creek area just beyond Horseshoe Bend (on the ridges, not the creeksides) has produced Chukar. So have some of the areas around Sykes Mountain in the Horseshoe Bend area, but these are difficult to reach. (If you are still hot for Chukars, you can try another option. Drive beyond the causeway over the south end of Bighorn Lake to the well-marked turnoff on the right for Crystal Creek about a mile-and-one-half beyond the causeway. This road goes all the way back to Greybull. You can check the first few miles in particular, especially along the drainages.)

Return to US 14, which, by the way, merged with US 16 and US 20 at Greybull, and continue westward toward Cody.

Clark's Nutcracker
Gail Diane Luckner

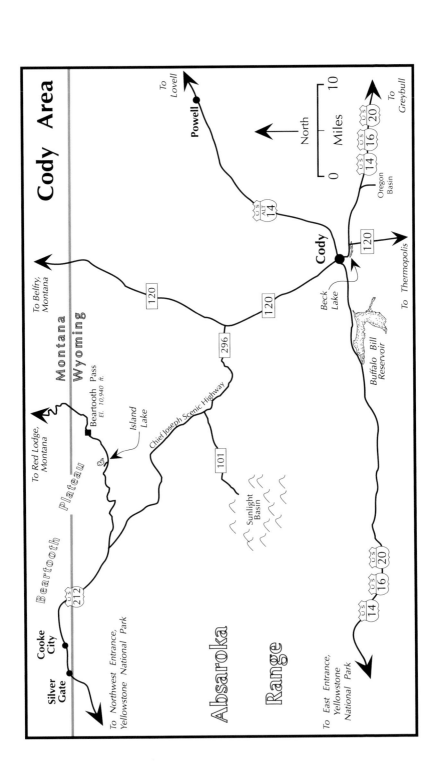

Cody Area

To Lovell

Powell

North

Miles

0 10

To Greybull

US 14 US 16 US 20

Oregon Basin

US ALT 14

Cody

120

To Thermopolis

Beck Lake

120

120

296

To Belfry, Montana

Montana

Wyoming

Beartooth Pass
El. 10,940 ft.

Island Lake

Chief Joseph Scenic Highway

101

Sunlight Basin

Buffalo Bill Reservoir

Beartooth Plateau

To Red Lodge, Montana

Cooke City

Silver Gate

US 212

To Northwest Entrance, Yellowstone National Park

Absaroka

Range

US 14 US 16 US 20

To East Entrance, Yellowstone National Park

18. CODY

Cody, founded by and named after Col. William F. "Buffalo Bill" Cody, is located at the base of the rugged Absaroka Range. The town, with a population of 8,000 and growing, serves as the gateway to Yellowstone National Park from the east inasmuch as those entering the National Park from the east, some fifty-two miles away, usually pass through here. This makes tourism an important part of Cody's economic life. A variety of habitats in the region, from high grasslands to alpine, offers good birding opportunities, and among them are the following:

1. **Oregon Basin and Loch Katrine**. If you are traveling west (from the end of the last chapter) on US 14/16/20 beyond Greybull, you will continue to cross the Big Horn Basin, a high-altitude desert. About 16 miles west of the junction of US 14/16/20 and State Route 30 you are in the middle of the basin, where Mountain Plovers are possible. This rather poor land is administered by the BLM and you can go anywhere you like. But, stay on the roads and leave gates as you found them. Some 26 miles from this junction there is a road (3FK) on the left which leads to Oregon Basin. (If you are coming from Cody, eastbound on US 14/16/20, Road 3FK is 6.9 miles beyond the Route 120 intersection.)

Oregon Basin is an 18-square-mile closed basin in an 8- to 10-inch precipitation zone, 5,125 feet above sea level. Loch Katrine, located in a Pleistocene lake-bed in the middle of the basin, is actually two lakes. The southern lake supports a dense community of bulrush and cattail as well as open water up to three feet deep. The northern lake is deeper by a couple of feet and is currently permanent, while the area covered by the southern lake may shrink considerably when the discharge of water from the nearby Marathon Oil operation is seasonally cut off. (This is a famous old Marathon Oil operation, and the water that is separated from the production of oil has no oil left in it.) If you see anybody, which is unlikely, tell them what you are doing.

Loch Katrine is the best shorebird and common-duck lake in the area. Nesting ducks include Lesser Scaup, Redhead, Gadwall, Northern Shoveler, and all three teal. It has Black-necked Stilts and lots of American Avocets as well as Wilson's Phalaropes and other shorebirds. There are plenty of rails—Soras and some Virginias. There are no nesting gulls. During migration all sorts of waterbirds occur. There are plenty of shorebirds, geese, and

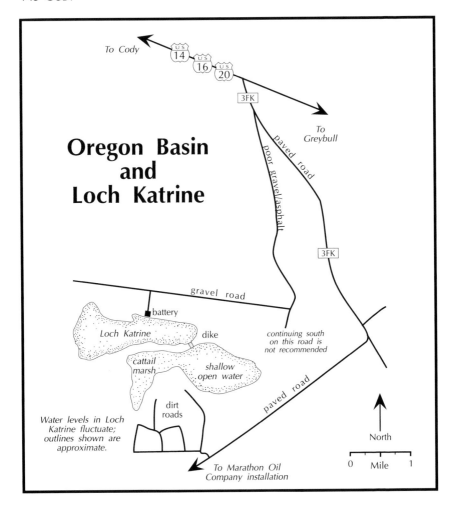

Oregon Basin and Loch Katrine

To Cody

US 14 US 16 US 20

3FK

To Greybull

paved road

poor gravel/asphalt

3FK

gravel road

battery

Loch Katrine

dike

continuing south
on this road is
not recommended

cattail marsh

shallow open water

paved road

dirt roads

Water levels in Loch
Katrine fluctuate;
outlines shown are
approximate.

North

0   Mile   1

To Marathon Oil
Company installation

ducks. Raptors in the basin can include Prairie Falcon, Northern Harrier, Golden Eagle, and Ferruginous Hawk, depending on the season.

BLM, which administers Loch Katrine and much of the land in the basin, is currently working on a cooperative project with the Marathon Oil Company and Ducks Unlimited to stabilize the water levels at the lake, improve waterbird habitat, and build facilities for public viewing and education.

To get to the lake area, drive south on Road 3FK for 0.5 mile from the US 14/16/20 turnoff. Bear right onto a poor gravel road. Check for sparrows as you drive 2.6 miles up and over the rim of the basin to a right turn onto a better gravel road. (The southbound continuation of the road which you were on deteriorates quickly and should be avoided.) In 1.0 mile you will see a track leading left toward a pumping facility, known as a battery, on the north shore of the north lake. Take this and park to the side of the road short of the battery. Walk in either direction along the lakeshore.

When you are through, you may turn around in the battery area, but *do not linger*. One of the byproducts of the pumping operation of the facility is hydrogen sulfide (HS). In small amounts this gas smells like rotten eggs, but large concentrations of it are odorless and are very dangerous to you. During a temperature inversion or on days when there is no air movement (most common in winter months), it is wise to stay a safe distance from oil and gas production-facilities. If you have any questions, contact the BLM office in Cody (1002 Blackburn, Cody, WY 82414; phone: 307/587-2216). They are very helpful to birders.

After visiting Loch Katrine, go back to US 14/16/20. You are now only 6.9 miles from the Junction of US 14/16/20 and State Route 120 on the outskirts of Cody.

2. **Beck Lake**. As you approach the junction of State Route 120 you will see Alkaline Lake on the left followed by Beck Lake. These are relatively small lakes but are good for ducks and some shorebirds. You will mostly find common ducks like Redhead, Lesser Scaup, and the tip-up ducks, but rarities like Harlequin sometimes show up. The common gulls such as Ring-billed, California, Franklin's, and Bonaparte's can also be seen here.

3. **Chief Joseph Scenic Highway and the Beartooth Plateau**. When you reach Cody, you might decide to try this interesting side-trip or use this route to enter Yellowstone National Park's Northeast Entrance at Silver Gate.

From Cody take Route 120 north for 17 miles to Route 296, Chief Joseph Scenic Highway, on the left. The road climbs steeply into the Absaroka Range with the views becoming grander at every turn. Many people feel that this may be the most spectacular or finest scenic highway in the contiguous 48 states. Along the rest of this route you will be driving through northern portions of Shoshone National Forest. In 13.5 miles you will reach Dead Indian Pass (El. 8,048 ft.). Turn into the parking area at the left for a breathtaking view. The road then switchbacks down quickly to a left turn onto Route 101 leading into Sunlight Basin. You are now 22.8 miles from Route 120. This good dirt road winds for a dozen miles and can be good for common riparian birds such as Red-naped Sapsucker, Warbling Vireo, and Lazuli Bunting. Return to Route 296 and continue west. This road follows Clark's Fork of the Yellowstone River. The Upper Clark's Fork is Wyoming's only "Wild and Scenic River". American Dippers nest along the river. This area can yield Golden Eagles, too.

There are reports that the US Forest Service is considering leasing some of the Shoshone National Forest in this area for development. I certainly hope that this doesn't take place; it would spoil the area.

A few miles beyond the Sunlight Basin turn-off, you will notice extensive burned areas on the ridges to the south of the road, a result of the wildfires of

1988. At one point, the Clover-Mist Fire was burning along a broad front in this area. To reach a burned area, turn left 7.4 miles from the Sunlight Basin junction onto Forest Service Road 114. Drive 2 miles or more to the top of the ridge where you can try your luck for woodpeckers. (While this road may offer an interesting diversion, there are *plenty* of opportunities to check out burned areas in Yellowstone National Park.) Also, watch overhead for raptors.

There is a gripping story about this area. In 1877 the Nez Perce Indians were trying to escape from the US Army and get into Canada. The Indians came through Yellowstone Park, over the Absaroka Mountains, down Trail Creek, into Crandal Creek, which in turn runs into the Clark's Fork. They went down Clark's Fork and out onto the plains through the gorge—a group of over 700 people and a large contingent of horses—baffling three US Army units that were trying to catch them. Looking at the terrain today, it is hard to imagine how they did it. You can't get through the gorge even now; the highway takes you over Dead Indian Pass instead.

After the turn-off for Forest Service Road 114, it is another 16.1 miles to the junction of Wyoming 296 and US 212. When you reach US 212, you may turn left toward Cooke City, Montana, 14 miles, and then through Silver Gate, 4 miles, and to Tower Junction in Yellowstone National Park, another 29 miles. (You can pick up the text from Chapter 15.) But to continue up the Beartooth Plateau, turn right. You might at least want to continue the 24 miles to the summit of Beartooth Pass to sample alpine species such as (Black) Rosy Finch and American Pipit. The last nine or so miles are in the alpine zone. This stretch is the only section of road in this book in the alpine zone.

On the way to Beartooth Pass a number of scenic turn-outs are available, and you will enjoy stopping at several. Looking back toward the west, you will note the strikingly beautiful panorama with Pilot and Index Peaks rising majestically. The scenic turn-outs also provide the opportunity to scan for hawks and eagles. This section of road may sometimes produce Northern Goshawk. A number of campgrounds and picnic areas are also available to the traveler along this route.

Pine Grosbeaks favor the higher areas in the mountains. Island Lake Campground, 12.4 miles from the Route 296 turn-off, is a particularly good area to check for this hardy species. Around the conifer stands of Lodgepole Pine, Subalpine Fir and spruce at Island Lake Campground, also look for Blue Grouse, Williamson's Sapsucker, Three-toed Woodpecker, Mountain Chickadee, Gray Jay, Clark's Nutcracker, Mountain Bluebird, and Dark-eyed Junco.

The drive to the summit of Beartooth Pass is well worth it. The pass (El. 10,940 ft.) is on US 212 14 miles beyond the entrance to Island Lake Campground. Here the road winds through great alpine habitat for the black race of Rosy Finch. Often, the Rosy Finches can be viewed from the car while driving past rocky outcroppings along the road. If you missed seeing them on the way up, try walking from the parking lot near the summit. A short walk to the rocky ridge-tops, where the species likes to nest in rock crevices, may produce the birds. Persistent searching should yield Rosy Finches along with American Pipits and Horned Larks. In this alpine habitat birds can often be found foraging on the edge of the melting snowfields. While "on top of the world" you will also want to take some time to enjoy the riot of alpine wildflowers. The peak of the blooming season is mid-July.

The best time to visit the Beartooth Plateau is from late May to September. Generally, the Beartooth Highway is open from Memorial Day through September. To best appreciate this wild country, try to travel this route on a relatively clear day. Also, be aware that snow can fall at any time.

4. **Along the North Fork**. Whether or not you decide to go up to the Beartooth Plateau, you may want to enter Yellowstone National Park directly west from Cody. To do this, drive along US 14/16/20 for 52 miles westward to the East Entrance of Yellowstone National Park. This route goes up through Shoshone Canyon. And you will drive through miles of the Shoshone National Forest, much of it along the North Fork of the Shoshone River. Some 4.6 miles from the beginning of the National Forest you will encounter the visitor center near the Wapiti Ranger Station. The birds along this route are the typical ones of the Douglas-fir and Lodgepole Pine forest which you have probably encountered before. Look for Gray Jay, Mountain Chickadee, Red-breasted Nuthatch, Yellow-rumped Warbler, Dark-eyed Junco, and Pine Siskin almost anywhere along the Forest road. There are a number of campgrounds and picnic areas on the Cody-Yellowstone corridor, and several warnings of the presence of Grizzly Bears.

This National Forest (as well as others in the area and the surrounding National Parks) also continues to play a part in the ongoing debate over re-introduction of the Gray Wolf in the greater Yellowstone area. The Gray Wolf was designated an endangered species in 1973, yet it was 1987 before a plan for Gray Wolf recovery was finally approved. An Environmental Impact Statement is currently being drafted with a final report due in 1994. While the greater Yellowstone area is full of Elk and Buffalo—Gray Wolf food—it also has substantial ranch livestock, and that is the problem. Strong objection to the wolf from ranchers in the region has so far blocked re-introduction.

From the Wapiti visitor center to the East Entrance of Yellowstone National Park is 26 miles. Here is your opportunity to pick up the text of Chapter 15 at the Fishing Bridge section and explore (or re-explore) Yellowstone National Park.

SOME CONCLUSIONS

As I wrap up the birdfinding portion of this book, I want to raise some issues concerning Wyoming's birding future. Some I've already raised in the birdfinding text; some will be mentioned in the annotated checklist; all, I think, deserve pointing out now. Below is a "wish-list" of nine developments that I'd like to see come true soon in my state:

1. *Some positive resolution on the long-term future of important bird habitat in the Casper area.*
Yant's Puddle needs a secure future; it is a superb place for birding, the best place by far in the state for waterbirds. Jackson Canyon's eagle roost must also be strongly protected.

2. *Security for the Yellowstone ecosystem.*
There is a growing realization that retirement income and especially self-employment in the service sector provide more economic horsepower than logging and mining in the Yellowstone area. Working from this assumption may mean getting the environmentalist-conservationist and business interests and government in the same room and knocking their heads together until they get some common sense. Sometimes this seems impossible.

3. *Less commercialism/less crowding in the Great Parks.*
The commercialism/crowding must stop. For example, the Fishing Bridge facility at Yellowstone National Park is plunk in probably the best Grizzly Bear habitat in Yellowstone Park. I would hope that readers will avoid using this facility unless they absolutely have to. In general, if we could get human facilities out of the Park and into surrounding places like West Yellowstone, Gardiner, Cody, and Flagg Ranch, Yellowstone would be far better for wildlife, and the Grizzly in particular might have a better chance for survival. (At the same time, we need to avoid the growth of some other developments *outside* Yellowstone National Park, such as the proposed lodge-complex in Sunlight Basin.)

4. *Finding better/more spots for birding in the state.*

There are probably many other important birding spots that remain to be uncovered in Wyoming. Here, I am especially focusing on migrant-traps and hawk-watching sites.

5. *A serious new effort on Atlasing the state.*

The Avian Atlas was done in 1982; it needs serious revision.

6. *A more understanding Wyoming Game and Fish Department.*

I would like to see a Game and Fish Department that would be more responsive to the needs of the large numbers of people interested in non-game birds.

7. *A concentrated effort to monitor neotropical migrants.*

There is a growing need to watch the status of key neotropical migrants. A broad variety of species, however, need watching in Wyoming, if only to compare and contrast with their numbers in other states. Perhaps more involvement in the Breeding Bird Survey program would be a good place to start.

8. *Enough feedback to re-do this book soon.*

As I wrote in the introduction to this book, there are errors that have undoubtedly crept into the work. The book will need revision, and that includes the annotated checklist which follows.

9. *More birders coming to enjoy the state.*

Birders are enjoying Wyoming in increasing numbers. And, this is not only in the popular Great Parks. Still, we need to assure that birders' recreation dollars are somehow tabulated; the state authorities should realize how much birders actually spend here. Visiting birders also need to make sure that their observations are recorded for the benefit of us all.

WYOMING
ANNOTATED CHECKLIST

To bring McCreary (*Wyoming Bird Life*, 1939) up to date at the present time is no easy task. Today we have lots of competent birders in the field who are constantly digging up either new birds, or birds that we thought were accidental or casual. It is also much more difficult to keep up than it used to be, and any list like this is obsolete before it is printed. Take the problem of warblers. Many of the eastern warblers that show up almost regularly in California probably went there via Wyoming. Therefore, we should theoretically see them all. At the present rate this will be true before very long. The number of vagrant eastern warblers seen in Wyoming has risen sharply in the last few years. In fact, 1991 was the first year in four that a new warbler for the state was *not* seen at the Fontenelle Trap.

We have another problem, which is our state Avian Atlas. There has not been time to investigate all the records which are in the Atlas. As a result it contains many records which are open to question. Perhaps the most remarkable is the Western Bluebird. From what the Atlas indicates, there are records for this species in many of our latilongs and even some breeding records. However, in 44 years of birding in the state and more intensively in the last 19, I have yet to find one or been shown one. Nor have I met anyone who has seen one well enough to document it, and this applies to most of the active birders in the state. We hope that the Wyoming Bird Records Committee will have time to clean up the Atlas. There are lots of good records in it, and we wish that that statement were true for the whole work. But just because a report is in the Atlas does not mean that it ought to be considered as legitimate for Wyoming avifauna at the present time.

On a more positive note, if readers find significant changes in birdlife or rare birds in their birding through Wyoming, please send details to the *American Birds* Regional Editor for the "Mountain West Region," Hugh Kingery, 869 Milwaukee Street, Denver, CO 80206. Also, send specifics on rare birds to the Wyoming Bird Records Committee, c/o Game & Fish Department, 260 Buena Vista, Lander, WY 82520. Your contribution toward documenting the changing bird scene in Wyoming will be much appreciated.

Finally, you should be aware of locations mentioned in this annotated checklist. The overwhelming majority of locations mentioned are found in the previous birdfinding chapters in this book. (For example: Yant's Puddle, Lake DeSmet, Lions Park, or the Fontenelle Trap.) So refer to them when necessary.

THE SPECIES LIST:

Red-throated Loon—*Casual.* The most recent reports are from Yellowstone, May 5, 1988, by Bill Schreier, and Lake DeSmet, May 15, 1988, by Helen Downing and others. There is an old report—well out of range and without many details—of a pair nesting in Yellowstone National Park in 1929 (McCreary, *Wyoming Bird Life*). One was taken out of an alkali pit at a trona plant west of Green River on October 26, 1975. These pits have since been cleaned up. Another was seen by Platt Hall on Lake DeSmet November 1-2, 1975. One was on Healy Reservoir just down the creek from Buffalo October 24-26, 1986, by Helen Downing and many others, including the author

Pacific Loon—*Rare.* It is seen every fall, and some years there are several. It has been reported from Lake DeSmet, Ocean Lake, Healy Reservoir, Keyhole Reservoir, and Yellowstone Lake, to mention a few. The dates are mostly October and November. No spring reports. One bird in breeding plumage spent most of the summer on Yellowstone Lake and the ponds near Fishing Bridge in 1990.

Common Loon—*Uncommon summer resident and common migrant.* Nests on lakes in the northwest part of the state, particularly on the southwest arm of Yellowstone Lake, and has nested as far south as First Creek, which is just south of Colter Bay in Grand Teton National Park. It is a common migrant on many lakes, such as Yellowstone, DeSmet, and Ocean, and on Glendo, Keyhole, and Healy Reservoirs. The largest concentration I have seen (over 20 Common Loons) was on Lake Cameahwait just west of Boysen Reservoir. However, Helen Downing has had 50 or more on Lake DeSmet. DeSmet is the premier place for loons in the state. The migration dates are April and early May in spring and in the fall mid-September through November.

Yellow-billed Loon—*Casual.* One was seen on Lake DeSmet November 1, 1978, and on several subsequent days by Helen Downing and Fred Harrington. Bill Hayes had one below the power plant at Grayrocks Reservoir on the Laramie River near Wheatland November 20,1988. He took an excellent picture of the immature bird. The bird was seen by Jim and Verna Herold later.

Pied-billed Grebe—*Uncommon summer resident.* Nests in small reedy ponds throughout the state and on larger lakes with reedy components. Migrates in April and the first three weeks of May in the spring and in September and October in the fall.

Horned Grebe—*Uncommon migrant.* Present in the spring mostly in April on a number of lakes, but especially on Glendo Reservoir, where groups of up to 50 have been found. In the fall they can be seen on many of our better lakes, such as Yellowstone, DeSmet, Keyhole, Yant's Puddle,

Bridger Ponds, etc., but not Glendo, which is largely drained by irrigation by the fall. The fall dates are mid-September through October.

Red-necked Grebe—*Casual.* Helen Downing and others had one on Lake DeSmet on October 8, 1982. There were three seen on Yellowstone Lake on September 29, 1986, by A. Siebecker. Another was seen on Two Ocean Lake in Grand Teton National Park by Sam Fitton and the author on July 19,1988.

Eared Grebe—*Common migrant and summer resident.* They like the smaller, shallower lakes and ponds for nesting, such as Loch Katrine out of Cody and Yant's Puddle near Casper, but they are found almost everywhere. They arrive from late March through April in the spring. Most are gone by late October in the fall and a few will stay until freeze-up in late November. They have been known to overwinter.

Western Grebe—*Common migrant and summer resident.* There are colonies at Ocean Lake, Loch Katrine, and many other smaller and shallow ponds. As migrants they can be found on all our deeper, larger lakes through April and the first half of May. In the fall they can be seen in the same areas in September through November—often in sizable numbers, such as 400 on Lake DeSmet November 5, 1987.

Clark's Grebe—*Uncommon migrant and summer resident.* Only recently has information on this bird accumulated. It has been found nesting on the Lovell Lakes, which lie just east of that town. Sam Fitton found this bird nesting at Ocean Lake. It has been found as a migrant on Lake DeSmet, Fontenelle Reservoir, and others. The dates appear to be the same as those for Western Grebe.

American White Pelican—*Common migrant and summer visitor,* but nests in only a few locations at the moment: Yellowstone Lake, Bamforth Lake northwest of Laramie, and an island in Pathfinder Reservoir on the North Platte River. The latter has been by far the biggest rookery. However, due to drought and the need for repair of Pathfinder Dam, the lake level may be too low, and the rookery location is now just part of the mainland and therefore not in current use. Many other lakes have numbers of non-breeding birds because it takes three years for a pelican to mature, so Ocean Lake, Wheatland Reservoir, Keyhole Reservoir, and Jackson Lake in Grand Teton National Park will have a group, along with a number of other lakes. Migration takes place in April and the first half of May in the spring and September and October in the fall.

Brown Pelican—*Accidental.* One was collected near Cheyenne by Frank Bond on July 12, 1899 (McCreary, *Wyoming Bird Life*).

Double-crested Cormorant—*Common migrant and summer resident.* The largest colony (of several hundred nests) is at Yant's Puddle. To name a few more places, there are also colonies on Yellowstone Lake, Pathfinder Reservoir, and Ocean Lake. Migration starts in March and lasts until mid-April in the spring and in September and October in the fall, but there is a scattering everywhere all summer.

American Bittern—*Uncommon summer resident and migrant.* Although no nests have been found in recent years, there are old records of nests; the species undoubtedly does nest in places like Hutton Lake National Wildlife Refuge and Table Mountain. It is seen in marshy areas all over the state but is not common. However, in the great new National Wildlife Refuge now being organized on the Bear River south of Cokeville, it is common. It seems to migrate in May and September. Once a bird showed up on a residential street miles from water during a mid-October snowstorm in the city of Casper.

Least Bittern—*Casual.* There are several old reports (McCreary, *Wyoming Bird Life*) but no recent ones.

Great Blue Heron—*Common migrant and summer resident.* There are colonies along all our major streams in Wyoming except the Yellowstone, which doesn't have much suitable habitat. One of the largest colonies is in the southern part of the Seedskadee National Wildlife Refuge on the Green River. They arrive in the last half of March and first two weeks of April and leave in October and November. Every now and then one winters over, probably successfully.

Great Egret—*Rare.* It has been seen almost every year somewhere in the state, but most of the records are from the eastern part in such places as just below Keyhole Reservoir Dam, Glendo Reservoir, and Goshen Hole. It has occurred from May through September.

Snowy Egret—*Uncommon migrant and summer resident.* It used to nest at Springer Lake in Goshen Hole south of Torrington but not in recent years. It has nested at Yant's Puddle just north of Casper and on the Laramie Plains near or on Hutton Lake National Wildlife Refuge. It is seen from May through September. Most of the birds probably nested somewhere else or are non-breeding adults. The most likely places to see them are the Laramie River near Laramie or in the vicinity of Lake Hattie west of Laramie.

Little Blue Heron—*Casual.* There was an adult seen at Hutton Lake National Wildlife Refuge by many people, including the author, for a week or more in early May 1977. This species has been seen as an immature at Yant's Puddle in September 1983, August 1985, and August 1989 by numerous people. Sam Fitton saw an adult on Horse Creek, a tributary of the Sweetwater arm of Pathfinder Reservoir on Route 220, April 26, 1989.

Cattle Egret—*Rare.* This bird is becoming much more common but probably should still be considered rare. It is now seen more than once a year. The first record for the state was in 1978 by the author and Steven Lund at Yant's Puddle, so although Wyoming may have been the last state where this species has been recorded, the number of records has certainly increased. There are no breeding records as yet.

Green-backed Heron—*Rare migrant.* It is seen almost every year somewhere in the state, mostly in the eastern half. I have seen it only four times in 44 years. Most of the records are from May or the first week of June.

Black-crowned Night-Heron—*Uncommon migrant and summer resident.* If there is adequate water, it nests at Hutton Lake National Wildlife Refuge southwest of Laramie and on smaller lakes like West Carroll Lake farther north on the Laramie Plains. It also nests at Yant's Puddle just north of Casper and at Table Mountain in Goshen Hole. It migrates in early May and September. It is less common in the western part of the state. There was a colony at Ocean Lake formerly, but it is rumored that personnel of the State Game and Fish Department destroyed the colony years ago.

Yellow-crowned Night-Heron—*Accidental.* It was seen by Helen Downing and others on July 27-29 and again on August 22, 1976, on the Tongue River near the canyon.

White Ibis—*Accidental.* One was reported to Helen Downing, who confirmed the identification northwest of Buffalo on Piney Creek on September 12, 1976. It was in a wet meadow.

White-faced Ibis—*Common migrant and summer resident.* Nests in places like Seedskadee National Wildlife Refuge, and the new wildlife refuge just south of Cokeville on the Bear River on the western edge of the state, where up to 900 were seen in August 1987. It migrates through most ponds and lakes in open country from mid-April to mid-May and during September.

Wood Stork—*Accidental.* There are two old records in *Wyoming Bird Life* (July 16, 1925, and June 28, 1930), one with photographs; there are no recent verified reports.

Tundra Swan—*Uncommon migrant.* Up to 50 or a few more regularly visit Yant's Puddle in the late fall from the end of October to solid freeze-up. If weather permits, they will linger into January. They will appear in Yellowstone National Park every fall. They can be seen occasionally on all our larger lakes. In spring they are a very early arrival—often before the end of February—and they will be gone usually by the end of March. In spring they are often seen on smaller ponds since most of the big ponds are still frozen.

Trumpeter Swan—*Locally common resident.* Trumpeters are common in Grand Teton and Yellowstone National Parks all year round. There are enough warm springs so that they have no trouble overwintering. The most famous place to see them through the year is Flat Creek on US 191 just north of the town of Jackson. This stream has warm springs and often has many swans on it in the fall and winter months. In summer there is often a nesting pair there. Another nesting-spot that has been used for many years is Christian Pond just across the highway from Jackson Lake

Lodge in Grand Teton National Park. Efforts to get Trumpeters to expand their range have had limited success. There is a pair near Boulder (south of Pinedale), but these great birds have trouble with power-lines and fences. Dave Lockman of the Wyoming Game and Fish Department says that 60 percent of the known mortality of Trumpeters come from these two factors. (The Whooping Crane re-introduction effort at Grays Lake National Wildlife Refuge just over the border in Idaho had the same problem.) Trumpeters have a nesting-spot also at Colony near Sundance in extreme northeast Wyoming. This is believed to be related to the Lacreek National Wildlife Refuge colony 150 miles east in South Dakota. There is another population extension in Star Valley (Afton) that appears to be successful.

Greater White-fronted Goose—*Uncommon along the eastern edge of the state.* Elsewhere, it is unknown. Game and Fish Department personnel assure me that this bird is seen every now and then in the Goshen Hole complex of Table Mountain, Springer Lake, and Bump Sullivan and Hawk Springs reservoirs. With others I saw a flock of 35 at Table Mountain on October 10, 1985. Platt Hall saw several over the years on Lake DeSmet. They migrate through in October and November. As yet there are few spring records.

Snow Goose—*Uncommon migrant.* They are seen on all of our larger lakes and at times in sizable numbers—more than a thousand. They usually don't stay long. They are more commonly seen in the fall than in the spring. Sometimes in the spring and fall they will be seen on Ocean Lake, Lake DeSmet, Yant's Puddle, and particularly Table Mountain (where thousands have occurred), to mention a few places. The time of migration varies a great deal from March to mid-May and September through early December.

Ross's Goose—*Rare migrant.* We used to think that this was an accidental, but there are so many records from recent years that it is now considered just rare. It is a late migrant—our fall records from Yant's Puddle are all in November. However, a group of us, including Paul Lehman of California, had one at Table Mountain May 10, 1985. There are records in April and May from Yant's Puddle as well.

Brant—*Casual.* There are no recent records, but Otto McCreary, in *Wyoming Bird Life*, saw quite a few, so it would seem that things have changed. He thought that all his records were of the West Coast subspecies.

Canada Goose—*Common resident.* They nest on all our major rivers and suitable lakes and ponds. The Wyoming Game and Fish Department makes every effort to increase their numbers. In most areas where they breed, Game and Fish has erected nesting-platforms, and every now and then one of these is used. Geese overwinter wherever there is open water—and there is a surprising amount in Wyoming although our winters are relatively long and severe. There are many warm springs and riffles on the rivers that stay open; geese also will stand on the ice of frozen lakes by day and glean in surrounding fields at night. Local birds are augmented by sizable flocks of migrants. The Game and Fish Department has established a large habitat for geese in Goshen Hole at Table Mountain Wildlife Habitat Management Unit and Springer Lake.

Wood Duck—*Uncommon migrant and summer resident.* The Wyoming Game and Fish Department has worked hard and with considerable success to get Wood Ducks to nest in the Rawhide area up the North Platte River from Torrington. They have lots of nesting boxes up, a few of which are used. For two years Wood Ducks have nested in my little ranch reservoir west of Casper. They have been seen over almost all the state except the southwest. They arrive in February and don't leave until November.

Green-winged Teal—*Common summer resident and migrant.* This bird is perhaps the second-most-common overwintering species of the surface-feeding ducks. Migration starts in early March and continues through April and starts again in late August and continues until freeze-up in November. Green-wings like smaller ponds and lakes that are shallow (such as Table Mountain and Loch Katrine) for nesting.

American Black Duck—*Very rare migrant.* There are only a few records, most of them old. The picture is a little bit confused because a waterfowl zoo of sorts in the Cody area was dissolved, and the Black Ducks there were released.

Mallard—*Common resident.* Mallards spend the winters on all our main rivers wherever there is open water from either riffles or warm springs. Also, they spend the winter on irrigation projects such as the one near Powell and on the Missouri Valley project north of Riverton. For instance, up to a thousand Mallards will rest on the ice at Yant's Puddle during the day, and spread out to glean on the nearby Kendrick irrigation project at night. Many thousand manage to overwinter, making this species our most common puddle-duck during that season. In summer they nest on all our ponds of any size. However, we probably have more in winter than summer. Larger numbers migrate through.

Northern Pintail—*Common summer resident and migrant.* Migration starts in early March or February if melting ice allows. Occasionally, they will overwinter if conditions permit. Spring migration lasts through April; fall migration starts in late August and lasts until freeze-up in November. Pintails nest on any of our larger lakes or even on small ones.

Blue-winged Teal—*Common summer resident and migrant.* Migration starts in early April and lasts until May and starts again in mid-August and is over by the end of September. For nesting, Blue-wings like smaller ponds that are shallow, such as at Seedskadee National Wildlife Refuge on the Green River or at Table Mountain at the bottom of Goshen Hole.

Cinnamon Teal—*Common summer resident and migrant.* The dates of the Cinnamon are just like those for the Blue-wing, but perhaps the Cinnamon is more plentiful. Anyway, they can often be seen earlier. They nest in the same locations.

Northern Shoveler—*Common migrant and summer resident.* They nest in virtually all our open-country ponds and lakes. Arriving in late March and early April, they are gone by November.

Gadwall—*Common summer resident.* Gadwall is probably our most common nesting duck. Greater numbers migrate through, and occasionally, one will overwinter. Gadwalls like all ponds and lakes with vegetation around them; lakes in forests without riparian plants won't do. Migration starts as early in March as melting ice will allow and lasts through April. In the fall it starts in late August and lasts until freeze-up, usually in November.

Eurasian Wigeon—*Rare migrant.* There are several recent records—almost one each year now. These are mostly in October and November although there are spring records from Jackson, the Kendrick irrigation project near Casper, as well as Grey Reef Reservoir south of that city.

American Wigeon—*Common summer resident and migrant.* In migration this is perhaps the most numerous of the surface-feeding ducks. It nests throughout Wyoming from Cokeville and Seedskadee National Wildlife Refuge to Table Mountain in Goshen Hole. It arrives in early March and stays until freeze-up in November. Occasionally, some will overwinter.

Canvasback—*Common migrant and uncommon nesting summer resident.* A few Canvasbacks are believed to nest at Cokeville and Yant's Puddle and possibly at other spots in the state. As a migrant they are common but don't occur in the numbers which most of the surface-feeding ducks do. They arrive a little later—about the third week in March—and leave by November. A good show of Canvasbacks would be over a hundred, while the surface-feeders show up by the thousands.

Redhead—*Common migrant and summer resident.* This is one of our most common ducks. If there is open water such as at Grey Reef Reservoir below Alcova on the North Platte River, they will start appearing in February. Spring migration lasts through April; fall migration goes from September to freeze-up, usually in November. Perhaps the greatest concentration during migration is at the west end of Lake Hattie west of Laramie, where there will be several thousand. It nests on all our marshy ponds and lakes from Cokeville to Table Mountain.

Ring-necked Duck—*Common migrant in the eastern part of the state and the most common nesting duck of Jackson Hole.* It usually arrives in April and leaves by freeze-up in November. It likes small ponds and is unusual on lakes. If the lake has a small appendage, however, look for Ring-necks in that area. This is true at Lake DeSmet and Yant's Puddle. I have a small ranch reservoir which is often visited by Ring-necks.

Tufted Duck— *Accidental.* Michael Gochfield and others had one at Hutton Lake National Wildlife Refuge southwest of Laramie April 10, 1966, as reported in *Condor* 70: 186-187, 1968. Since the author reported Greater Scaup, which are thundering rare, with the Tufted Duck, there has been much debate about this sighting. The chances of the Tufted Duck being an escapee are very high.

Greater Scaup—*Rare migrant.* This is one of our rarest ducks. However, with more and better observers in the field in recent years, we have had reports of the bird almost every year, mostly in March and April.

Lesser Scaup—*Common migrant and summer resident.* Nests in numbers in all our big duck-nesting areas such as Cokeville, Seedskadee, Yant's Puddle, and Table Mountain. Spring migration is in March and April and fall migration lasts from September to freeze-up in November.

Harlequin Duck—*Rare nester* on the bigger streams of the Bighorn and Wind River Mountains. Some places are the Middle Fork (Red Fork) of the Powder River, Shell Creek in the Bighorns, and Dinwoody Creek above the Dinwoody Lake in the Wind Rivers. In Yellowstone National Park there are two mating areas that are accessible. One is LeHardy Rapids on the Yellowstone River below Fishing Bridge, and the other is on the Yellowstone River near the bridge just east of Tower Junction. The latter is now the more reliable of the two. The Park authorities built a boardwalk to LeHardy Rapids and virtually ruined the place for Harlequin Ducks. Now, often there is none there, whereas in the good old days this was a great place to see them.

Oldsquaw—*Rare migrant.* This species has been seen almost regularly at Yant's Puddle for the last ten years, usually late in the season—not long before freeze-up. In fact, one year there was a rift in the ice, so the bird stayed into the new year. Oldsquaw has been seen on Lake DeSmet, Bridger Ponds, and Yellowstone Lake. Most of the reports are from late October on.

Black Scoter—*Casual.* Platt Hall had one November 1, 1972, at Lake DeSmet and another one on the same date in 1975 at the same place. The author had one at Yant's Puddle October 27, 1957, and another one at the same place November 6-7, 1982, which was also seen by many others.

Surf Scoter—*Rare migrant.* However, it is seen every year somewhere—at places like Creighton Lake in Hutton Lake National Wildlife Refuge, Yant's Puddle, Lake DeSmet, Bridger Ponds, or Healy Reservoir east of Buffalo.

White-winged Scoter—*Uncommon migrant.* This bird is a little more common than the Surf Scoter but is found in the same places. The fall migration is from the middle of October to freeze-up, which is sometimes as late as December. Our only spring records come from the Bridger Ponds.

Common Goldeneye—*Common winter visitor.* This duck competes with the Mallard as our most common wintering species. It is predominant on our major streams where there are open rifts in the winter even in the coldest weather, such as the North Platte, Tongue, etc. Common Goldeneyes show up in early October and can be found well into April. Occasional non-breeding birds will stay with us throughout the summer. In the last part of the fall migration this duck will be the most common species on many of our lakes before freeze-up. In addition, it is perhaps our most common wintering duck on any remaining open water.

Barrow's Goldeneye—*Common resident in western Wyoming and uncommon winter visitor in the rest of the state.* It nests on many small ponds in the Jackson Hole area, such as the Sawmill Ponds near Moose and the little pond on the right one-half mile from the Teton Park Highway on the road up Signal Hill. Elsewhere in the state Barrow's are found uncommonly in the winter on open riffles of our major rivers. Places like Seedskadee National Wildlife Refuge have them in the spring in impoundments along the Green River.

Bufflehead—*Common migrant.* A common winter visitor in open areas such as Flat Creek on the National Elk Refuge just north of Jackson and the Glenrock Power Plant on the North Platte River. It nests rather commonly in Yellowstone on embankments on Yellowstone Lake and on the Yellowstone River and its tributaries above the lake.

Hooded Merganser—*Uncommon winter visitor and migrant.* Wherever there is open water in the winter, such as at the Glenrock Power Plant or Grey Reef Reservoir on the North Platte River or on Flat Creek at Jackson, one may find Hoodeds. The largest number reported is seven on the Snake River above Jackson Lake in March. They also were seen on Lake DeSmet fairly often in May by Platt Hall. There is an old breeding record of a female with two downy young along the Green River June 4, 1929, south of the city of Green River (McCreary, *Wyoming Bird Life*).

Common Merganser—*Common resident.* In winter they occur in almost all open water in the state whether it be riffles on our major rivers or open water from warm springs as on Flat Creek at Jackson in the National Elk Refuge or Grey Reef Reservoir on the North Platte at Alcova. In summer they nest on smaller permanent streams like LaPrele Creek at Ayres Natural Bridge or the Hoback River south of Jackson. During spring and fall, both migrants and our resident birds can be found on most of our lakes.

Red-breasted Merganser—*Uncommon migrant.* While over the state this an uncommon migrant, they can be common in certain favorite lakes. Ocean Lake, particularly in the spring, has lots of them. They arrive in the last week of March and stay through April. The fall migration is not so well documented, but it is from late October until freeze-up.

Ruddy Duck—*Common summer resident.* These ducks nest in most of our marshy lakes from Table Mountain to Cokeville and Seedskadee. They are numerous, arrive about the first of April, and stay with us almost to freeze-up.

Turkey Vulture—*Common summer resident in the eastern two-thirds of the state; uncommon to rare in the western part of the state.* Nests on cliffs in places like the south side of Casper Mountain or the Mendicino Hills north of Guernsey. They arrive in April and leave by mid-October.

Osprey—*Common summer resident of the northwest; elsewhere, it is almost uncommon but increasing.* There was a nest on the top of an old derrick at a unused sand-and-gravel operation within the city limits of Casper. It was the tallest thing in Casper. In 1989 the derrick was removed, and three young birds were dumped into the nearest ashcan. A friendly person found them and sent them to Lois Layton's Bird Hospital in Casper, where they did well and were later returned to the wild. The parents are still around; they have a less-conspicuous nest downstream. There is a famous nest on a special power-pole on US 87 near Story which has been there for about 17 years. There is another beside US 191 in Boulder just south of Pinedale. From the headwaters of the Green River and its tributaries around Pinedale northwest through the Great Parks (Grand Teton and Yellowstone), the Osprey is just plain common. You will see them everywhere on the streams and larger lakes. They start arriving in the second half of March and go south in September and the first half of October.

Black-shouldered Kite—*Accidental.* One was seen in Grand Teton National Park by many people from August 20 to September 14, 1982. It was first seen east of Moose by H. and B. Johnson, and then it moved to Willow Flats, where it was seen by a host of others. Another was seen by Charlie Scott early in June 1989 on the irrigated hay meadows on Bates Creek just south of Casper Mountain off US 487. Over the next two months it was occasionally seen briefly flying by a number of birders either on the south side of Casper Mountain or just south of it.

Mississippi Kite—*Accidental.* Pete Widener and Helen Downing had one at Ash Creek near Sheridan on June 11, 1987. They documented it with a good photograph.

Bald Eagle—*Uncommon resident.* There are a number of active nests in Yellowstone and Grand Teton National Parks—one each on Shoshone Lake, Yellowstone Lake, and the Snake River below Jackson Lake in Grand Teton. There are five nests on the North Platte River, one east of Casper, one at the Bighorn Canyon National Recreation Area, and others south of Saratoga. However, the nest-tree of the pair east of Casper blew down in the winter of 1989-90, and they didn't nest there in 1990. There is another nest on the Bighorn River near Greybull. This mentions several but not all of the nesting sites. There are also a number of nests that have been abandoned due to human encroachment. All Bald Eagle nests are by rivers or lakes. In winter the situation is different. Bald Eagles stay on our larger rivers wherever there is open water. There are a number of winter roosts and gathering-places. The largest gathering-place is Woodruff Narrows on the Bear River just below the reservoir north of Evanston and just east of the Utah state-line. However, they don't seem to stay there. This is a mixed eagle roost with Goldens and Balds, as are most of the winter roosts, although the Bald is the predominant bird. The North Platte River has several roosts. The largest roost is usually in Jackson Canyon southwest of Casper, where up to 40 birds have been counted, a very spectacular sight. There is a roost in Boxelder Canyon in the hills south of Glenrock. There are numerous other roosting-places, but they seem to be much smaller. The number of eagles in a given roost on a given night is highly variable, depending on the weather and the wind direction. On mild nights the eagles may not bother to go to a roost. A few years ago a banded young Bald Eagle in Jackson Canyon seen by Steve Lund was found to have been raised in Northern Saskatchewan. Probably most of our wintering birds are from north of Wyoming.

Northern Harrier—*Common migrant and summer resident.* These birds start being seen in the last half of March; however, most of the migration takes place in April. They stay until November and in warm spells can be found in the winter months. They nest in most suitable marshes in the state. A pair on the way into Ayres Natural Bridge is quite reliable. In Wyoming when conditions are just right there can be tremendous irruptions of grasshoppers over relatively small areas. In 1960 in late July there was such a concentration of hoppers on the Kendrick irrigation project northwest of the Casper International Airport. I counted 50 Northern Harriers there at once. This was the largest concentration I have ever seen.

Sharp-shinned Hawk—*Uncommon resident and migrant.* They nest in all forested areas in the state but are not common. During migration in both spring and fall there are more of them, but at no time could you call them common. There are no real migration sites like Pennsylvania's Hawk Mountain that are known in the state. However, there is a north-south path from the Bighorn Mountains south across a gap to Pine Mountain just south of the hamlet of Powder River, and thence down the Emigrant Anticline to Casper Mountain, the north end of the Laramie Range, and then down that range to Colorado. In migration this is probably the best we have. This path has been little studied, but we don't think that it is especially spectacular.

Cooper's Hawk—*Uncommon resident and migrant.* Everything said about the Sharp-shin applies to the Cooper's as well. Which species is more common is hard to say. Both species are seen in the winter almost as often as in spring and fall. When they are nesting, they are seen the least.

Northern Goshawk—*Uncommon resident.* This is the least common of the accipiters. Some people feel that they are more common in the northwest mountains of Yellowstone and Grand Teton National Parks, but probably this is because the observers are not familiar with the rest of the state. East of the mountains of the northwest the Gos is seen more often in winter than at any other time. It nests as do the other two (Sharp-shinned and Cooper's). However, it can be seen on the high plains almost as much as in the forests.

Broad-winged Hawk—*Rare migrant in the eastern half of the state; almost non-existent west of the Continental Divide.* However, in the Casper and Cheyenne areas it has been seen almost every year in April and May for the last 15 years or more. Before that we didn't have the observers. There are a few fall records, also. There are no known nesting-reports. There are a number of reports from Glendo Reservoir of this migrant and recently it was reported in Yellowstone National Park.

Swainson's Hawk—*Common summer resident.* This is a candidate for our most common big buteo in the state in summer. Swainson's start to arrive in the third week of April, and usually they are gone by November 1. There are old stories of over 1,000 birds being seen in a day in Goshen Hole in migration, but no such numbers occur today. One would be lucky to see 20 to 30. The largest concentration I have seen was at Merna, a hamlet about 25 miles west of Daniel Junction, which is near the Green River. Merna is in a large area of native hay, which is cut and baled in early August. The cutting and baling uncovers a large crop of mice, which Swainson's Hawks hunt from perches on the big round bales. Each third or fourth bale has a perched hawk, so one can see perhaps 100 birds in the area. There are no recent winter records. Many of us feel that the few winter reports which do exist are probably of misidentified Rough-legs.

Red-tailed Hawk—*Common summer resident.* There are numerous winter records, so one could almost call this a resident species. Actually, they usually show up in mid-March and stay through November. You don't find them out on the plains. They stay and nest in the forested mountains and riparian zones. In the forested areas they are usually the only big buteo. In numbers they rival the Swainson's statewide, but this impression may be an illusion since most of us live in or very near forested or riparian areas.

Ferruginous Hawk—*Common summer resident.* This is the common buteo of the plains where there are virtually no trees—just grass, sagebrush, and outcrops of rock. They nest on rock pinnacles or sometimes just flat on the ground. How they avoid predators like Coyotes I don't know, but since they are a successful species they must get away with it. They arrive in early March and stay until late November. There are a number of winter records. Since bird hospitals have become more common, there has been increased contact with caged wild birds, and we have insights on many species which we didn't have before.

Rough-legged Hawk—*Common winter visitor, but variable.* Usually they show up in the plains country in October and sometimes stay until April. These are mostly young birds. If we have very dry conditions, there will be few of them; at other times we may have them in great numbers. They will inhabit the riparian areas as well as the open country, so Jackson Hole has them, as well as the rest of the state.

Golden Eagle—*Common resident.* This is our more common eagle by far. They nest everywhere in the state, and in the winter we have a large population from the north, such that in 1973 by aerial surveys it was estimated that we had 10,000 birds in the state. These surveys were done by the state and the National Audubon Society. We believe that the numbers have diminished somewhat since that time. They nest on cliffs and in trees. They also have the habit of making several nests before they choose one. If someone tells you there are so many nests per mile, beware: they won't all be active. In winter when the eagles are hungry because the jackrabbits are scarce, they can attack sick, weak Antelope successfully. Wyoming has enormous numbers of Antelope—the latest estimate is about 350,000. These attacks have been recorded on film. I have seen the process myself.

On a very wintery day in January I saw a small group of Antelope trotting leisurely along a fence line. For some reason one of them lallygagged behind. Along came a pair of Golden Eagles and started dipping by turns at this animal but not touching it. The Antelope got tired of this, stepped on the gas, and quickly joined the others. The eagles sat down on the nearest fence-posts. How different this story would have been if the Antelope had been in such poor shape that it couldn't rejoin the others. The Wyoming Game and Fish Department doesn't worry about this predation since these weak animals are going to die anyway.

Golden Eagles can eat carrion of Antelope, deer, and sheep, but not cattle. The hide of the latter is too thick, and the eagles can't get through it unless somebody opens it up for them. Once we had a veterinarian do a postmortem on a cow. Of course, he had to cut it open. Within thirty minutes after he left, there were eagles feeding on the carcass. On the other hand, I lost 26 cattle through the ice in the North Platte River one Christmas and spent the rest of the winter hauling them out onto the bank. There were lots of eagles around, and they even sat on the carcasses while watching the river but never could they feed on them.

The story with sheep is different. Sometimes it becomes rather technical. For instance, does a tail-ender lamb that is going to die anyway lie down and gasp his last before the eagle jumps on him, or does the eagle jump on him before he has his last gasp? However, some sheep-herders insist that a lamb has to be dead two weeks before an eagle will eat it. Since a ewe has two and occasionally more lambs while often she can take care of only one, there are going to be dead lambs scattered behind any band of sheep that has recently lambed. Some predator will eat these, and certainly the Golden Eagle is one of the common ones. Hence the theory from some sheepmen that eagles kill sheep, particularly lambs. This leads some bureaucrat who sits in Cheyenne to call up some sheepman who believes most losses are due to eagles. The bureaucrat gets the figure, and he knows how many sheep there are supposed to be in the state. From here he extrapolates and comes out with some horrendous figure on the losses to the sheep industry by eagles, thereby trying to justify his existence in predator control. Of course, now the eagle is protected by law. Extending enforcement of the laws to the remote corners of Wyoming is difficult, but public opinion here now is on the side of the eagle, which is perhaps more important than the law. Most informed sheepmen don't pay attention to eagles because they don't feel that they are a problem—which would seem to be the actual case. There is another important factor. The total number of sheep in Wyoming has been dropping for decades. Whereas there used to be five million or more, now the figure is 775,000 and still falling.

American Kestrel—*Common almost-resident.* Winter records are really fairly frequent and regular in Goshen Hole. The bulk of kestrels start arriving in the last week of March and stay until November. They nest wherever there is open country with trees nearby. This means that most of our mountain areas have lots, as well as areas that have riparian trees not too far away.

Merlin—*Uncommon resident and migrant.* Most are seen in migration (spring and fall), but there are almost as many in winter. They are least common in summer. They nest in tree holes in almost all parts of the state, however, they are not consistent. They are most common in the Green River valley above the town of Green River. The gray form is seen in all parts of the state but perhaps more frequently in the western half. The dark form is the more common.

Peregrine Falcon—*Rare resident.* Peregrines are seen at all times of the year. Due to the re-introduction program it is hard to generalize about this bird. It goes back to its historical aeries, which are scattered all over the state but perhaps more in the northwest mountainous portion, including the Great Parks. In Wyoming, however, there is hardly a place where one can't see forested mountains in the distance. There are mountains everywhere.

Gyrfalcon— *Rare winter visitor.* Almost all the records are from the Sheridan area along the east side of the Bighorn Mountains. Among other records Platt Hall had a white Gyr at Lake DeSmet. Helen Downing has had one north of Sheridan several years. These birds are not seen every year, but there are more sightings than just casual reports. There is one report from the west side of the Bighorn Mountains in Shell Canyon.

Prairie Falcon—*Common resident.* These birds nest on rocky cliffs—Wyoming abounds in such places. One can expect to see this bird any day one goes out and sees a fair amount of country. Perhaps there are more around in winter, spring, and fall than in summer, but there isn't a great deal of difference. These falcons can be seen anywhere in the state, mountain or plain. In winter in the deep snow country, as in Grand Teton and Yellowstone National Parks, they may be missing, but this doesn't apply to the rest of the state. Keeping a checklist of the birds for over forty years, I often see my first Prairie Falcon on the first day of January.

Gray Partridge—*Locally common.* The greatest concentration of these birds is in the Sheridan/Story area. Bird Farm Road off US 87 is a good place, or any of the rural dirt roads in this area can be good. The Bud Love Game Preserve north of Buffalo has some, and the roads leading to it are likely areas. As is the case with most of the gallinaceous birds, it is difficult to know where they will be at a given moment. Farther south in the Casper region they are more scarce, but the Bolton Creek Road which turns off State Route 220 south of the Route 487 turn-off and just before you get to the bridge over the North Platte River is a good area. Finding them anywhere in central Wyoming is possible. From mid-June to mid-August they are very hard to find unless you stumble upon a nesting-area. Where I live and work, a ranch southwest of Casper, I will bump into these birds several times a year, but I can never guess when this is going to happen.

Chukar—*Locally common.* When I think of Chukar, I think of the Big Horn Basin. The Wyoming Game and Fish Department has stopped stocking them, so they are not so common as they used to be. In recent years State Route 172 (the Black Mountain Road) leading east from Lucerne (which is north of Thermopolis) has been a hot spot. This is a paved road, but you have to go out 21 miles to where there is a fork to the right and the paved road turns left. Another spot is the Corbett Dam Public Fishing area on US 14A, 4.5 miles east of the junction of Route 120 and US 14A in Cody. Chukars can be found in any place in the drier parts of the state. In recent years I have seen them at FMC Park south of Green River and at Pavillion near Ocean Lake. Like the Gray Partridge they are almost impossible to find between mid-June and mid-August. Fortunately, they say their name when disturbed—which is different from the harsh cackles of the Gray Partridge. It is hard to tell these two species apart when they are flying away from you but the head area of the Chukar is gray while the head area of the Gray Partridge is brown. Their red tails appear to be identical.

Ring-necked Pheasant—*Common locally.* Irrigation projects in the Big Horn Basin have them in numbers. The Sheridan area has them, and they are everywhere east of the Bighorns and the Laramie Range—particularly where there is irrigation. They also occur in the irrigated areas around Riverton, Ocean Lake, and the Big Horn Basin. The western part of the state where there is little irrigation has few if any. The Wyoming Game and Fish Department still releases them. In the irrigated and watered area near Ayres Natural Bridge they have even introduced "green" Pheasants, a Ring-necked variation.

Spruce Grouse—*There is some argument at the moment as to whether this species belongs on the list.* There are old records cited in McCreary from Yellowstone National Park and Teton County.

Blue Grouse—*Common resident of all our heavily forested mountain ranges.* In Yellowstone and Grand Teton National Parks as well as the rest of the northwest mountains the Richardson form (which has no or very little white on the tip of the tail) prevails. The rest of the mountain ranges have birds with good white tips to their tails. In general they are hard to find, but if you walk the back trails in the Tetons and Yellowstone you will bump into them eventually. In the Tetons avoid trails like the Cascade Canyon Trail which runs from the west side of Jenny Lake past the Cascade up the canyon and then forks to the right to Lake Solitude. Swarms of people take this walk to the poorly-named Lake Solitude. A much better bet is the Paintbrush Canyon Trail, which leaves nearby String Lake and doesn't have nearly as much human traffic. In general the lowland trails with more open areas and deciduous trees are going to have the Ruffed Grouse rather than the Blue. Look for the Blue in any of our mountain ranges, the more remote the better.

White-tailed Ptarmigan—*Uncommon resident of the alpine zone in Wyoming.* They are hard to find. I have seen them most often on the Snowy Range west of Laramie, but even there it may take a great deal of effort to rout them out. According to old records in McCreary, they also occurred on the top of the Bighorn Mountains as well as the Wind Rivers, and in the remote northwest mountains of Yellowstone. The Tetons don't have them. In recent years there has been some doubt as to whether they still exist in the Wind Rivers, Bighorns, and the northern mountains of Yellowstone. Personally, I feel that they still do.

Ruffed Grouse—*Common resident of all the forested areas except the Laramie Range.* I have never missed them on the Valley Trail in Grand Teton National Park which runs from the Whitegrass Ranger Station along the face of the Tetons to Taggart Lake and eventually to the bottom of the Avalanche Trail. For a gallinaceous bird this is a remarkable statement. These Park birds are different. If you come across an eastern Ruffed Grouse, it will jump with a bang to scare you and then put a tree between you and itself immediately. These western birds will move out of your way slowly, grousing all the time. They deeply resent your intrusion into their domain. In fact, I once had a hen with chicks in the Black Hills attack me. They can and will fly, but they certainly prefer that you get out of their way. Another good place to see them in Grand Teton National Park is Two Ocean Lake, but they can be found anywhere in the lowlands of the Park. One can hear them drumming through early July. There are a fair number in Story and the Black Hills. The juniper forests of central and southern Wyoming don't have any.

Sage Grouse—*Common in the sagebrush country.* The hereditary strutting-grounds are scattered all over the state; every town has one near it, and some of the residents go out each spring to see the show. Since the bird isn't very wary, it can be seen easily. Perhaps the most convenient and reliable strutting-ground is the one near Casper off the Hat Six Road. The strutting starts in early March and reaches its height in the first two weeks of April; by mid-May it is really finished. Occasional birds hang on until June, but there is no show. This is one of the greatest shows in nature, and if you have never seen it you should make a special effort to take it in. These strutting-grounds are almost cast in concrete. It is very hard to move them at all. They wax and wane depending on the number of birds in the area. A graduate student at the university at Laramie studied one of these leks and found that 90 percent of the hens were bred by 10 percent of the cocks in the center of the ring. This seems like a poor system. At any rate they are unwary as far as humans are concerned, but with their natural enemies it is a different story. They are normally wary. This great courtship-and-mating show goes on from dawn to sunup. As soon as the light get good and strong for photography, they disperse. Some people will tell you that you don't have to get up at the crack of dawn—you can go there in the evening. This is twaddle. There are some birds in the evening, but there is no zip and little happens. The real thing is at daybreak. The two great concentrations of Sage Grouse in the state are around Bates Creek Reservoir (well south of Casper), which is impossible to get to in early spring due to snow and mud, and the Farson area, which is approachable all year round. Go north on US 191 three miles from Farson and take any of the tracks and roads to the east toward Big Sandy Reservoir. This is perhaps the best area, but all of the local roads are fine. The Bates Creek area also has large numbers of leks, but it is essentially unapproachable.

Greater Prairie-Chicken—Formerly, these birds got into the eastern edge of Goshen Hole on the Nebraska Line (McCreary, *Wyoming Bird Life*), but there have been no reports for the last 40 years at least.

Sharp-tailed Grouse—Common in northeastern Wyoming from the foothills of the Bighorn Mountains east through the Black Hills to the border. South of this they are uncommon as far as Goshen Hole. There is a sizable population south of Rawlins in the foothills of the Sierra Madre. Formerly, this bird ranged over most of Wyoming. It requires native grasses, so it is absent wherever there has been sod-busting. The best places to see them are Wagon Box Road south of Story, Bird Farm Road south of the hamlet of Big Horn, and on State Route 335 west of Big Horn. You will note these are all in the foothills of the Bighorn Mountains. Another spot is paved Route 112 from Hulett to Alzada, Montana, on the edge of the Black Hills. The strutting-grounds of the Sharp-tail are almost as spectacular as those of the Sage Grouse, but they are not as firmly set. They can be moved, so they are more difficult to find. Near the old cemetery on Wagon Box Road I have seen a Sharp-tail strutting on the top of a haystack, but it was an individual performance. One can see individual performances along roadways rather commonly.

Wild Turkey—*Locally common.* There are sizable numbers in the Black Hills such that there is a hunting season on them. I used to think that turkeys require oak trees, but the turkey has been successfully introduced in many places where there are no oaks and never have been. There are numerous Wild Turkeys above the fish hatchery in Story along the east face of the Bighorns. There are turkeys in numbers to the north and east of Laramie Peak in the Cottonwood Creek drainage and around Esterbrook. There has been a successful plant on the Bates Creek drainage south of Casper which is now extending to Casper Mountain and its drainages. All in all, they are in a great many places in northeast and east-central Wyoming where there are coniferous forests that aren't too dense or high.

Northern Bobwhite—*Repeated introductions.* Sooner or later our winters exterminate them, but they are continually reintroduced just the same. Originally, there never were any Northern Bobwhites here. It is possible that around Torrington on the eastern boundary in the North Platte valley some could persist for a while. You may see one in Wyoming, but it won't last long.

Scaled Quail—*Repeated introductions.* Here we have about the same story as for the Northern Bobwhite. They can't survive our winters, but they have not been as popular as the Bobwhite so they have been introduced less. I haven't heard any reports of them in quite a number of years now. In any case the result is the same: no Scaled Quail.

Yellow Rail—*Accidental.* Platt Hall had one on State Route 336, the Wyarno Road, in August 1968.

Virginia Rail—*Uncommon summer resident and migrant.* Normal migration is the last week of April through May. Not too infrequently they winter where there are marshes with open water in the cold months. In Wyoming there are a number of marshes with warm springs—Flat Creek Marsh just out of Jackson and the little Piggery Marsh in Casper, to mention a couple. Fall migration is in September and the first half of October. They nest in a number of marshes, such as Table Mountain, Saratoga, Cokeville Meadows National Wildlife Refuge, and Flat Creek Marsh near Jackson.

Sora—*Common summer resident and migrant.* Sora are much more common than Virginia Rails and nest in much smaller marshes as well as the big ones, but they don't winter over except very rarely. In fact, any small marsh is likely to have nesting Soras—such as the little Piggery Marsh in Casper. They arrive from the last week in April through the middle of May, and leave in September. Loch Katrine near Cody has lots of them, as well as Seedskadee National Wildlife Refuge and a host of other locations.

Purple Gallinule—*Accidental.* One was picked up dead near Leazenby Lake by the Red Buttes Biological Research Station south of Laramie September 24, 1986. Dr. Bill Eddleman, formerly of the Denver Museum of Natural History, confirmed the identification of the juvenile gallinule.

Common Moorhen—*Accidental.* One was seen May 11, 1982, at Seedskadee National Wildlife Refuge by James Alfonso. Another was at Hutton Lake National Wildlife Refuge on June 10, 1985, observed by Bill DeBaets of Illinois.

American Coot—*Common nester and summer resident.* It nests in all our larger marsh areas from Table Mountain to Cokeville. It arrives early in March and stays until freeze-up. In migration it occurs in large numbers (several thousand) on suitable ponds and lakes, and is sort of a nuisance. Not infrequently it overwinters where there is open water, such as Flat Creek at Jackson or the Dave Johnson Power Plant near Glenrock.

Sandhill Crane—*Common summer resident in western Wyoming and uncommon migrant in eastern Wyoming.* It nests at Cokeville and in all large damp meadows to the north and east, such as the large meadow west of Pinedale and around Merna. There are usually several nesting pairs in the National Elk Refuge north of Jackson, and in Willow Flats and the marsh below Two Ocean Lake in Grand Teton National Park, to mention only a few places. That wild grating cry of theirs can be commonly heard all through the lowlands of Grand Teton National Park and suitable areas of Yellowstone National Park like Hayden Valley. In eastern Wyoming occasional single birds can be seen on lake shores in migration. Sandhills move from their nesting-grounds to staging-areas like the Cokeville Marsh in September, but migration is mostly in April and October. In eastern Wyoming sizable flocks of up to 300 birds can be seen flying through in migration. There has been a short open season on these birds in western Wyoming in spite of there being a few Whoopers in the area. Our western population are the Greater Sandhills whereas it is likely that the eastern birds may be Lesser Sandhills.

Whooping Crane—*Uncommon summer resident in western Wyoming.* The experiment of taking Whooper eggs from either Patuxent, Maryland, or from the wild flock in Wood Buffalo National Park in Alberta and putting them in Sandhills' nests at Grays Lake National Wildlife Refuge, Idaho, went on from 1974 to 1988. There was never a breeding pair, and the project has now been abandoned. When these Whoopers fledged, most of them moved next door to Wyoming, where most of the suitable habitat lies. Grays Lake is just over the border west of Star Valley (Afton). The young Whoopers have had a very high mortality rate by flying into fences and power-lines and almost anything else. There was an imbalance between females and males, most being females. There was a mature male at Grays Lake, so they took females in Wyoming to the male but the ladies all promptly went home. In a species of this kind the logical thing to do would be to move the male to the females, but this hasn't been done. One wonders if that horrible curse of the bureaucracy called *turf* hadn't reared its ugly head. The Whooper experiment was an Idaho project.

Black-bellied Plover—*Uncommon migrant.* They migrate through in May in the spring with the migration finished here by June 1. The fall is more leisurely, but most pass through in September. However, an occasional bird can be seen from the third week of July well into October. Eastern Wyoming has many more of these birds than the western half. They are not rare in the west, however. Keyhole Reservoir on the Belle Fourche River on the edge of the Black Hills is probably the best place to see them. Yant's Puddle at Casper is a close second.

Lesser Golden-Plover—*Rare migrant.* I have seen this bird only once in spring in 44 years of birding in Wyoming, and that was at Keyhole Reservoir in May 1988. In the fall they pass through in the latter half of September in the eastern half of the state. Again, Keyhole and Yant's Puddle are the best places to see them. I have yet to see them in breeding plumage in Wyoming. In western Wyoming they are plumb rare.

Snowy Plover—*Rare migrant.* Snowies have been seen almost every year with most of the reports from the eastern part of the state. I have seen them only three times: twice at Goldeneye, a BLM-maintained lake 20 miles north of Casper off US 20/26, and once at Table Mountain. These records were all in May, but it has been seen in summer as well. Certainly, this is one of our rarest birds. However, in 1990 a pair successfully nested in the dry alkali back pond at Bridger Ponds in southwest Wyoming. These birds were discovered by Forrest Luke.

Semipalmated Plover—*Uncommon migrant.* In the eastern half of the state they are often rather common but are scarce in the western half. They arrive about the third week of April and are gone by June 1. They reappear in the third week of July and will be gone by mid-September like most shorebirds. Usually they are a little later than most other shorebirds and are more common in later August and early September. Lake DeSmet, Table Mountain, Keyhole, Yant's Puddle, and Hutton Lake National Wildlife Refuge are great places to see them.

Piping Plover—*Rare migrant in the eastern half of the state.* In the '60s and '70s Piping Plovers were seen in May at the lower end of Lake DeSmet. In the late '70s Texaco, the lake's owner, raised the level of Lake DeSmet, and Piping Plovers haven't been seen there since. The observers were Tom Kessinger, Platt Hall, and Helen Downing. This plover has been seen many years at Yant's Puddle in August and the first half of September such that we believe that it occurs regularly. In fact, the one year when Fred Broerman went there dutifully morning and evening during migration, he found Piping Plover, later seen by others. We wonder how many other places it would be found in the eastern part of the state if we had more observers.

Killdeer—*Common summer resident and migrant.* It occasionally overwinters at warm springs. Killdeers arrive in the last week of March and don't leave until early November. They nest in any open gravelly spot. There are lots of such places in Wyoming, so Killdeers are a very common bird. They almost surpass the American Robin in numbers. Killdeers are the most common shorebird on our ponds and lakes, also.

Mountain Plover—*Uncommon summer resident and migrant.* Wyoming has more nesting Mountain Plovers than any other state. They are most common on the Laramie Plains and its northern extension, the Shirley Basin. They are also rather common on the Red Desert north of Interstate 80. They occur in lesser numbers on the high grasslands around Cheyenne, a feature which extends southward to give Colorado its well-known Pawnee National Grassland. Mountain Plovers also nest in the Powder River Basin, the Green River Basin, and the Big Horn Basin. They arrive in the latter half of April although most of the migration is in May, and then leave by the end of the first half of September. After the nesting season they gather in groups, but the largest number I have seen together was in August in a large depression south of State Route 130 west of Laramie where there was a loose concentration of 23. I have rarely failed to find them on the track on Shirley rim between State Routes 77 and 487. The greatest concentration of nesting is in the area around West Carroll Lake northwest of Laramie.

Black-necked Stilt—*Uncommon summer resident.* There is a nesting-colony at Yant's Puddle and another at Loch Katrine near Cody. There used to be a few at Ocean Lake. Otherwise, they are very scarce in the state. They migrate in from mid-April through early May and leave by the end of

August. Since the Yant's Puddle colony is relatively new, it may be that there are other colonies, too.

American Avocet—*Common summer resident.* Spring migration starts about April 1, and some birds will linger into September. This is a candidate for our next-most-common nesting shorebird after the Killdeer. American Avocets won't nest or frequent lakes in the woods unless there are lots of flats, but every wet place in open country will have them. The drier the area and the shallower the pond the better. Some of the heaviest concentrations are in the few lakes in the Red Desert. Because the Great Parks, Yellowstone and Grand Teton, have little open country, avocets sometimes are uncommon there, but Hayden Valley will have them in Yellowstone or the flats on Jackson Lake in Grand Teton. After the nesting season they wander around locally.

Greater Yellowlegs—*Uncommon migrant.* In the spring they move through in April and May. The returning birds come back from mid-July to the end of August, but some linger until close to freeze-up in November. They prefer the little ponds and lakes but can occasionally be found on the larger ones from Table Mountain to Seedskadee National Wildlife Refuge. Farm ponds are particularly to their liking. I have seen these birds every year, but compared with the next species they are uncommon.

Lesser Yellowlegs—*Common migrant.* A candidate for our most common summer shorebird after July 15. They migrate through in April and May going north and then are with us from mid-July through October, but the bulk leave Wyoming by the end of the first week in September. They are most common on the larger shallow lakes like Table Mountain and Yant's Puddle or Loch Katrine and Bridger Ponds. However, they can be found almost anywhere there is shallow water. The Great Parks have few good shorebird areas. The upper end of Jackson Lake has flats, but since this is a irrigation storage project with big variations of water-level there is little food for shorebirds. Hayden Valley in Yellowstone is good, but Pelican Creek is probably the best area in that park.

Solitary Sandpiper—*Uncommon migrant.* This bird is rare in spring, but what records we have are in May. From mid-July to the end of August they occur sparingly in small ponds with vegetation around them. Farm ponds or Beaver ponds are ideal for them. Every now and then they can be found on the edge of one of the bigger lakes like Yant's Puddle. I manage to see them every year, but often it takes considerable effort.

Willet—*Common migrant and nester in the eastern half of the state.* In spring they arrive in the latter half of April and are present until the third week of May. In suitable lakes and marshes in the eastern part of the state they nest at such places as Yant's Puddle and the ponds on the eastern part of the Red Desert. Migrants appear again in mid-July and leave by the end of the first week in September. This is the western subspecies, *inornatus,* with pale underparts.

Spotted Sandpiper—*Common summer resident.* They can be found nesting on rocks along lakes or in rocky stream-beds throughout the state. At Yant's Puddle there is an artificial causeway made of rocks on which they nest regularly. Once the snow melts in the spring, there are lots of rocky stream-beds throughout the back country that are just right for them. Jackson Hole is loaded with such streams. They arrive in May and are gone by the end of the first week of September.

Upland Sandpiper—*Uncommon migrant and nester in the eastern half of the state.* They like the higher, drier plains. They can be found on the plains west of the Black Hills around places like Oshoto and east of Gillette around Rozet—also on the plains south of Van Tassel and around Prairie Center south to Torrington. They can be found in Goshen Hole at least in migration. They nest on the high plains north of Shirley Basin around the headwaters of Bates Creek where it is dry but where there are wet spots near spring seeps. I see them regularly in migration on my alfalfa fields west of Casper in late July and early August and again in late August. They occur in the alfalfa fields southwest of Sheridan in migration, also. They appear in May and stay until the end of August.

Whimbrel—*Rare migrant.* Virtually all the records have been in May. Most of the records are from the eastern part of the state—Table Mountain, Glendo Reservoir, Yant's Puddle, Goldeneye Reservoir, Keyhole Reservoir, Lake DeSmet, the farmlands southwest of Sheridan, and the Big Horn Basin near Otto and Basin. However, there is a record from the southwest part of the state.

Long-billed Curlew—*Uncommon summer resident.* They arrive about the end of the first week of April and are gone by mid-September. They used to be much more common than they are now. Urbanization has driven them from a number of nesting-sites in the Casper area. The greatest concentrations now are in the western part of the state, particularly in the large meadows west of Pinedale and Daniel Junction, and Cokeville Meadows National Wildlife Refuge. They are usually on the National Elk Refuge just north of Jackson. In the grasslands below the east side of the Bighorn Mountains, there is a scattering of nesting-sites. However, they can be seen almost anywhere.

Hudsonian Godwit—*Casual migrant.* In 44 years I have seen them only four times, mostly in spring and in full breeding-plumage. One was at the pond below the Wyoming Hereford Ranch in Cheyenne at a dammed-up large pond which has been subsequently destroyed by a cloudburst. This was May 19, 1968, at a time when many shorebirds were gathered there—of unusual varieties that ordinarily migrate to the east of us. Another observation was at Ocean Lake May 21, 1972. Two birds were at Yant's

Puddle on April 27, 1990, one of which was not in breeding-plumage. All these observations were with a number of other people. There are three records from Lake DeSmet before Texaco raised the water-level and none since. These records were August 5, 1970, by Tom Kessinger and Platt Hall; another September 22, 1971, by the same people; and the third on August 17, 1976, by Platt Hall and Helen Downing. There was also a report from Keyhole Reservoir in 1988. The most recent report was a bird seen in late August and early September 1992 at Yant's Puddle.

Marbled Godwit—*Common migrant.* They arrive in mid-April and are gone by late May and then reappear in mid-July and stay until mid-September with a few remaining through October. They occur on all our major shallow lakes where there are plenty of shorebirds from Loch Katrine to Table Mountain. Usually, they occur in small numbers. Rarely does one see a flock of 15 or more at once.

Ruddy Turnstone—*Rare migrant.* One is seen at Yant's Puddle about every other year in late August or early September. Platt Hall had one on September 20, 1969, at the lower end of Lake DeSmet before Texaco raised the water-level.

Red Knot—*Rare migrant.* These have been seen almost every year at Yant's Puddle, usually in the last half of July but sometimes in August. Our first record was on a May 30th in the early 1950s, but that was before Yant's Puddle was built. It was seen at what is now called Goldeneye Reservoir of the BLM and at Lake DeSmet before Texaco raised the water-level. It also has been seen once in Jackson Hole.

Sanderling—*Uncommon migrant.* They are seen mostly in the eastern half of the state, arriving in May going north and reappearing in late August. Sanderlings are usually gone by mid-September, but they are essentially a late shorebird migrant. They like sandy beaches, which are in short supply in Wyoming. We have plenty of alkali flats but little sand. They are seen regularly at Table Mountain, Yant's Puddle, and Lake DeSmet but are not common. With more observers a number of other places will surely be found to have them regularly.

Semipalmated Sandpiper—*Common migrant.* Although this is a common bird, they are probably the least common regular "peep." They arrive in May and leave before the end of the month and in spring are seen only in small numbers. They reappear by mid-July and are present until the end of the first week of September. Any of the shallow lakes will have them, such as Table Mountain, Yant's Puddle, Bridger Ponds, or Loch Katrine.

Western Sandpiper—*Common migrant.* They appear about the last week of April and have gone north by June. They are seen again by mid-July in fine breeding-plumage, which fades out in August. Most are gone by the end of the first week of September, but some will linger on to the end of the month. Westerns are found along any shore that is suitable for shorebirds.

Least Sandpiper—*Common migrant.* These are perhaps the commonest of our "peep." They arrive by mid-April and move on by the end of May. In the spring their numbers are limited. When they reappear in mid-July, they are very common and are distributed more widely than the rest of the "peep." Hence, one can see them on almost any shore of ponds or lakes in the state. They stay until September, but a few will linger through October.

White-rumped Sandpiper—*Rare migrant.* If they are seen at all in the spring, it will be in the last week of May. Twice I have seen them in numbers in the little ponds beside the road east of Yoder, where there were about 24 in late May two years running. They have also been seen at Yant's Puddle and Keyhole Reservoir at the same time of year. They have also been seen at Healy Reservoir southeast of Lake DeSmet. There are few records from the summer and fall migration, but most are in August as is the record from Healy Reservoir above.

Baird's Sandpiper—*Common migrant.* Baird's competes with the Least as our most common "peep." They arrive in the last week of April and are gone by the end of May. Occasionally, non-breeders will remain. They reappear in mid-July and stay until the end of the first week of September; a few will remain through October. They are found singly or in small flocks that are usually mixed with the other "peep." Any shore in open country will do for them. All our big lakes like Table Mountain, Yant's Puddle, Bridger Ponds, Keyhole Reservoir, and Loch Katrine, as well as hosts of smaller lakes, will have them.

Pectoral Sandpiper—*Uncommon migrant.* These are later migrants which usually appear in late August and stay until late September and often longer. Since they like little, grassy, wet areas like those preferred by snipe, they are often harder to find on the big lakes although Yant's Puddle has them regularly. In the fall, there is a flooded bottomland in Bessemer Bend that is ideal for them as well as for snipe; the area is just a field the rest of the year. Bessemer Bend is 11 miles west of Casper on Route 220 and is on the Goose Egg Circle Road off the Bessemer Bend Road, County Route 308.

Dunlin—*Rare migrant.* They have been seen almost as much in the spring as in the fall, but that's still not often. The reports have been from about every other year. Spring sightings have mostly been in April; fall ones, in September. Bridger Ponds, Lake DeSmet, and Yant's Puddle have accounted for most of the reports.

Stilt Sandpiper—*Uncommon migrant.* Sizable flocks in full breeding-plumage have been seen in the spring. There once was a flock of 70 at Table Mountain in May and lesser numbers in other years. Hutton

Lake National Wildlife Refuge has had good-sized flocks in the spring. The Stilts are gone by the end of May and reappear in mid-July. In the fall migration most are seen in late August. Yant's Puddle has had them in numbers—as many as 30 in a flock. By mid-September they are usually all gone. They are not so common that you can count on seeing them annually.

Buff-breasted Sandpiper—*Rare migrant.* Most of our reports are from Yant's Puddle, which may mean only that this spot is more closely watched than others. The species was seen occasionally at the lower end of Lake DeSmet before the lake level was raised, but none since that time. Most of the sightings are from the last week of August and the first week of September, however, there are a few scattered reports from earlier in the summer. This bird is seen almost every year somewhere in the eastern part of the state.

Short-billed Dowitcher—*Rare migrant.* The only reports we have are from Yant's Puddle in late July. However, they have been seen for several years. It may well be that they occur in a number of places but haven't been observed because the identification is not easy.

Long-billed Dowitcher—*Common migrant.* They arrive as early as the 10th of April and have moved north by the end of May. They reappear by mid-July, and a few stay until almost freeze-up in November. The bulk of them will have gone through by the middle of September. They usually occur in flocks, and their distribution throughout the state is widespread. They take to any wet irrigated field or ponds and lakes that have suitable shorebird habitat. They are particularly common at all the principal shorebird lakes, such as Table Mountain, Yant's Puddle, Keyhole Reservoir, Bridger Ponds, Hutton Lake, and Loch Katrine.

Common Snipe—*Common resident.* Wherever there are warm springs with vegetation, snipe will overwinter. Wyoming abounds in such places, so a lot of snipe overwinter. They will also nest in most of our marshy areas, which are numerous. My favorite little marsh to hear winnowing snipe is on the road in to Ayres Natural Bridge. Big or little marsh, the snipe are there.

American Woodcock—*Accidental.* We have had no reports from recent years, but there are specimens from earlier years (McCreary, *Wyoming Bird Life*).

Wilson's Phalarope—*Common summer resident.* They arrive in mid-April and leave by the end of the first week in September. They nest around any small pond and are probably as numerous as American Avocet, or more so. If there is suitable habitat, they will nest in our larger lakes also, but certainly smaller lakes and ponds are preferred. In mid-August after the nesting-season they stage on some of our larger lakes, such as Ocean Lake and Yant's Puddle, and then migrate; however, always a few remain.

I have seen over a thousand congregate at Yant's Puddle. They are distributed everywhere in the state. Flat Creek, just north of Jackson in the National Elk Refuge, has them.

Red-necked Phalarope—*Common migrant.* They are almost always in flocks. They arrive in the last three weeks of May and are gone by June 1. They reappear in late August and stay around until the last week of September. They are usually found on our larger lakes like Table Mountain, Yant's Puddle, Ocean Lake, Hutton Lake, and Bridger Ponds.

Red Phalarope—*Casual migrant.* There was one at Ocean Lake October 8-10, 1988, found by Sam Fitton and also seen by Jim and Verna Herold. On July 21-23, 1987, Arthur R. Clark of Buffalo, NY, had one in breeding-plumage at Sawmill Ponds near Moose in Grand Teton National Park. A good photograph was taken. Bert and Meg Raynes of Jackson also saw it. Platt Hall had one on November 7, 1973, at the lower end of Lake DeSmet. There is an old report of a specimen taken September 14, 1897, by C. W. Gilmore (McCreary, *Wyoming Bird Life*). This specimen is in the University of Wyoming collection.

Pomarine Jaeger—*Accidental.* One was seen in full breeding-plumage at Goldeneye Reservoir off US 20/26 north of Casper on May 16, 1980, by Jim and Verna Herold, and was confirmed by many others, including the author. The bird flew overhead at a low altitude, affording the best view of a Pomarine Jaeger I have ever had, and I have seen many.

Parasitic Jaeger—*Rare fall migrant.* Almost every year Parasitics have been seen somewhere in Wyoming in the fall, mostly in late August, September, and October. They have been seen a number of times at Yant's Puddle. Other areas are Lake DeSmet, Bridger Ponds, and Ocean Lake. There is one trouble with this distribution pattern: these are the areas where we have our best observers at the moment, so the species may actually have a more widespread distribution than is here indicated.

Franklin's Gull—*Common migrant.* This is the most common black-headed gull in Wyoming and can be seen on most of our lakes and ponds, particularly in the open country in the eastern part of the state. They arrive in April and May and return in August and September.

Common Black-headed Gull—*Accidental.* One was seen and photographed by B.J. Rose of Omaha, Nebraska, and others at the marsh at Saratoga November 9, 1989. It was with Bonaparte's Gulls.

Bonaparte's Gull—*Common migrant.* These gulls arrive in April and May and show up again in August through October. In fact, flocks of them are more likely in late September and October. They occur on any of the ponds, lakes, or streams throughout the state with no east/west bias.

Heermann's Gull—*Accidental.* One immature was seen September 26, 1984, at Yant's Puddle by Bob South, Bud Stratton, and the author.

Another was seen on October 13, 1991, in the same area by the author and several others.

Mew Gull—*Accidental.* There are two old records. One specimen now in the National Museum was taken by Vernon Bailey at Lake Fork in the Wind River Mountains on August 28, 1893, and another was taken near Laramie by A.E. Lockwood. Both these records are in McCreary's *Wyoming Bird Life.* There are no recent records.

Ring-billed Gull—*Common migrant and uncommon nester.* They arrive early in March and are gone by the end of May. They start back in late July and stick around until almost two weeks before Christmas. In fact, they have been seen on Christmas counts. They are the common late gull, staying much longer than the California Gulls. They are very common, often being seen in large numbers. Scott Finholt pointed out that there are a number of Ring-billed nests within the huge colony of Californias at Yant's Puddle. It is quite likely that they have been overlooked elsewhere.

California Gull—*Common summer resident.* They arrive in early March as soon as there is open water in abundance and leave by October. There is a huge colony of up to 2,000 nests at Yant's Puddle. They are dependent largely on the Casper Landfill dump but will often forage in the surrounding countryside if grasshoppers are plentiful.

One year I had a terrible infestation of grasshoppers on my 100-acre alfalfa field west of Casper. When I walked out into the field, so many grasshoppers took flight that I couldn't see the ground there. It was about the 10th of July, and it seemed obvious that my second cutting of alfalfa was going to be destroyed. There were a few gulls flying around that day, but by the next morning the field was white, as if it had snowed during the night. On closer inspection the field was covered with about 350 or more gulls. They were gorging themselves on grasshoppers, and their capacity was immense. I am about 10 miles west, as a gull flies, of the Yant's Puddle California Gull colony. I have a hand-moved, overhead irrigation system that must be moved twice a day. Under the artificial rain the grasshoppers clung to the alfalfa plants and didn't move. The gulls enjoyed the rain, and these sharp-eyed birds got every grasshopper under these circumstances—but they did well elsewhere too. In ten days there were practically no grasshoppers left, and I got a good second cutting.

Then there is the famous old California Gull colony on Molly Island in Yellowstone Lake. There are also numerous smaller colonies on several of the lakes on the Laramie Plains, Ocean Lake, and any lake that has an island without much vegetation. In general, a gull in Wyoming in the summer is a California until proven otherwise. There is a sizable colony in Pathfinder Reservoir when the reservoir is full enough so that a promontory southwest of the dam across the reservoir to the west turns into an island.

Herring Gull—*Uncommon migrant.* Regularly in the late fall (usually November or October), first-year birds will show up. They can be seen occasionally in the spring in May and every once in a while one can see an older bird, but I have never seen one in full adult plumage in the state. Herring Gulls are more commonly seen in the eastern half of the state. They are usually with other gulls, and are widely distributed.

Glaucous Gull—*Casual.* There is an old specimen in the University of Wyoming collection taken November 23, 1933, by Elmer Isberg (McCreary, *Wyoming Bird Life*). Another was seen at Yant's Puddle April 10, 1982, by the author and many others. On March 11, 1991, Verna and Jim Herold and many others had one at the Casper Landfill dump, which is close to the North Platte River.

Black-legged Kittiwake—*Casual.* There is an old record of one collected near Douglas on November 18, 1898, by Mortimer Jeserum (McCreary, *Wyoming Bird Life*). Mary Back had two near Dubois on the Wind River October 22, 1974. Bob South and Jim Gaither saw an immature with a black collar on the back of its neck at Yant's Puddle November 11, 1988.

Sabine's Gull—*Rare migrant.* One is seen practically every year somewhere in the state, and sometimes there have been several. Very rarely one has been seen in the spring; most of the sightings are from late August through October. Over the years many have been seen at Yant's Puddle. There have been several at Lake DeSmet, Goldeneye Reservoir, and several other areas, so it can be looked for on any of our lakes and reservoirs.

Caspian Tern—*Uncommon migrant and nester.* A few nests are found in the area of Yellowstone Lake's south arm. The biggest colony has been on the island on the west side of Pathfinder Reservoir—opposite the dam, but a little to the southwest. This island has a large number of waterbirds nesting, including 25 or so Caspian Tern nests. Unfortunately, in 1988 the reservoir level was down and the "island" was a peninsula on the west side with no nesting. For a number of years before this the peninsula was an island, and we hope that this condition will shortly return. There have been some small colonies elsewhere in the state, such as at Yant's Puddle and along the road to Lake Hattie west of Laramie. Caspians arrive in May and leave by the end of September.

Common Tern—*Rare migrant.* The spring reports are from May and the fall ones from late July through September. I once asked Jim Lane how he distinguished the Forster's from the Common Tern in breeding-plumage and he said, "Wait until fall when it's easy!" Wyoming doesn't have that option—by fall they are all gone. If there were a easier way of telling these two birds apart, we might find that we have more Commons than we thought we had.

Forster's Tern—*Common migrant and nester.* Forster's nest in reedy ponds and lakes throughout the state. There are more such ponds on the Laramie

Plains (like West Carroll and Bamforth Lakes) than elsewhere. This is the common tern of Wyoming. They arrive in May and leave by the end of September.

Least Tern—*Formerly nested on islands in the North Platte River from Fort Laramie east.* There have been no reports of them in the last forty years that I know of except that Jean Adams had one at Keyhole Reservoir in northeast Wyoming on April 23, 1989, seen again on May 2. This sighting is not too surprising since Least Terns nest near Miles City, Montana, to the north. Forrest Luke, Rick Steenberg, and others had one on June 16, 1991, at the boat dock on the west side of Hawk Springs Reservoir in Goshen Hole. This is not far from the North Platte River, so perhaps they will nest by the river again.

Black Tern—*Common migrant and uncommon nester.* Black Terns nest on the Laramie Plains at Bamforth Lake and others. They are believed to have nested at Yant's Puddle, but we have few reports of it as a nesting bird. However, as a migrant they are common, arriving in the last half of May and showing up again in late July and staying with us until the end of the first week in September. They can be seen flycatching on most of our larger lakes such as Ocean Lake, Table Mountain, and Loch Katrine. Sometimes sizable flocks of 100 or more birds are seen.

Ancient Murrelet—*Accidental.* It is hard to believe that an alcid is ever seen in Wyoming, and I can assure you that it is quite an accident when it does happen. Bert Raynes picked up a half-dead Ancient Murrelet at the Moran Ranger Station in Grand Teton National Park in November 1971 in a storm. It subsequently died; the specimen is with the Game and Fish Department in Lander. Another was found in a storm in November 1972 on the main street of Lander by Leonard Sierdiuk of the Game and Fish Department. It apparently thought that the wet pavement was water. After appropriate pictures were taken, it was released at the local sewage-ponds and flew away. The pictures are in the file of the Non-Game Bird office at the Game and Fish headquarters in Lander.

Rock Dove—*Common resident.* The Rock Doves in the nesting-colonies on Devils Tower and in the north end of Wind River Canyon have reverted to their ancestral habit of nesting on cliffs. Of course, they also nest on buildings in our cities and towns. There are also lots of dove-fanciers in the state, so whether a given bird is "wild" or not is always a question.

Band-tailed Pigeon—*Rare.* In regard to its status in Wyoming, this is a problem bird. It has been seen at Battle Creek Campground in the Sierra Madre just north of the Colorado line several times in late August and early September. There are scrub oaks there, one of the very few such areas in Wyoming, and the oak is a principal source of food for the Band-tailed. Do the birds nest at Battle Creek Campground? Nobody seems to know. Other visits to the campground in early September have not found the bird. Elsewhere in the state Band-tails are very rare, while they are relatively common to the south in Colorado.

White-winged Dove—*Accidental.* One was seen in a chicken-yard by the author in what was then a rural area on the south side of Casper on October 29, 1954, and for several days thereafter. It acted wild, but was it?

Mourning Dove—*Common summer resident.* Mourning Doves are one of the most common birds in the non-forested areas. They nest in deciduous trees or on the ground, often in sagebrush in most of the lowland areas where it isn't too dry. They arrive in early April and leave by the end of October. There is a hunting season on them, but most hunters in this state disdain such trifles. The idiots who do take to the field will shoot most anything. The ranchers take a dim view of those who shoot up everything including their power-lines, so many ranches are off-limits. In general, the dove hunter is a low form of life. (Texans, take note.)

Passenger Pigeon—*Extinct.* Apparently there used to be a fair population in Wyoming during part of the year. See McCreary, *Wyoming Bird Life.*

Black-billed Cuckoo—*Uncommon summer resident.* These birds nest in the deciduous-tree and brush areas throughout the state but are much less common in the west. Due to their shy habits they are not seen a great deal. One summer when we lived in Casper we had a small backyard with an apple tree shading the back porch. Along came a sudden stiff wind and down came a bunch of young cuckoos. We had no idea that we had a nest within a few feet of our living-space. Black-bills arrive in late May although I usually don't see or hear them until June; they leave by the middle of September.

Yellow-billed Cuckoo—*Rare.* They occur regularly in the eastern half of the state in deciduous-tree areas but are not commonly recorded. We are reasonably sure that they nest in the state. They arrive in June and probably leave in August, but we really don't know if they nest here or not.

Barn Owl—*Rare.* There is a population in the North Platte valley from Casper east, but they are not often seen. The bird hospital in Casper has received several injured Barn Owls. There are few observers in the area, and most efforts to see the bird from Casper have been fruitless, but one was seen in an abandoned ranch shed north of Casper in June 1988 by Jim and Verna Herold. Nests have been found in the past but only rarely. It is believed that the population is resident.

Flammulated Owl—*Casual.* Judy Ward found a Flammulated Owl that had been picked up dying in a snowstorm in October or November 1982 on Willow Creek, which is about 7 miles northwest of Muddy Gap (Three Forks) on US 287. The specimen was sent to the Denver Museum of Natural History, where the identification was confirmed and where the specimen remains. Another was seen in Jackson Hole by Bert Raynes and others on October 8, 1982. It subsequently was found dead.

Eastern Screech-Owl—*Rare.* There is considerable interest in the distribution of the Eastern and Western Screech-Owls in Wyoming. Easterns have been seen in the vicinity of Casper, and in the past have nested in the city. They also nest regularly in City Park in Wheatland and in Sybille Canyon on Route 34 (between Wheatland and Bosler) just east of the Game and Fish installation. Eastern has been seen in Sheridan. Some say that Westerns also occur there but there are disagreements. Sam Fitton, who has had considerable experience with Wyoming's owls, feels that the Western does not occur in Sheridan. One of our troubles is that there are too few observers knowledgeable about owls and their calls. Furthermore, the almost complete dominance of the scene by the Great Horned Owl over most of the state makes owling rather difficult.

Western Screech-Owl—*Rare.* Sam Fitton called in a Western at New Fork Lake north of Pinedale after he had heard it calling. There are several other records for Westerns in the western part of the state that we believe are accurate. (See Eastern Screech-Owl, above.)

Great Horned Owl—*Common resident.* About every mile or two along our rivers and creeks there is a nesting pair of Great Horned Owls. They will also nest on cliffs if there is a small ledge. They are common in our forested areas, and manage to sneak into our cities and towns to nest. They are a very successful species with lots of food available in the form of mice and small rodents in our grass and sagebrush lands.

Snowy Owl—*Rare winter visitor.* Most years there is at least one report of a Snowy Owl, always in the open-plains areas of the state. In 44 years of birding in the state I have managed to see this species only twice. The records have been in December through the middle of March. The birds don't seem to stay in the same place. They move on.

Northern Hawk Owl—McCreary includes winter sightings for this species, but most Wyomingites do not regard these sightings as credible.

Northern Pygmy-Owl—*Rare resident.* Although a nest has not been found, it is presumed that these birds nest in our western coniferous forests. I have seen the species once in the back country of Yellowstone and twice in Grand Teton National Park. One of these records was of a pair. The species was seen on a Christmas Count near Lander in the Wind River Mountains, so we presume that it is resident. Sam Fitton had one just north of the Colorado state line near Harriman in the Laramie Range in 1988. However, most sightings come from the coniferous forests of Jackson Hole.

Burrowing Owl—*Uncommon summer resident.* They nest in prairie-dog holes all over Wyoming's open country, and are probably much more common than is generally supposed. There are nests in a good prairie-dog colony at Yant's Puddle just north of Casper. If you drive in the evening east of Interstate 25 on Ormsby Road (some 12 miles north of Casper) during migration in late August, your headlights will pick up a dozen or more owls scattered along the road over a course of about 10 miles. There is another Burrowing Owl location out the 33 Mile Road in the Casper area. Burrowing Owls should be looked for in all prairie-dog towns in Wyoming. Helen Downing mentions (in her *Birds of North-Central Wyoming and the Bighorn National Forest*) the Prairie Dog Road off Interstate 25 south of Sheridan. The owls arrive in the third week of April and leave by mid-October.

Barred Owl—*Accidental.* One was taken in the Bear Lodge Mountains of the Black Hills in March of 1905 (McCreary, *Wyoming Bird Life*). There is also a tape of a bird that sounded like a Barred Owl from Jackson Hole on September 21, 1982. Whether the rather similar-voiced Spotted Owl was eliminated is not clear. Theoretically, the Spotted Owl is a possibility in that location.

Great Gray Owl—*Uncommon resident of Jackson Hole and Yellowstone National Park.* There is a fairly sizable population of these owls in Yellowstone and Grand Teton National Parks, described in the birdfinding portion of this book. That area has had nesting Great Grays for the last 50 years that I know of. In fact, years ago Roger Peterson saw a Great Gray just behind the old headquarters (now the Beaver Creek service area) which may have been his first. Great Grays like to nest in snags, which are high stumps of great trees that have been broken off well above the ground—perhaps 20 feet. They are likely to nest in the same place for a few years and then move on. Sometimes one of the personnel at the Moose headquarters will know where they are located. I have seen them around Emma Matilda Lake and Two Ocean Lake. Hiking around these two lakes will take you a day, but it is a great wilderness walk with lots to see. Yellowstone can have Great Grays almost anywhere. One of the best areas is in the meadows along the road from Canyon to Norris Junction.

Long-eared Owl—*Rare resident.* Groups of Long-ears have wintered in the state. The last group that we know of was in a small copse of half-grown cottonwoods on the Green River just above Flaming Gorge Reservoir. They stayed there two winters. There was a similar spot on the North Platte River not far from Alcova years ago. They are known to nest almost all over the state but only sparsely. They move around particularly in the fall, so it is not clear whether they all are residents or some are partly migratory. At any rate, it is an event if you see one. Sam Fitton showed me a nest in the juniper country on Powder Rim, but most seem to be in deciduous brush and trees along water-courses. In general, in the juniper country if it isn't a Great Horned, it is a Long-eared.

Short-eared Owl—*Uncommon resident.* They nest in the meadows and grasslands throughout the state but not commonly. Occasionally, there are outbreaks of mice in the sagebrush and grass country, and then the Short-ear becomes common. A few years ago there was an outbreak of mice on the high meadows and sagebrush land above Shirley Basin, and soon there were a half-dozen nests within perhaps a five-mile radius. The National Elk Refuge just north of Jackson is a good place to see them or the area around Prairie Center in the grassland south of Van Tassel near the Nebraska border. We are not sure that a number of our birds are not migrants, but the fact is that you can see a Short-eared at any time of year in Wyoming.

Boreal Owl—*Rare resident.* Either we have more and better observers or the status of this bird has recently changed. Recent studies in Grand Teton National Park have produced a number of sound records. In the past few years there have been a number of sightings. There have also been reports from Yellowstone National Park. There has been a population in the front range of Colorado just south of Wyoming, and this deme appears to have stretched north into Wyoming. In June 1988 Bill Hayes, a graduate student at the University of Wyoming, heard a Boreal at Lake Marie at the top of the Snowy range. Later in early August he and Verna and Jim Herold found an immature bird being fed by an adult about a mile away from that location. About 10 days later a lot of other people including Sam Fitton and the author relocated the same birds. Brad Hammond and others from Idaho Falls found them in March 1992 a half-mile down on both sides of the summit of Teton Pass on Route 22 west of Wilson. This species has also been reported at Togwotee Pass on US 26. (For a discussion of this species in Wyoming see Garber, Wallen, and Duffy, 1991.)

Northern Saw-whet Owl—*Uncommon resident.* There are several old records of nesting, and they have nested in Jackson Hole. They have been seen in all months of the year. Saw-whets have been seen mostly in the coniferous forested areas, but certainly have been found in deciduous areas as well. With more observers seeking owls we might find we that have had more of these little birds than we thought. On a spring evening in the Bridger National Forest near the Salt River Range in western Wyoming Sam Fitton and Dave Lockman on snowmobiles found six Saw-whets. The forests of the northwestern part of Wyoming, including the Great Parks, probably have lots of them.

Common Nighthawk—*Common summer resident.* They nest on any rise in the plains or any bare hill—of which Wyoming has great numbers. Their booming can be heard all June and much of July. Whether it is due to insecticides, such as grasshopper-spraying, which has been widely done in Wyoming, or some other reason, these birds are much less common than they used to be. But they are still common. They arrive in the first week of June and leave by mid-September. From late August on they often gather in sizable flocks.

Common Poorwill—*Common summer resident in the drier eastern and southern parts of the state.* They are confined to the dry, partly wooded hills. For instance, the foothills below Devils Tower can be a good place for them, where they may be heard from the road not far from the visitor center. They are very nocturnal and much more common than is generally believed. Their plaintive call can be easily missed. For about a dozen years I ran a Breeding Bird Survey off the 33 Mile Road about 40 miles north of Casper. The route started at the bottom of a rise with a few sparse trees—perfect Common Poorwill habitat. Common Poorwills regularly called there, but they quit about 5 minutes before the official starting time of the survey, so in those years I never got them on the count. My alfalfa fields are adjacent to some dry, sparsely vegetated hills where there are a number of Common Poorwills, and at night they come down onto the dirt road leading into the fields. Their red eyes are easily spotted, and when they fly their flight reminds you of a butterfly. On my grassy summer range, which is up in the hills almost surrounded by trees, I have often heard up to three Common Poorwills calling at the same time. They start calling by mid-May and stop by October 1. Nothing is known of their migration.

Chimney Swift—*Uncommon summer resident.* They have been regular apparent nesting birds in downtown Cheyenne for many years. Over the rest of the eastern boundary of the state they are less reliable in the few towns there, but are seen fairly often in Wheatland and Torrington. Occasionally, they have been seen as far west as Casper, but whether or not they really nest there is not clear. The same is true of Sheridan. They arrive about the first of May and are gone by mid-August.

White-throated Swift—*Common summer resident.* They nest in colonies on cliffs, mostly in the eastern half of the state. Ayres Natural Bridge has a colony, and there is another at the mouth of Tongue River Canyon north of Sheridan. One colony on the front face of Casper Mountain at the top is easily seen from the turn-out on the highway leading up the mountain. They arrive about the middle of April and leave by mid-September.

Magnificent Hummingbird—*Casual.* There was one at Brooks Lake July 15-22, 1988. Bert Raynes and Jay Foott had a Magnificent July 2-8, 1982, at Jay's feeder at Wilson just north of Jackson. A year later on June 26, 1983, Jay saw a female. Then there was the fellow who had a feeder on Casper Mountain much frequented by the local Broad-tails. He once said to me, "About two weeks ago I had a great big green hummingbird for a few days. Never saw anything like it before. I thought of calling you." I resisted my impulse to choke him on the spot.

Black-chinned Hummingbird—*Uncommon summer resident.* These occur along the western boundary of the state. Marie Adams of Evanston showed

Black-chins to several of us at a feeder south of Evanston about 2 miles from the Utah line. They also occur in Star Valley (Afton) and Jackson Hole. They arrive in early June and leave by mid-August. East of the western boundary area Black-chins are unknown.

Anna's Hummingbird—*Accidental.* Marian Collins had one at her feeder in Story from August 1 to September 15, 1973.

Calliope Hummingbird—*Common summer resident.* They occur in the mountainous areas of the state, and are a candidate for the commonest hummer in Jackson Hole. They are silent as well as being the smallest hummer; Broad-tails are noisy. As you enter Hoback Canyon down-river from Bondurant on US 191 less than a mile from the first bridge, you encounter Cliff Creek Road on the left. There is alder marsh running a half-mile up the road. This is an excellent place to see Calliope Hummers at close range. It hasn't failed me in years. The males love to perch on the top of a dead alder twig to patrol the area. These feisty mites will drive almost anything away. Almost any alder swamps in the high country are good for Calliopes. Look for them at Willow Flats in Jackson Hole and in the Story area. They arrive in late May and leave by the first of September.

Broad-tailed Hummingbird—*Common summer resident.* These are our common hummers throughout the state. They are confined to hill-and-mountain country that is vegetated. They are often in the riparian areas along streams coming off the higher ground. Since they are noisy, they are easy to find. They arrive about the middle of May and are gone by the end of the first week of September.

Rufous Hummingbird—*Common summer visitor.* They occur in all our mountainous areas or near them, as well as in towns, since most of our towns are near mountains. There are perhaps more in Jackson Hole than elsewhere. Another good place to see them is the top of Signal Mountain in the center of Jackson Hole if there are flowers in bloom there. There are no breeding-records for the state. They arrive about the first of July and are usually gone by mid-August over most of the state. In Grand Teton National Park and the Jackson area they sometimes linger longer.

Belted Kingfisher—*Common resident.* They nest in mud-banks all over the state. There are more in the summer than in winter so some must be somewhat migratory. However, there are some places where there are warm springs that regularly have open water all winter; in such places, kingfishers stay all winter.

Lewis's Woodpecker—*Uncommon summer resident.* They are not often found in the heavily forested areas. Look for them in the cottonwood riparian habitats or open forests where the trees are more scattered. There is more of this sort of country in the eastern part of the state than in the western sections. They have nested along Ash Creek out of Sheridan for years. The fall is the best time to see them. In late August and early

September they gather in scraggly flocks of up to 50 birds altogether. The road up beside Boxelder Canyon (Boxelder Road) is an excellent place for them. This road leads off to the south about two miles east of Glenrock. Another good spot is on the Esterbrook Road, Route 94, leading south from Douglas at the west end of town. At 20.9 miles up this road (a few miles beyond the end of the pavement) one comes to a creek with a lot of cottonwoods by the road; this is a great place for them. Lewis's arrive in May and are gone by the end of September. They seem most numerous in the last two weeks of August and the first two weeks of September.

Red-headed Woodpecker—*Common summer resident.* They are common on the eastern edge of the state in deciduous growth in places like Torrington and the valley of the Cheyenne River above Mule Creek Junction. The farther west one goes, the less common they are. Lander is about as far west as they get. They have been recorded in Jackson Hole and Yellowstone National Park but are thundering rare there. They arrive in May and leave in September.

Acorn Woodpecker—*Accidental.* One was seen near Moose (Blacktail Ponds) June 20, 1975, in Grand Teton National Park by Bill DeBaets and party, confirmed by a park ranger, and supported by an excellent photograph. Forrest Luke had one on July 15, 1989, on Pine Mountain 80 miles south of Rock Springs.

Red-naped Sapsucker—*Common summer resident and migrant.* They nest in aspen and cottonwood groves throughout the state, but most commonly in Grand Teton National Park. In fact, in Grand Teton they are hard to miss. They arrive in the third week of April; the migrants are gone by mid-May. In the fall they leave in September and October.

Williamson's Sapsucker—*Uncommon mountain summer resident.* Williamson's occurs in all the mountain ranges of Wyoming except the Laramie Range and the Black Hills. It really is rare except in Yellowstone and Grand Teton National Parks. In 44 years of birding I have never missed it in the areas around Lupine Meadows south of Jenny Lake in Grand Teton. They can be found in the first three-quarters of a mile on the trail around the south end of Jenny Lake or the south end of Lupine Meadows at the start of the trail up the Grand Teton. The first mile of the Valley Trail is the best before it starts to rise very much. Another fine place is Blacktail Plateau Scenic Drive in Yellowstone National Park. They arrive in May and leave by the first week of September.

Downy Woodpecker—*Common resident.* Downies can be found at lower elevations mostly—often in riparian vegetation. Sometimes they can be found in the mountains, also. They occur throughout the state, but are less common in the high forests.

Hairy Woodpecker—*Common resident.* This is by far our most common woodpecker. One might say that all woodpeckers are Hairies until proven otherwise. They are the woodpecker which you will see on the higher ground predominantly. In recent burns they can become abundant. On a burn on Casper Mountain we counted 50 in half of a square mile the first year after the burn.

White-headed Woodpecker—*Accidental.* There is one old record from Jackson Hole by Alexander Klots on October 27, 1924 (McCreary, *Wyoming Bird Life*). None has been found recently.

Three-toed Woodpecker—*Uncommon resident.* They occur in all mountain ranges of Wyoming except the Black Hills, where they are replaced by the Black-backed. Look for them in recent burns; they can almost be guaranteed in such areas. The tremendous amount of insect life underneath the bark of a dead tree attracts Three-toeds as well as Hairies and Downies. In a recent burn it is hard to get out of hearing of a woodpecker. Woodpeckers are little interested in trees where the bark has been entirely burned off, but that isn't the way a fire burns. Many trees will still have their bark after a burn. A burn is good for woodpeckers for at least ten years in this region. Our National Forests are run for the most part as tree farms where there are few dead trees, but our National Parks are different, and the recent policy of "let it burn unless it bothers park facilities" has allowed some wonderful burns in Grand Teton National Park. Three-toeds have become common in such places as the Beaver Creek burn. Even the Superior Point Fire of 1975 is still pretty good, but you have to contend with the new forest growing up. The recent conflagration in Yellowstone National Park may allow the woodpeckers to increase for the next ten years, but huge burns like this may act differently. However, some caution needs to be observed, as for instance in a nice burn on Casper Mountain which was on Bureau of Land Management land. The BLM promptly salvaged all the big trees with bark, leaving the small barkless ones. This policy ruined the burn as far as Three-toeds were concerned.

Black-backed Woodpecker—*Uncommon resident.* In theory the Black-backed occurs only in the northeast in the Black Hills. Actually, there are a number of them in the northwest in the Great Parks, also. The best place in the northeast to find them is at Devils Tower. They are in the old burn area on the left as you go up to the tower. By sticking to the road you may miss them, but they actually have nested here. To find them may require a walk into the burned woods. In the northwest they occur in all the good burns along with the Three-toeds—although the Three-toed is the more common. In the rest of the state they are absent.

Northern Flicker—*Common resident.* Very common in the riparian areas and in towns, they can be found in open forests as well. Most of our flickers are Red-shafted, but we have many "Orange-shafted" as well as a few Yellow-shafted.

Pileated Woodpecker—*Probably casual.* I have never personally known anybody who has seen this bird in Wyoming, but one of the personnel in Grand Teton National Park, Bob Wood, has. It also has been reported in Yellowstone.

Olive-sided Flycatcher—*Uncommon resident.* A denizen of the high-mountain forest—almost all the mountain ranges of Wyoming qualify except the Black Hills. A good place to see these birds is Brooklyn Lake in the Snowy Range west of Laramie. Olive-sideds are really common in Grand Teton National Park between Leigh Lake and Jenny Lake and surrounding areas. They arrive in the last week of May and leave by the last week in September.

Western Wood-Pewee—*Common summer resident.* They nest throughout the state from the deciduous riparian zones through the mountain forests. They are the commonest of our flycatchers. Some of the guide books say that there is trouble telling the Eastern from the Western, but I don't think that this is true. The Western has a heavy band right across the chest which the Eastern does not have, and, of course, their calls are totally different. Some of the cities and towns in Wyoming , including Casper, spray for mosquitoes and have eliminated the wood-pewees from those areas. Elsewhere, they arrive in mid-May and leave by October 1.

Eastern Wood-Pewee—*Accidental.* There was one on Matheson Creek 11 miles southwest of Casper behind the author's house, identified by the author and several other people on July 9, 1975. This bird was constantly calling but remained only a few hours.

Willow Flycatcher—*Uncommon summer resident.* This bird is practically common in high-altitude alder marshes. There are numerous suitable marshes in Grand Teton National Park. It can often be found in Willow Flats and at the big marsh below Two Ocean Lake. It arrives about the first of June and leaves by mid-September.

Least Flycatcher—*Common summer resident.* It occurs in the eastern half of the state, usually near water-courses. It is common in the Black Hills and can be found at the campground at Devils Tower. It is fairly common as far west as the Sheridan/Story area. There are spots for them along the North Platte River, such as Edness Kimball Wilkins State Park just east of Casper and the Rawhide area between Torrington and Lingle. They arrive in mid-May and leave by mid-September.

Hammond's Flycatcher—*Rare summer resident.* There are some in the northern part of Yellowstone, and a few in Grand Teton National Park—mostly high up on the mountains near tree-line but occasionally lower. They have been rarely identified on migration, but we presume that they arrive about the first of June and leave by September.

Dusky Flycatcher—*Common summer resident.* Duskies nest in various habitats, to paraphrase McCreary, such as pine forests, aspen groves, bushy ravines, or along streams. They are particularly common in Grand Teton National Park in the vegetated bottomlands as well as on the lower slopes of the mountains. They can be found in the Happy Jack area near Vedauwoo or on Muddy Mountain south of Casper Mountain. They arrive in mid-May and leave in September with the rest of the *Empidonaces* that are difficult to identify at that time of year.

Gray Flycatcher—*Common summer resident in its restricted habitat.* These birds are confined to the dry juniper forests south of the Rock Springs/Green River area and similar habitat on Powder Rim, and there are also a few east of Highway 789 to Baggs in the same juniper habitat. There are other juniper areas of the state, but they don't have these birds. They arrive in the last week of May and leave by September.

Cordilleran Flycatcher—*Common summer resident.* They are sparse but can be found in all forested areas except the juniper country, usually along water-courses. They are most common in the Laramie Range. Casper Mountain, the north end of the Laramie Range, often has one on an upper branch of Elkhorn Creek. The Esterbrook area south of Douglas is a good place to look for them. Brooklyn Lake in the Snowy Range west of Laramie is another good place. Gros Ventre Campground in Grand Teton National Park has them. They arrive in the last week of May and leave in mid-September.

Eastern Phoebe—*Rare migrant.* There have been attempted nestings in the Black Hills but with no success as far as we know. Below Keyhole Dam a nest was built, but only one bird was present. Elsewhere in the eastern part of the state a bird will show up, sing frantically for a week or so, and then disappear. This is most likely to happen in June.

Say's Phoebe—*Common summer resident.* They nest throughout the state but are much less common in the forested areas of the northwest, the Great Parks of Yellowstone and Grand Teton. They prefer deserted sheds and outbuildings, of which there are plenty. There is a deserted school-house with sheds on the way into Ayres Natural Bridge that has had a pair for years. They can also be found on the right just after you turn into the road to Ayres Natural Bridge. They like open country and can nest on cliffs, too. Most gullies in Wyoming will have steep open banks or cliffs. These birds arrive in early April and leave in October.

Vermilion Flycatcher—*Accidental.* On July 5, 1986, there was one at the edge of the Beaver Creek burn of 1985 in Grand Teton National Park. It was seen by Sam MacDonald, R. Hawke, and others, including Bert Raynes.

Ash-throated Flycatcher—*Uncommon summer resident.* They are confined to the juniper country south of Rock Springs/Green River. A good place to find them is in the Little Firehole area. Another good area is along Powder Rim. They are tree-hole nesters, and the older junipers have a lot of holes. In other juniper areas, such as the rather extensive area south of Casper, they are rare and not regular. They arrive in the third week of May and leave by September.

Great Crested Flycatcher—*Casual migrant.* Ken Diem had one at Jackson August 7, 1979. Lois Layton found one in Casper September 29, 1981.

Cassin's Kingbird—*Uncommon summer resident.* They occur in the eastern part of the state. For many years a pair has nested along Lance Creek in a grove of trees north of the hamlet of Lance Creek. You go 2.8 miles east of town on Route 270, then 10.5 miles north on Route 272, and then walk across the creek to the east. The creek is just a trickle. They are seen infrequently in the Sheridan area, whereas the Casper region has not reported them yet. Farther east they are much more common with many older records and nests in the collecting era. In the fall I have seen them travel with small groups of Western Kingbirds. They arrive by mid-May and leave by mid-September.

Western Kingbird—*Common summer resident.* Many of the farmyards in the eastern part of the state have nesting Western Kingbirds. Where there are Easterns, too, the Western predominates. As one goes west, the Western becomes more scarce until one gets to Jackson Hole and Yellowstone, where they are practically rare. They can be expected from the 10th of May on and leave by mid-September.

Eastern Kingbird—*Common summer resident.* These birds are a little more plentiful than the Western, and they occur over more of the state although they are less common the farther west one goes. They love to eat grasshoppers, and, since Wyoming has always had more than its share, they do very well. They arrive about the 10th of May and leave by the end of September.

Scissor-tailed Flycatcher—*Rare visitor.* In recent years there have been more sightings, with at least three in 1988. One bird remained for a month. There have been no reports of nesting to date. Since we are north of their range, we can't call them "migrants"; they seem to be just wanderers. The reports have been between late May and late August.

Horned Lark—*Common resident.* This is a very common bird in Wyoming. They nest in all the drier areas—which covers most of the open country. They can be found in all months of the year, but a heavy snowfall will drive them out. Wyoming winters are characterized by high winds and dry snow. To those who are not familiar with dry snow, it is snow that comes down in very cold weather as very fine particles. It is then subjected to high winds and blown to smithereens; the resulting drifts made of the finest of particles are practically solid. (This is the kind of snow which you can make an igloo out of.) This drifting results in bare spots almost all winter, and it is in these snow-free areas that Horned Larks feed. Since the birds are attracted to bare ground, spring snows that leave only the highways open will cause the slaughter of horrendous numbers of Horned Larks. At times highways can be made slick from the bodies of these birds. Unlike the meadowlarks, they don't seem to get out of the way fast enough. The recent tendency to allow cars to go faster makes matters worse. However, there are still plenty of Horned Larks.

Purple Martin—*Rare visitor and possible nester.* Brad House saw one at Douglas in the 1940s. Since then there has been only one report: Helen Downing had a pair at Worland in the Big Horn Basin August 7, 1978. With more observers perhaps this paucity of sightings will be corrected. Otto McCreary in his *Wyoming Bird Life* of 1939 cited several records, including a nesting at the junction of Chugwater Creek and the Laramie River. Since Utah has Purple Martins, Wyoming should have them, too.

Tree Swallow—*Common summer resident.* They nest throughout the state where there are trees—which means mostly in the riparian areas in the eastern part of the state. They arrive in mid-April (although I have seen them as early as late March) and leave in September.

Violet-green Swallow—*Common summer resident.* They are colonial and like high cliffs on which to nest, such as the cliffs opposite Slide Lake on the Gros Ventre Road out of Jackson Hole or Tongue River Canyon or the top of the front face of Casper Mountain. In fact, they are plentiful throughout our many mountain ranges, probably more so than the Tree Swallow. In migration Violet-greens are plentiful everywhere else. They arrive about the end of the first week in May and leave in August in the huge exodus of swallows.

Northern Rough-winged Swallow—*Common summer resident.* More common in the east than the west and probably the least common of our regular swallows. They are not colonial and nest in holes in banks, usually along streams. They arrive in early May and leave with the rest of the swallows in August, when great mixed flocks gather, usually in the vicinity of lakes.

Bank Swallow—*Common summer resident.* They nest in holes in banks all over the state, preferably near streams and ponds, where there is more food for them. There is a fine bank for them near the fish hatchery at the north end of the National Elk Refuge north of Jackson. They pick any bank even if it is very small, such as at Yant's Puddle, since the amount of food available there is tremendous. The refinery that owns the place has used a bulldozer to smooth things out, much to the swallows' distress. They appear early in May with the other swallows and leave in late August.

Cliff Swallow—*Very common summer resident.* This is by far our most common swallow. They nest anywhere. Any steep bank or cliff in a gully will do, or a rock cliff—of which Wyoming has enormous numbers. Also, bridges are used and sometimes the wall of a building. In many areas these birds are abundant. One year they decided that the back of my house looked like a good place to nest, and about 60 pairs set about building nests. The noise and disturbance went on all day and night. I thought that either the birds or I were going to have to leave. Fortunately, after three days they decided it was a poor place and left. I heaved a sigh of relief and unpacked. Normally they arrive in early May but don't get numerous until about May 10; they leave in August. They usually are the principal component of the great swallow flocks that gather in August before going south.

Barn Swallow—*Common summer resident.* They can be found throughout the state but are more common at lower elevations and in the east. Their favorite nesting-site is under bridges. They arrive in the third week of April and leave in September.

Gray Jay—*Common resident.* They are common in the forested areas of the state, particularly in Grand Teton and Yellowstone National Parks. They are common in the Bighorns and can often be found at Devils Tower. They are scarce in the Laramie Range but elsewhere common. They live up to their name of Camp Robber here as elsewhere. The campground at Green River Lakes has more than its share.

Steller's Jay—*Common resident.* While they are a common resident over most of the state, they do not occur in the Black Hills, they are scarce in the Bighorns, and they are somewhat uncommon in Yellowstone National Park. They are confined to the forests but in winter will come to bird-feeders in nearby towns. It would be hard to miss them in Grand Teton National Park, or at Brooklyn Lake in the Snowy Range west of Laramie.

Blue Jay—*Uncommon resident.* This species is confined to the eastern half of the state. In the North Platte Valley around Torrington Blue Jays are common. Their numbers have been steadily increasing, and they are now rather common in both Cheyenne and Casper. As you go west, they become rare. The Black Hills have always had some.

Scrub Jay—*Uncommon resident of the southwest juniper forests.* With Sam Fitton we found a nest on Powder Rim in July 1988, but they occur regularly in the juniper forest south of Rock Springs/Green River. Very rarely they have been found elsewhere in the state. One occurred at the base of Casper Mountain during the winter of 1950. However, they are one of our less easily found residents. They seem much more common in summer.

Pinyon Jay—*Common resident.* They are often found in the juniper country, particularly south and west of Casper and south of Green River/Rock Springs. Much of the time, except when nesting, they travel in flocks. They can be found in Ponderosa Pine forests of the east and south part of the state, so the only parts of the state where they are not found are the Great Parks of the northwest and the surrounding areas. Also, they are not found in the high forests in the rest of the state. They nest in April and May.

Clark's Nutcracker—*Common resident.* This colorful, noisy "Mountain Crow" is found everywhere in coniferous forests in Wyoming, however, it is scarce in the Black Hills. Their numbers vary with the size of the cone crop. They usually are found in small groups. When nutcrackers are absent from some small area, due to a poor local cone crop, they will be still plentiful over the state. All forests are in mountainous areas and all mountainous areas are pierced by roads, so one can't miss seeing these birds.

Black-billed Magpie—*Very common resident.* Whether it be plains, rough country, foothills, or mountain forests, the magpie is there. They eat anything, everywhere, at any time. They survive our worst winter weather when other birds can't. Their nests are big round piles of sticks that are very obvious. They line the bottom inside with a heavy layer of mud which dries and becomes brick-like. Various local "sportsman" organizations have gone on magpie-extermination programs and go around shooting up these nests. Little damage is done to the magpies inside their brick-bottom houses. My garage is very close to the house with a Chinese Elm between. One spring the magpies built a huge nest in the elm, and fledged seven young in good flying condition. On the day when the young emerged, our two dogs stood below barking at the tops of their lungs, and jumping at them with the two adult magpies just out of the dogs' reach. The seven young were just above that point, imitating their parents. The result was pure bedlam. Except for the noise no harm was done. The ubiquitous magpie survives everything very well.

American Crow—*Locally common resident.* Also a common migrant in the eastern half of the state. The Sheridan area has lots of them and they are common in the Big Horn Basin. In winter there is often a huge roost of them in the Big Horn Basin north of Thermopolis near US 20 where a big cliff comes down close to the Bighorn River on the east side. Sam Fitton estimated 10,000 birds here, but this is not a consistent roost. Elsewhere in the state they are scarce with only a few pockets of them. One is along Mormon Row in Jackson Hole, which is off the road to Kelly east of Black Butte. In the eastern half of the state they can be seen as migrants in March and April and again in October and November.

Common Raven—*Common resident of western Wyoming.* From Riverton and Cody west, this is the common corvid. In the Great Parks of Yellowstone and Grand Teton, ravens may appear to be the most prominent species of bird. They also occur in the Bighorn Mountains as well as the Snowies and the Sierra Madre. There is a pocket of them about ten miles east of Moneta on US 20/26. Moneta is one of these towns where you had better not blink as you drive by; otherwise, you will miss it. There is another small group at Tie Siding on US Route 287 south of Laramie. Ravens are by no means confined to mountains. They can be found in the valleys as well. They are absent in the juniper forests of the state, however.

Black-capped Chickadee—*Common resident.* They can nest at higher elevations, but generally this is a lowland bird that is common wherever there are trees—which means in riparian areas and in towns. Yellowstone National Park is the only part of the state where they are rare, because of the Park's high elevation.

Mountain Chickadee—*Common resident.* Nests in all our mountains in numbers and can be found in the mountains at all seasons. In winter there are fewer at high elevations; at that season they often can be found down with the Black-capped Chickadees. They come to feeders as easily as the Black-caps. Their note is somewhat similar to that of the Black-capped Chickadee but is very nasal and can be identified with ease.

Plain Titmouse—*Uncommon summer resident of the southwest juniper area.* Elsewhere, even in juniper country, there are almost no records. South of Rock Springs/Green River they nest in numbers but are hard to find when they are very quietly nesting in late May and June. They arrive in late March and are most noisy in April, when you appreciate how common they are. They are easier to find in late summer. They leave in November, however, they may remain all winter and actually be residents but not often. This is, of course, the grayer interior population.

Bushtit—*Irregular visitor and nester in the southwest juniper forests.* They have been found in the juniper area south of Rock Springs/Green River and on Powder Rim. Occasionally, they will nest. They move in small flocks, and when they do breed there is more than one nest. Forrest Luke of Rock Springs found a group once in February, and they have been seen in many other months. Most are seen in summer, but of course that is when most observers are around. The juniper forests seem particularly bleak and lifeless in winter, and Route 191 which traverses the area south of Rock Springs/Green River is often closed at that time.

Red-breasted Nuthatch—*Common resident.* A common nesting-bird of the mountain forests. From time to time they invade the lowland deciduous areas—primarily riparian, but also in the towns. Usually, this is in the fall.

White-breasted Nuthatch—*Uncommon resident.* These birds' numbers can be variable. Sometimes they are quite common, but most of the time they are a little hard to find. They are distributed throughout the state wherever there are trees. It doesn't matter whether the habitat is in the mountains or in riparian areas on the plains.

Pygmy Nuthatch—*Uncommon resident.* Pygmies are limited to Ponderosa Pine forests in the eastern part of the state. They can be found at Story, but are scarce. They seem regular at Glendo Reservoir. In the big

Ponderosa Pine forest north of Laramie Peak they can be found regularly. They are on Casper Mountain most years at all seasons, but there seem to be more in summer than in winter.

Brown Creeper—*Uncommon resident.* They are found throughout the state wherever there are trees. However, they are distributed sparsely, and although one gets to see one almost every year, one cannot count on it. They nest everywhere but mostly in old-growth trees, where their needs are best met.

Rock Wren—*Common summer resident.* Wherever there are rocks there are Rock Wrens—and there are lots of rocks in Wyoming. Small cliffs and talus slopes attract them but not big cliffs. They also like gullies, and much of Wyoming's grasslands are made up of rolling hills with steep-sided gullies with lots of Rock Wrens. In a Breeding Bird Survey in the eroded grasslands of eastern Wyoming, the second most common bird is likely to be the Rock Wren. (The first will be the Western Meadowlark.) In rocky hills and lower mountains it is hard to be out of hearing of Rock Wrens. They arrive in the last week of April and are all gone by mid-October.

Canyon Wren—*Uncommon summer resident.* We have seen them on a Christmas Count in the Casper area and found them singing in February at Ayres Natural Bridge, so we are not sure that they are a summer resident only. In Wyoming one cannot find them consistently in many places. I have found them at Devils Tower, but not regularly. I have found them at Sand Creek near Beulah in northeast Wyoming in the Black Hills, but again not regularly. Wyoming has a tremendous number of spectacular canyons where one would expect to find Canyon Wrens. Some of the canyons will have the wren some of the time, like Tongue River Canyon, Fremont Canyon on Alcova Lake southwest of Casper, Shell Canyon on the west side of the Bighorns, several of the canyons in the juniper country south of Rock Springs/Green River (particularly Minnie's Gap near the Utah line on US 191), Bighorn Canyon in central Wyoming, and on it goes. Perhaps the most consistent place has been Ayres Natural Bridge canyon. They arrive in March and probably leave in November.

Carolina Wren—*Accidental.* One was seen on Matheson Creek, eleven miles southwest of Casper behind the author's house, on May 8, 1977, for several hours. It was observed by several other Casper birders.

Bewick's Wren—*Common summer resident in the juniper forest south of Rock Springs/Green River.* It also occurs on Powder Rim and has been seen in junipers east of Route 789 north of Baggs. It has not been recorded in other juniper areas of the state. It is one of the most common of juniper birds where it does occur. It arrives in the middle of April and is gone by October 1.

House Wren—*Common summer resident.* One of the commonest birds in the state. They occur wherever there are deciduous trees and brush. In the riparian areas one could expect a pair almost every eighth-of-a-mile. They arrive in the last week of April and leave by the first of October.

Winter Wren—*Rare resident.* It used to be that one could go along with the mob of tourists up Cascade Canyon from Jenny Lake in Grand Teton National Park to the fork in Cascade Creek. The south fork goes to Alaska Basin. Alaska Basin in about the first week of August is one of the most beautiful spots in the Rocky Mountains, carpeted with flowers of every hue. The north fork goes to Lake Solitude. Above the roar of the fork one could hear the voice of the Winter Wren. Then, after a few years, they were no longer there. Another spot has been about three miles up the trail from the parking area on Swift Creek behind Afton in Star Valley. The trail forks, and they have been found in that area. I have found them three times in 44 years in winter in the Casper area, all near the open water of warm springs. Other observers have had much the same experience.

Sedge Wren—*Accidental.* One was collected by Frank Bond near Cheyenne April 14, 1889 (McCreary, *Wyoming Bird Life*). Deborah Finch had one in a grassy meadow on Sherman Hill (Laramie Range) east of Laramie June 1, 1982.

Marsh Wren—*Common in large marshes,* of which Wyoming has relatively few. There are good colonies at Table Mountain, Ocean Lake, Seedskadee National Wildlife Refuge, and Flat Creek Marsh just upstream from the town of Jackson in the National Elk Refuge. Presumably, there are Marsh Wrens on the great marsh south of Cokeville on the Bear River, an area that is to become our newest National Wildlife Refuge. At present it is so difficult to get access that I really don't know if Marsh Wrens occur there or not. Marsh Wrens not infrequently overwinter. They usually arrive by mid-April and are gone by the middle of October.

American Dipper—*Common resident.* Many people prefer the name Water Ouzel. They nest early at lower elevations. One of the best places to find them nesting is Ayres Natural Bridge. The young fledge by early May. However, later one can find these extraordinary birds nesting up into July in the high country near white-water. Most permanent streams with fast water have them. They winter over on smaller streams wherever there is open water. This means warm springs which, as mentioned before, the state has in great numbers.

Golden-crowned Kinglet—*Uncommon resident.* They nest in the mountains very sparsely. One of their favorite places is high in some very large and tall Douglas-fir on the west side of Jenny Lake not far from Hidden Falls, a cascade. It is very difficult to see them there. One will find them in the summer occasionally in most of our higher mountain ranges. The rest of the year the best place to see them is the area around the fish hatchery in Story, but they are found occasionally almost anywhere except in the high mountains.

Ruby-crowned Kinglet—*Common summer resident.* This is a candidate for the commonest nesting bird in our conifer forests. There are a few reports of their being seen on Christmas Counts. Our winters seem much too severe for Ruby-crowns, and it seems likely that the reports may have been of Golden-crowns instead. The Ruby-crowns are nearly everywhere that appropriate habitat is available in migration and very common. They arrive about the last week of April and are gone by the end of October.

Blue-gray Gnatcatcher—*Common summer resident in the juniper country south of Rock Springs/Green River.* Elsewhere in the juniper areas they are uncommon to rare as a nesting-bird. In migration they are rare except in the juniper areas. For some reason the Cheyenne area has them rather commonly. It is no surprise that Yellowstone National Park has perhaps only one record. Grand Teton National Park, however, has had them. They arrive by the last week of April and are gone by mid-September, or so we think.

Eastern Bluebird—*Rare nester and wanderer in the eastern half of the state.* Jean Adams of Sundance has put out a large number of nest-boxes on Route 876 (between Route 585 and the Moskee Road). Almost every year since 1985 she has had one or more boxes used by Eastern Bluebirds. Generally they have had two broods. Otherwise, we have had no breeding records since the '30s (McCreary, *Wyoming Bird Life*) except a possible nesting-area just up river from Torrington. Outside of Jean Adams's birds I have only seen them four times in 44 years. One of these was in the city of Casper in January. The few other birders in the eastern half of the state have seen them only once or twice. It is apparent that this bird was never common in Wyoming but probably was formerly more common than it is today. If more nest-boxes were put up, we might have more of these birds than we do now. Usually, they arrive in April and leave by October.

Western Bluebird—*Casual.* No recent records. About 15 years ago Florence Spring told me that she had one in Rock Springs. Otherwise, we have to go back 50 years, when there were a number of records (McCreary, *Wyoming Bird Life*). There is too little information to make a guess as to when or where they might be in the state at present. The state Avian Atlas lists many records. These must be old for they have nothing to do with the present situation. Like most birders in Wyoming I have never seen the bird in the state, and I probably have been more active statewide for longer than any other current birder. With the increased numbers of good observers we may be able to shed more light on this situation.

Mountain Bluebird—*Common summer resident.* They nest from the lowlands to tree-line on the mountains. One of our commonest birds statewide. Occasional severe blizzards will decimate them. About five years ago we had a terror of a blizzard over the eastern half of the state in the last week of April, following which they were found dead in piles on Casper Mountain. Bluebirds at lower elevations survived in spite of temperatures in the low 20s and 70-mile-per-hour winds that blew snow horizontally for three days. (Incidentally, the sheep losses in the same storm were catastrophic while cattle losses were moderate.) Mountain Bluebirds arrive as early as the first week of March and sometimes earlier. They leave by November but occasionally are seen in the winter months.

Townsend's Solitaire—*Common resident.* It nests in the mountains throughout the state but more commonly in the eastern and southern mountains such as the Laramie Range, Snowy Range, and Sierra Madre. It is least common in the Great Parks of the northwest, though easy to find at Mammoth Hot Springs in winter. In fall, winter, and early spring the solitaires are confined to the juniper areas, where they eat the berries. They don't require a lot of junipers, so in these areas they are common. An amusing common sight in winter is the defense of a berry tree by a single Townsend's Solitaire against a flock of 50 to 100 Bohemian Waxwings. The waxwings pay absolutely no attention to him and proceed to eat his berries while he flounces around scolding loudly trying to drive them off, the picture of anger and frustration. He could handle a few, but he is so outnumbered that his protests make no difference. Usually there are plenty of berries, so this is a tempest in a teapot.

Veery—*Uncommon summer resident.* They nest in lowland spots of deciduous growth in the eastern half of Wyoming; elsewhere they are rare. There are numerous places in the Black Hills that have them, such as along Houston Creek and the road over Bear Lodge Mountains. Story has a lot of them, as does Muddy Creek as it goes through Three Forks. They arrive in the second week of May and are gone by mid-September.

Gray-cheeked Thrush—*Rare migrant.* It is likely that this bird has been overlooked; it may be more common than believed. It is rarely reported, and the records are from only the eastern half of the state. Our reports are all in May. Thrushes tend to be silent in migration, and I have never heard this bird's distinctive song in Wyoming.

Swainson's Thrush—*Common summer resident.* This is our most common thrush. It nests in all our mountainous country, so the Great Parks are well supplied with them. In migration in the second to third week of May it can be the most numerous bird present. In the fall they are gone by October 1.

Hermit Thrush—*Common summer resident.* This bird is not as common as the Swainson's, but it does occur in all our mountain ranges. They are particularly common on the southern end of the Laramie Range, on Green Mountain west of Three Forks, and in the lowest forests at the base of the Tetons in Grand Teton National Park. In migration they are everywhere.

They arrive earlier than the other thrushes. The first birds are here in the last week of April; they usually leave by the end of October.

Wood Thrush—*Rare migrant.* When I was first in Wyoming in Casper sitting at my desk working one early May morning, the beautiful song of the Wood Thrush came through the window. I shortly went out and found the bird. On asking around about Wood Thrush, I met a lady who said that we had lots of Wood Thrushes. She had a cabin in the Bighorn Mountains and they were all over the place. Therefore, on my first checklist of the birds of Wyoming the Wood Thrush was listed as "common." Well, I later found out that this lady had the logical notion that all thrushes in the woods were Wood Thrushes. It was over 20 years before I found another Wood Thrush. Now with more and better observers we are doing better, but it is still a very rare bird most seasons. Most sightings are in the fall, and to date all are in the eastern half of the state.

American Robin—*Abundant resident.* Wherever there is plant life bigger than sage, there are robins. However, I don't think that they are all residents. My guess is that the legions of nesting birds migrate from the south, whereas the not-so-common wintering birds come from the north. In winter they eat the juniper berries and Buffalo berries along the riparian areas and the planted Russian Olives which are used as wind-breaks near homes in town and out. There are really lots of available berries, native or otherwise.

Varied Thrush—*Rare winter visitor.* All reports that I am aware of have been in late fall or winter. One would think that the northwestern part of the state would see the most since that area is nearer their wintering-ground, but that area is high and snowbound. Most of the records come from the eastern towns—Cheyenne, Casper, Sheridan, Rawlins, etc. We now have a sighting almost every year. One of the occurrences in Casper came from a Christmas Count, and the bird was seen by many people.

Gray Catbird—*Uncommon summer resident.* Catbirds nest in the riparian areas in the eastern half of the state but are rarer in the western half. This means they are confined to deciduous habitat, but they still are not common. They arrive after the 10th of May and will leave by October. However, along with the rest of the mimic thrushes, very occasionally they are found in winter.

Northern Mockingbird—*Rare nester and visitor.* These birds show up occasionally anywhere in the state. More often they are seen in the southeast from Cheyenne as far north as Casper and west to Laramie and east to the state line. In this block they will sometimes nest. Not infrequently they show up in autumn and spend the winter where there is plenty of food. They are seen somewhere several times a year. McCreary gives their dates as arriving in May and leaving in September, but I have seen them in all months of the year.

Sage Thrasher—*Common summer resident.* These birds are found wherever there is extensive sage. This means that they are found in huge areas of the state. They don't mind a mixture of greasewood, either. They are particularly common in the Green River valley, so a ride over Route 28 on the new road from Farson to the Green River or up Route 372 from the town of Green River to Fontenelle will produce a number of Sage Thrashers. Even Yellowstone National Park has them in the right habitat. They arrive in mid-April and leave by the end of October, but there are a number of wintering-records for Sage Thrashers.

Brown Thrasher—*Uncommon summer resident.* They can be found in the lowland deciduous riparian areas like the Gray Catbird. They can be found in appropriate habitat in the eastern half of the state, but there are almost no records in the western half of the state. They arrive in the last week of April and leave by October, but there are winter records also.

American Pipit—*Common summer resident.* They are very common above the treeline in the alpine zone. Beartooth Plateau is probably the easiest place to see them on their nesting-ground, and Medicine Bow Peak is a close second. Any alpine zone will do, however; try looking on Mount Washburn in Yellowstone National Park and above Powder River Pass in the Bighorns. There is a trail from Old Faithful in Yellowstone which goes down to the Beckler River to southwest Yellowstone that goes through a bit of alpine zone that is heavily used by American Pipits. Incidentally, if you are a backpacker, the trip down the Beckler River is probably the best in Yellowstone with two big, little-known waterfalls plus beautiful wild country, the 1988 fires notwithstanding. In migration in April and May, American Pipits can be found in meadows and fields and along lake shores and streams, and again in September and October.

Sprague's Pipit—*Rare migrant.* Since this bird nests in Montana, there have been a number of attempts to find them nesting in northern Wyoming but with no success to date. As a migrant they are rare except for the Lake DeSmet area, where they have been seen several times in May and September. Helen Downing has also found them on some of the lower grassy shoulders of the Bighorn Mountains.

Bohemian Waxwing—*Common winter visitor.* They are erratic. Occasionally, there are years when there are very few, and some years we have them by the thousands. Usually they come in flocks of up to several hundred and clean out any remaining berries or fruit such as old crab-apples. They are relatively tame and don't hesitate to come into towns and pour into front yards and back yards, making quite an impression on the local populace. As mentioned under American Robin, there are lots of berries both in towns and in the countryside for them. Waxwings are much more common in the eastern part of the state, east of a line from Cody to Lander to Rawlins. The flocks often start arriving in November and stay as late as the first week in April.

Cedar Waxwing—*Uncommon resident.* Calling them "resident" may be stretching it, but the fact is that in early winter there are a few Cedars mixed with the flocks of Bohemians. In late winter the Cedars fade out, but by March they often can be found again, this time not necessarily with Bohemians. During migration in April and May, Cedars become most common, but they do nest here. Cedars seem very variable but are not as erratic as Bohemians.

Northern Shrike—*Uncommon winter visitor.* We regularly have these birds throughout the state although some years there are more than others. The House Sparrow is one of their favorite foods. When the sparrows get out of town they are more at risk, since they are not quite so quick as the native birds. At times, however, the shrikes will appear in town trying to get them. Of course, the House Sparrow isn't the Northern Shrike's only food. The Northerns arrive any time from November 1 on and can stay up until the middle of April.

Loggerhead Shrike—*Common summer resident.* They nest in any brushy area and don't mind very dry country. They like greasewood, but don't look for them in coniferous forests. Therefore, they ought not to occur in Yellowstone National Park and ought to be very rare indeed in Grand Teton National Park. They start arriving in early April and are all gone by the end of November. I used to say that all you need to identify a shrike was a calendar. All after April 1 are Loggerheads and those after November 1 are Northerns. However, there is some overlap and early April and mid- to late October birds ought to be carefully identified by field marks. With a lot of relatively inexperienced birders taking to the country on Christmas Counts there is trouble with the identification which isn't easy. The usual trouble is reports of winter Loggerheads. Unless there is a good photograph with a detailed description and confirmation by an experienced birder, Helen Downing, our regional editor, has kindly removed them from the counts. So far no Loggerheads have made it through.

European Starling—*Common resident.* For the last 40 years these birds have been steadily increasing in the lowlands. You won't find them in the conifers. It used to be that one would see just a few, but now we have flocks of several hundred. They are rare in Yellowstone, but Grand Teton has a few in the deciduous bottoms. Elsewhere in the riparian areas there are too many.

Solitary Vireo—*Common summer resident of the Black Hills.* Also found on the east side of the Bighorns and the northern part of the Laramie Range. They are uncommon nesting birds in the southwest juniper country. The subspecies of Solitary Vireo in Wyoming is the *plumbeous*. Devils Tower has several pairs, as does Sand Creek. They are an uncommon migrant over the eastern half of the state. They start arriving in the last week of April and are gone by October.

Yellow-throated Vireo—*Accidental.* I heard and saw one with a group of other people June 1, 1958, about five miles southwest of Casper.

Warbling Vireo—*Common summer resident.* One of our most common nesting birds. They particularly like aspens, in fact, no aspen grove is complete without a Warbling Vireo. However, they are often found in other deciduous trees whether they are riparian or otherwise. They arrive about the third week of May and leave in September.

Philadelphia Vireo—*Rare migrant.* This bird has been seen in the Sheridan area several times in May and at least twice in the Casper area in September. It has not been recorded elsewhere.

Red-eyed Vireo—*Common nesting summer resident over the eastern fringe of the state and in the Sheridan area. Elsewhere it is an uncommon migrant.* Places like Sundance, Newcastle, and Torrington have them as breeding birds commonly. They are confined to deciduous trees. They arrive in late May and are gone by the end of September. There have been a few later dates.

Warblers

With the advent of more and better observers, it is apparent that all of the eastern warblers that have been seen in California will have been seen in Wyoming also. In the last few years we have had a rash of first sightings of eastern warblers, so any remarks here may soon be obsolete.

Golden-winged Warbler—*Rare migrant.* This bird was recorded for the first time on May 18, 1985, in Lions Park in Cheyenne by a lot of people, including the author. Since then there have been several sightings, all in May.

Tennessee Warbler—*Rare migrant.* These warblers are seen every year mostly in the eastern half of the state, but one cannot be sure of seeing them at all. They are seen going north largely in the first half of May and going south in late August and September. Usually a cold front stops them in the spring so we get to see them, and the same is true in the fall.

Orange-crowned Warbler—*Common migrant and uncommon summer nester.* They nest in rather high moist areas in deciduous growth. These areas are difficult to get to in most cases such as the headwaters of Corral Creek on Muddy Mountain, which is the mountain immediately south of Casper Mountain in the northern Laramie Range, and near Battle Lake in the Sierra Madre west of Encampment, where some were seen by Dorothy Waltman (McCreary *Wyoming Bird Life*). All nesting is in the eastern half of the state. As a migrant they are rare in western Wyoming including the Great Parks. However, in the eastern half of the state they are one of our commonest warblers and a relatively early arriver, often in the last days of April and through the first half of May. In the fall they start moving south in late August and are gone by the middle of October, so they are almost the last warblers to leave.

Nashville Warbler—*Rare migrant.* While they have been seen very rarely over most of the state, for some reason more are seen in the Green River Valley than anywhere else. Some years the species is merely uncommon in the Green River Valley. In general, it has been seen somewhere every year. The records are from May and September.

Virginia's Warbler—*Uncommon summer resident.* Forrest Luke reports nesting at Minnie's Gap on US 191 near the Utah/Wyoming boundary, as well as on the Little Firehole. It also has been found just below Seminoe Dam on the North Platte River in a dry gulch on the east side. Virginia's stick to dry gulches. It has been regular for a number of years on the Garrett Ranch in mid Bates Creek at the east end of Bates Hole southwest of Casper—likewise in Lesser Jackson Canyon on the west end of Casper Mountain. These are some of the better-known nesting-sites. It has not been reported on migration. McCreary did not mention this bird.

Northern Parula—*Rare migrant.* One of our rarer warblers. There are three old records listed by McCreary, including a specimen taken by Frank Bond in 1888. In recent years there was one in Audubon Park in Casper May 16, 1964, and again May 10, 1980. There was one below Fontenelle Dam on June 2, 1976, and again in 1990, plus one near Pine Bluff in 1990. There are several other records but not at the rate of one a year. All our records so far are in May and early June.

Yellow Warbler—*Common summer resident.* They nest in brushy riparian areas and particularly in towns. Yellowstone National Park has little habitat for them, and they do not occur in the juniper forests, but otherwise they are very common throughout the state. They arrive in the first week of May and are scarce after September 1 but can be found occasionally up to October 1.

Chestnut-sided Warbler—*Rare migrant.* This bird is more common than many of our other rare warblers. They have been see over all of the eastern part of the state, and below Fontenelle Dam. They have been seen in Cheyenne more than anywhere else, particularly in Lions Park, the Horticultural Station (the High Plains Grassland Research Station, as it is officially known), and the headquarters of the Wyoming Hereford Ranch. They go through in May and late August and again in early September around Labor Day. They usually are reported at least once a year.

Magnolia Warbler—*Rare migrant.* Almost every year more than one Magnolia is seen somewhere in eastern Wyoming—usually where there are more observers, such as in Cheyenne, Casper, and the Sheridan/Story area. However, Forrest Luke has had these birds for several years at the

Fontenelle Trap. He has shown them to me on at least two occasions. All reports, including the old ones in McCreary, have been in May.

Cape May Warbler—*Casual.* One was observed by Steve Gniadek June 16, 1975, at Tower Junction in Yellowstone National Park. Another was seen by many observers below the Fontenelle Dam for over two weeks in late May 1990.

Black-throated Blue Warbler—*Rare migrant.* This is another of the more common rare warblers, seen almost every year. Sometimes there is more than one sighting per year. These have been seen in the fall as well. Most of the reports are from Cheyenne, Casper, and the Sheridan/Story area. There is one report from Jackson Hole and none from Yellowstone National Park. The sightings are from May and September with at least one in the second week of October.

Yellow-rumped Warbler—*Common summer resident.* In the conifer forests of Wyoming all warblers are Yellow-rumped until proven otherwise. This statement is particularly true of Grand Teton and Yellowstone National Parks. The Yellow-rumped is our most common warbler; the resident bird is the "Audubon's" plumage. In migration they are everywhere. The first birds are likely to have the "Myrtle" plumage with a lot of mixtures, followed by those in "Audubon's" plumage. They arrive in the last week of April and are gone by November.

Black-throated Gray Warbler—*Common summer resident in the juniper forests.* In the juniper country south of Rock Springs/Green River and the sizable juniper area south of Casper, they are rather common. They haven't been reported elsewhere. In migration they can be found anywhere. They arrive in the second week of May and leave by the end of September.

Townsend's Warbler—*Uncommon migrant and rare nester.* Townsend's are more common in western Wyoming and the Green River Valley in particular, where at times it is plentiful. There are some old records of its nesting in Evanston and Yellowstone National Park (McCreary, *Wyoming Bird Life*), but no recent records. In migration, over the rest of the state they are variable. Some years they are hard to find while in others they are more common. In spring they are rare. They arrive in May and leave in August and September.

Hermit Warbler—*Accidental.* One was seen in the Fontenelle Trap May 26, 1990, by Forrest Luke, Marie Adams, and Rick and Janis Steenberg.

Black-throated Green Warbler—*Rare migrant.* This is one of the rarer warblers, though with more observers in the field there are reports almost every year. Most have been seen in the Cheyenne area. All reports are from May. There are no fall reports yet.

Blackburnian Warbler—*Rare migrant.* Another quite rare warbler, which has been seen in Cheyenne, Casper, and Sheridan. My first one was at the old ranch headquarters, now a small oasis of trees, just south of Laramie May 18, 1977.

Yellow-throated Warbler—*Accidental.* One bird was seen May 25-27, 1983, at Laramie by Doug Inkley, David Mozurkewich, and Craig Thompson. Another was seen in Green River May 18-19, 1989, by Forrest Luke and many others.

Pine Warbler—*Rare migrant.* This bird has now been seen in Casper, Douglas, and Gillette. All reports have been in September, except the remarkable bird from Gillette which for two weeks or more came to peanut butter in the bark of a tree in December 1988. This individual was seen by Verna Hays and many others, including the author.

Palm Warbler—*Rare migrant.* It has been seen in Casper, but mostly in Cheyenne. This bird is not seen every year, but there are now a number of records. All recent reports are from May. There is an old one from 1937 (McCreary) from Laramie on November 3 and 14. There is one recent record from Casper Mountain on September 27, 1989 (the eastern race).

Bay-breasted Warbler—*Casual migrant.* Verna and Jim Herold had one on the Gros Ventre River north of Jackson on June 8, 1980. Another in excellent plumage was seen in Garden Creek Park in Casper by Lucy Rognstad and Bud Stratton and his class on May 24, 1990. On June 2, 1990, there was one in the Fontenelle Trap seen by Forrest Luke and Marie Adams. The description is that of a female.

Blackpoll Warbler—*Uncommon migrant.* Blackpoll is found in the eastern half of the state every spring and fall, but it is never common. They have been found in almost all the communities from Lander east. They are less often seen in the fall. The spring dates are generally in the middle of May. In the fall they can be found from late August up to the third week of September.

Black-and-white Warbler—*Rare migrant.* They are more common than many of the other rare warblers. They have also has been seen in both spring and fall, but not necessarily every year. Again, all the records are from the eastern part of the state. The greatest number have been seen in Casper and Cheyenne. They go through in May and again in September.

American Redstart—*Common summer resident locally and common migrant.* Redstarts nest on the east side of the Bighorns in Story in some numbers and also in the Black Hills, particularly in the Sand Creek area. They used to nest in the Laramie Range and may still do so. In migration they show up in the last half of May and leave by the end of September.

Prothonotary Warbler—*Casual migrant.* Lucy Rognstad and Verna Herold had a male on August 27, 1985, in Audubon Park in Casper. Marie Adams had one at FMC Park on the Green River just below the town of Green River on September 2, 1986. There are two old records: one from

Yellowstone National Park September 10, 1931, by Charles H. Rogers and another October 31, 1938, by Arthur Mickey and Otto McCreary (*Wyoming Bird Life*).

Worm-eating Warbler—*Casual migrant.* Jim and Verna Herold had one at the Poison Spider School, a small oasis of trees, on the Zero Road west of Casper on May 11, 1981. Bill Hayes, a graduate student at Laramie, found one at the Wyoming Hereford Ranch outside of Cheyenne May 11, 1989. Another was seen for about two weeks in late May 1990 in the Fontenelle Trap by Forrest Luke and a host of others, including the author.

Ovenbird—*Common summer resident in the Black Hills and Story on the east side of the Bighorn Mountains.* There are also a few nests in the northern end of the Laramie Range. Elsewhere Ovenbirds are rare migrants only. Devils Tower has them, and they are common all through the Bear Lodge Mountains. The Fish Hatchery at Story has lots of them. They arrive about the end of the first week in May and leave by the end of September.

Northern Waterthrush—*Uncommon migrant.* I have heard Northern Waterthrush sing way into June in Willow Flats, so they probably nests sometimes but not consistently in Grand Teton National Park. As a migrant they come through about the second week of May and can be found almost to the end of that month. In the fall they are seen from the middle of August to the last week of September. The most consistent place to see them is Sloan's Lake in Lions Park in Cheyenne. They are rarer in the western part of the state.

Kentucky Warbler—*Accidental.* Lucy Rognstad had a Kentucky Warbler in Audubon Park between 23rd and 25th Street on Garden Creek in Casper on May 15, 1981, a bird confirmed by many others, including the author. Fred Lebsack and others found one at the High Plains Grassland Research Station outside Cheyenne on May 17, 1989.

Connecticut Warbler—*Accidental.* One was seen in the catch-all just below Fontenelle Dam on the Green River by Forrest Luke, Marie Adams, and several others on May 28, 1988.

Mourning Warbler—*Accidental.* Forrest Luke and the author had one in the Fontenelle Trap on May 27, 1989.

MacGillivray's Warbler—*Common summer resident.* They nest in brushy areas along streams throughout the state. Often they are hard to see, but one of the easiest places to observe them is around Jenny Lake in Grand Teton National Park. Another good spot is Sand Creek in the Black Hills, or Garden Creek Falls at the foot of Casper Mountain. These places all have easy access. They arrive about the middle of May and leave by the end of September, but are most common in August.

Common Yellowthroat—*Common summer resident.* No cattail marsh in Wyoming is complete without a Yellowthroat, and the marsh doesn't have to be very big. They arrive in the first week of May and leave by the end of September.

Hooded Warbler—*Casual migrant.* The author was shown one in the city of Casper on May 16, 1961, by Mrs. Dean Morgan. Another was found in sagebrush near Gillette on May 5, 1975, by J.L. Tate, Jr. Tim Manolis found one at Farson on August 14, 1982. Josephine Larson and Mr. and Mrs. Boevers had a female in the Fontenelle Trap on May 19, 1990.

Wilson's Warbler—*Uncommon spring migrant, summer nester, and common fall migrant.* They nest in the high alder marshes of the state such as Willow Flats, and in other marshes in Grand Teton National Park. They also nest in Yellowstone and the Bighorn Mountains. Over the eastern part of the state they are uncommon migrants in spring, but they are common at that season in Jackson Hole and the Green River Valley in western Wyoming. In the fall over the state they are very common. In the last week of August and the first two weeks of September Wilson's is our commonest warbler. At that time there are more of them than all the other warblers combined. They arrive in the last half of May and can be found also in the first week of June. In the fall movement they start in the middle of August and last until mid-October.

Canada Warbler—*Accidental.* There was one May 24, 1964, near the North Platte River on what is now the Lusby River Access off State Route 220 several miles north of Alcova. The bird was seen and heard by the author and a number of others at an Audubon Breakfast Picnic. Another was seen in the Fontenelle Trap by Forrest Luke and Rick Steenberg on June 6, 1990. This latter bird was probably a female.

Red-faced Warbler—*Accidental.* One was found in the town of Green River in May 1989. It was identified by Forrest Luke, Marie Adams, Sam Fitton, and many others from Utah and Colorado, as well as Wyoming.

Yellow-breasted Chat—*Common summer resident.* All the low sizable brushy spots along streams in Wyoming have chats. They arrive about the middle of May and are gone by mid-September.

Hepatic Tanager—*Accidental.* Frank Layton took some excellent pictures of a female Hepatic Tanager in his bird-bath just west of Casper on October 7, 1972. Another record was for May 22, 1977, by Jack Palma at Cheyenne.

Summer Tanager—*Rare migrant.* This bird has been seen a number of times in both Casper and Cheyenne, but most of these sightings have come from Cheyenne. The first one that the author saw was at the High Plains Grassland Research Station on May 14, 1966. This appears to be the first state record. All records so far are from May except one. The one exception to May is from Cody on July 8-19, 1977, by Kay Flora.

Scarlet Tanager—*Casual migrant.* There are a few records. One was on May 30, 1977, on the Garrett Ranch on mid Bates Creek south of Casper seen by a group including the author. Another sighting was on May 18-21, 1977, at Cheyenne by Lulu Corbin. A Scarlet Tanager was killed on June 27, 1977, by hitting a window in Burns near the Colorado border. There is a photograph of this one by Sue Adams. On June 9, 1982, there was one in an aspen/willow Beaver pond habitat near Rawlins by K. Hepworth. A female was seen at the Laytons' residence west of Casper on October 6, 1989, by the author and several others.

Western Tanager—*Common summer resident.* This is one of our more common summer birds statewide. They nest in conifers and in heavy riparian deciduous growth as well. There are a number of them around Jenny Lake in Grand Teton National Park, to name one typical place. They arrive in the last half of May and leave by October 1. I haven't distinguished their song from that of the Scarlet Tanager. Both sound to me like an improved American Robin that has a frog in his throat.

Northern Cardinal—*Rare visitor.* There are no breeding records. If they show up in winter they are likely to stay for the duration at feeders. However, they show up only about once in four years or so. They should be more common on the eastern border, particularly in the valley of the North Platte. While most of the records are from the eastern half of the state, one was seen in Pinedale in western Wyoming.

Rose-breasted Grosbeak—*Uncommon migrant.* There have been occasional nesting reports. Rose Forrister found a nest in June 1983 on Garden Creek in Casper near Audubon Park. There were young in the nest, and both parents were seen feeding the young after they had fledged. Gibson Peterson was sure that he had a nesting pair once on Elkhorn Creek, another stream on the north face of Casper Mountain. Rose-breasts have been seen as migrants almost all over the state, but they are seen most often in the eastern half. They arrive about the end of the first week of May and can be seen for a couple of weeks. In the fall they are seen less often, usually in September.

Black-headed Grosbeak—*Common summer resident.* They are confined to the deciduous areas in towns and in riparian zones. They are common throughout the state except Yellowstone National Park, which has little suitable habitat. The eastern part of the state has the best areas for them. They arrive in the last half of May and are gone by the end of the third week of September.

Blue Grosbeak—*Rare summer resident except in the North Platte valley downstream from Alcova southwest of Casper, where it is just uncommon.* They have been reported from most areas in the eastern part of the state, such as Rawlins, Cheyenne, Sheridan, and Lander. They arrive in very late May or early June, will sing even into early August, and are gone by the end of the first week in September.

Lazuli Bunting—*Common summer resident.* They require riparian areas but also commonly come into towns where there are deciduous trees and shrubs. They are really very common, and there isn't a creek or bigger stream with vegetation without a supply of these birds. They sing into the heat of the day and later in the season than most birds, usually into late July. Yellowstone particularly lacks the proper habitat, so they are somewhat uncommon there. Grand Teton National Park has more of the proper deciduous areas. They first arrive by the end of the first week of May but are much more common a couple of weeks later. They leave by the first of October.

Indigo Bunting—*Uncommon summer resident along the eastern edge of the state.* Most common in the Black Hills. There are hybrids between Lazuli and Indigo Buntings but from studies at Fort Collins, Colorado, there are not as many hybrids as one would expect considering the number of individuals in the overlapping zone of the species, so they ought not to be lumped. Rarely Indigo Buntings have been found nesting west of the eastern fringe of the state. For several years there was a male acting like a nesting bird in the author's woods on the North Platte River west of Casper, but we have never found a nest in this area. In migration Indigo Buntings can be found west of the nesting areas in the eastern part of the state and very rarely in the western part. Sand Creek near Beulah in the Black Hills is an area likely to produce Indigo/Lazuli hybrids. The migration dates for the Indigo are the same as for the Lazuli.

Painted Bunting—*Accidental.* May Hanesworth had one at her yard feeder May 23-26, 1956, in Cheyenne where it was observed by many. There was another observed at a feeder in Sundance on May 17, 1991, by Ernest Miller, who got a good videotape of this bird.

Dickcissel—*Uncommon summer resident on the eastern edge of the state.* They are most commonly found in the Black Hills and the lower North Platte Valley from Fort Laramie south. Even in these places they are not regular. West of the eastern edge of the state, around Sheridan and Story, they may occasionally nest. But here they they sing for just a few days and then move on. The same behavior is seen on the Kendrick irrigation project near Casper, but there are as yet no nesting records. Furthermore, these observations from the Casper area are for late in the season, often in July. Seemingly, these are lone males beyond their normal range seeking a mate. Having no success, they move on. They normally arrive in May and leave by mid-September.

Green-tailed Towhee—*Common summer resident.* This is the predominant species of the higher hills and the mountain sagebrush country throughout the state. Grand Teton National Park has lots of them, while Yellowstone has little suitable habitat. They arrive about the end of the first week of

May and leave by mid-October. Occasionally, they have wintered over, or at least made the attempt.

Rufous-sided Towhee—*Common summer resident.* They nest on brushy hillsides and riparian areas that have plenty of undergrowth but no sagebrush. This means that they are confined to the hill country and mountainous areas. The classification of this bird has always bothered me. It has a different call-note, song, and appearance from those of the Eastern Rufous-sided Towhee. I think that it ought to be a different species. Someday the A.O.U. committee could split it from the Eastern bird, as it used to be. The towhees arrive in the last week of April and leaves by the end of October. However, there are a number of records from Christmas Counts. It not infrequently tries to overwinter.

Cassin's Sparrow—*Casual summer resident.* Craig Faanes of the U.S. Fish and Wildlife Service had one on June 8, 1978, a few miles south of Midwest (*Western Birds* 10:163-164, 1979). On June 28, 1990, William H. Howe of the U.S. Fish and Wildlife Service, while doing a Breeding Bird Survey, found four singing, skylarking males at a spot east of Torrington three miles north of US 26. They continue to breed in this area.

American Tree Sparrow—*Common winter visitor.* They are distributed statewide except in the forested mountains. They arrive as early as late October and are usually gone by April 1. Older reports of Chipping Sparrows on Christmas Counts by very inexperienced birders were presumably of this species. However, we have this identification heresy well stamped out by now.

Chipping Sparrow—*Common summer resident and migrant.* They nest in all the forested areas of the state, perhaps more commonly at the lower elevations. They occur in the juniper areas as well. They migrate in flocks, sometimes with a few Clay-colored Sparrows. The farther east you go the more Clay-coloreds there are. Chipping Sparrows start to arrive in the last week of April and stay until about the end of October.

Clay-colored Sparrow—*Uncommon migrant.* There are no nesting records for the state. Along the eastern boundary they are more common; perhaps 25 percent of the birds in Chippy flocks are Clay-coloreds. By "eastern boundary" I mean the Black Hills, Newcastle, the North Platte Valley from Fort Laramie downstream, and from Wheatland and Cheyenne east. As you go west, they become scarcer, and by the time you get to Jackson Hole they are rare although there are a number of records for that area—perhaps because it is better covered. Now there is a record at north Yellowstone (in the Mammoth area) with a good photograph. They migrate with Chipping Sparrows.

Brewer's Sparrow—*Common summer resident.* They nest in the sagebrush in the lower lands between the hills and mountains, so Grand Teton National Park has a lot and Yellowstone National Park does, too, although it has much less proper habitat. Over the rest of the state, which has vast amounts of sagebrush, they are very common but can be spotty at times. They arrive about the last week of April and are gone by mid-October.

Field Sparrow—*Rare migrant.* They have been seen on the eastern edge of the state, south of Van Tassel and at the Wyoming Hereford Ranch. They are rare enough that they are not reported every year. Field Sparrows have been seen only in April and May.

Vesper Sparrow—*Common summer resident.* They occupy the lower sagebrush zone throughout the state although in some areas their distribution is spotty. This is true in northeast Wyoming. In general, however, these are very common birds. They arrive after the middle of April and leave by November. Only once have I found one on a Christmas Count, and that count was at least a week before Christmas. After Christmas that particular bird was gone.

Lark Sparrow—*Common summer resident.* Along the eastern edge of the state this becomes the predominant sparrow. This is true particularly in the lower North Platte Valley around Torrington, but they are still common over the eastern half of the state. In western Wyoming they are uncommon. They arrive about the first of May and are gone by October.

Black-throated Sparrow—*Rare summer resident.* They have been seen on the sagebrush flats between Farson and the Green River. They also have shown up at a private residence on White Mountain just north of Rock Springs. It is presumed that they are still here in summer, but in recent years no one has taken the time to find them. Reports of them west of Farson are from June. McCreary has three old sightings from the eastern part of the state at Guernsey, Fort Steel, and Laramie.

Sage Sparrow—*Common summer resident.* This sparrow is the commonest bird in the sagebrush of the southwestern part of the state. They also get into the western edge of the Big Horn Basin but are uncommon there. The Green River Basin has lots of them wherever there is sagebrush. Old reports in McCreary give a much greater distribution throughout central Wyoming and even up to Sheridan and east to Cheyenne. They can no longer be found in those areas. They arrive in April and leave by the end of October.

Lark Bunting—*Very common to almost abundant summer resident.* This bird is odd, for it is practically colonial in nesting—and the nesting locations vary from year to year. For instance, in doing a Breeding Bird Survey under proper guidelines, we had Lark Bunting often flying over the territory, but then one year there were 25 nests of them in 80 acres. As one goes west in the state, Lark Buntings diminish so they are almost uncommon in western Wyoming. Dry years in eastern Wyoming will send more of these birds into western Wyoming, providing that it is wetter in the west; and if the east is wet and the west drier, the birds will remain in the east. They arrive in flocks, skimming through the country from May 1 to almost the end of the month; they leave by October.

Savannah Sparrow—*Common summer resident.* They are confined to wet meadows and damp areas around lakes and ponds throughout the state, but in this sort of habitat they are plentiful. They arrive in April and leave by the end of October.

Baird's Sparrow—*Uncommon migrant along the eastern boundary of the state.* There are no known nesting records yet. However, I have been shown singing birds on the 4th of July just north of Cheyenne. We have had singing males acting as if on territory in late May and early June—only to find they had disappeared a week or two later. They are found in migration in the grasslands south of Van Tassel, around Cheyenne and west to Laramie, and north to the Black Hills. They are very rare in the Sheridan and Casper areas. They arrive in May and early June, and in the fall they are seen in September and up to the middle of October.

Grasshopper Sparrow—*Uncommon summer resident in the eastern part of the state.* We have more of them in wet years. The first time I did a Breeding Bird Survey north of Lance Creek in a very wet year, I had 21 of them. In the 20 years since, I have had nowhere near that number and in most years none at all. (However, in the particular spot where I had the most, there has been much deterioration of the range.) They can be found south of Van Tassel, and on Bird Farm Road south of Big Horn, and the Black Hills, or anywhere on the eastern grasslands. Look for them in good grass or poor alfalfa fields. I used to have them nesting in my alfalfa fields, but the quality of the fields has been improved and now I have none. They arrive in the last half of May and leave by the end of September.

Le Conte's Sparrow—*Accidental.* There were two records by Platt Hall and Helen Downing at the south end of Lake DeSmet in the fine stand of Beach Grass before Texaco raised the lake level. Those occurrences were on April 20, 1977, and May 9, 1978, respectively. There is no Beach Grass there now.

Fox Sparrow—*Uncommon summer resident of the high altitude marshes of the state.* They can be found in Willow Flats, where the auto traffic is a problem. The big alder marsh below Two Ocean Lake is a better place. Both of these spots are in Grand Teton National Park. There are probably some Fox Sparrows in the Bighorns, also. Except in the northwest, there are few marshes that are suitable. They probably arrive early in April and leave in October. As a migrant they are rare but can be seen almost anywhere in the state in damp areas.

Song Sparrow—*Common resident.* In the semi-arid part of the state, which is most of it, they like moist brushy habitat along streams, around marshes, and beside ponds. Jackson Hole has a lot of this type of area and there they are common, but Yellowstone is high with much less habitat to their liking and there they are scarce. In winter they stay if there is some open water as there is around springs and warm springs.

Lincoln's Sparrow—*Common summer resident and migrant.* The Beaver pond is their typical habitat. Wyoming has lots of Beaver ponds and lots of Lincoln's Sparrows, but any very moist area on the high ground will do. In this type of habitat they are distributed statewide. They are common migrants in late April and May and again in September and into October.

Swamp Sparrow—*Rare migrant in the eastern part of the state.* Whether they nest or not is not clear. They have been reported more in the Black Hills than anywhere else. Sam Fitton had one at Long Point on Ocean Lake, and they have been seen in the Sheridan area. Reports are from May and September, but their status is not well known.

White-throated Sparrow—*Uncommon fall migrant.* Occasionally, these birds will overwinter at feeders. Rarely they are seen in spring. In the eastern half of the state they are somewhat regular in the fall, particularly in October, in association with other sparrows. An active birder will not miss them.

White-crowned Sparrow—*Common summer resident and migrant.* They nest in the high brushy areas of all our mountain ranges. One very accessible place is on Highway 130 as it goes over the top of the Snowy Range west of Laramie. These are the Gambel's subspecies. As a migrant they are very common, sometimes abundant, in May, September, and October. They migrate from April through May and again in September into November, and there are numerous winter records. Grand Teton and Yellowstone National Parks have them in large numbers.

Harris's Sparrow—*Uncommon winter visitor in the eastern half of the state.* They come to feeders all through the eastern half of the state in small numbers—usually singly but sometimes two of them. They come in their winter and immature plumages in October and leave singing in their breeding-plumage in the first week of May. In the western half of the state they are rare.

Dark-eyed Junco—*Common resident and migrant.* We have most of the subspecies. The "White-winged" nests in the Black Hills. It should have been called the "White-tailed" since the white wing is hard to see. The Laramie Range and other southern ranges have the "Gray-headed." The "Montana" is mostly a migrant. The "Pink-sided" nests in the Bighorns primarily. The western mountains, including the Great Parks have "Oregons" (Schufeldt's). The "Slate-colored" is also a migrant. Then, of course, there are intermediates. The result is a slew of different-colored juncos in every flock in migration and winter. They nest in all our forested mountains. In winter they come down to lower elevations, particularly to riparian situations. Also, they come to brushy spots and areas of trees around buildings. They readily come to feeders where they are very common. Perhaps it is because we have long winters, but Wyoming does seem to have more feeders per capita than most states. The Audubon Society alone peddles 12 tons or more of sunflower seeds in Casper, a town of 50,000.

McCown's Longspur—*Common summer resident.* On the Laramie Plains they are more common than the Horned Lark in many areas. They require native grasses. On the grasslands south of Van Tassel they are also common, and in this area the nesting ranges of the Chestnut-collared and McCown's overlap, so both can be found nesting in one field. They are common on the high grasslands around Cheyenne, and they can be easily found on US 85 northeast of Cheyenne. Fortunately, the Wyoming Plateau extends south over the boundary into Colorado, making the Pawnee National Grasslands possible, so Colorado has some McCown's, too, but if you want to see the birds in numbers come to Wyoming. As one goes north, they are less common in the Powder River Basin. At Yant's Puddle just north of Casper, where the native grasses have been allowed to return and flourish, there is a new colony. They don't seem really colonial, yet their proper habitat is spotty, so they appear colonial. This fact would make some "colonies" consist of one nest. West of the Bighorn Mountains and the Laramie plains they become rare. They arrive in April when large flocks can be found along the eastern boundary of the state, particularly on the grasslands south of Van Tassel. In the fall they disappear during October.

Lapland Longspur—*Uncommon migrant and winter visitor.* They are rather confined to the eastern part of the state, and are rare in western Wyoming. By the middle of October they are almost guaranteed to be at Yant's Puddle just north of Casper. They will remain there for at least another month, but by Christmas Count time they are no longer regular. All the eastern grasslands have them, and they can occur in large flocks on the Laramie Plains. By February many are changing into their spring plumage. By March they are often mixed with flocks of Horned Larks. They arrive in mid-October and are gone by April.

Smith's Longspur—*Accidental.* Observed by K.C. and Bobbie Roberts and the author on September 26, 1992, south of Van Tassel on the grasslands.

Chestnut-collared Longspur—*Uncommon summer resident.* They can be found on US 85 northeast of Cheyenne, but they are not as common as McCown's. They are common south of Van Tassel. There are some in the Powder River Basin but most nest in Montana. The Laramie Plains rarely have any. In migration they can be found as far west as Sheridan and Casper but are not common. Big flocks can be seen on the eastern boundary in the same areas as McCown's. They arrive in April and leave in September and October.

Snow Bunting—*Uncommon winter visitor.* They probably occur regularly in the depths of winter but often in inaccessible places. They occur throughout the state. They prefer high grasslands, but in bad weather they can be found at lower elevations. Shirley Basin is a high grassland which probably has them almost every winter. The Sweetwater Plateau is another place where they often occur. If the weather is severe enough with cold, snow, and blow, they will come down into feed-lots and weedy places near towns. We have found them mixed with flocks of Horned Larks in February and early March. They are more regular in the Sheridan area than farther south. They arrive after severe weather sets in during December and will stay around until mid-March.

Bobolink—*Uncommon summer resident.* They can be found regularly in fields southwest of Sheridan and on the Wagon Box Road just west of Fort Phil Kearny. Occasionally, they can be found in the Black Hills, and I have seen them on the northern part of the National Elk Refuge in Jackson Hole but not regularly. As a migrant they can be found rarely over the eastern half of the state. They arrive in May and leave by September.

Red-winged Blackbird—*Common resident.* Quite a few overwinter, often at feeders. They will nest in any marshy bit throughout the state, but they are somewhat limited because the colonies of Yellow-headed Blackbirds pre-empt the best cattail marshes and exclude the Red-wings. Most Red-wings arrive in March and leave by November.

Western Meadowlark—*Abundant summer resident.* This is Wyoming's most common bird. Over the eastern grasslands of the state they are everywhere in great numbers. As you go west, they are not so common. Yellowstone and Grand Teton National Parks list them as uncommon. This status would be true of the juniper country in the southwest, also. In the lower North Platte Valley and extreme southeast Wyoming one suspects that a fair number overwinter at times. By the time of the Christmas Count a few are lingering in feed-lots over the eastern half of the state, but they rarely stay or survive the winter. They arrive in the last half of March and mostly leave by December.

Yellow-headed Blackbird—*Common summer resident.* Most good cattail marshes in Wyoming have colonies of Yellow-heads—Ocean Lake, Loch Katrine, Table Mountain, and Hutton Lake National Wildlife Refuge to mention a few. They arrive in early April and leave by the end of October.

Rusty Blackbird—*Rare winter visitor.* All records so far have been from the winter, probably because that is when we can recognize them most easily. Brewer's Blackbirds are so numerous in spring and summer that it would be like finding a needle in a haystack. However, the Rusty Blackbird occurs to the north of us in the Canadian Shield and Alaska, so we ought to have migrants. Rusties have been found scattered all over the state, but not every year. I have found them only twice in 44 years in the Casper area, but the Sheridan area has done much better than that. Green River in southwestern Wyoming has also had them.

Brewer's Blackbird—*Common summer resident.* A few have overwintered from time to time, and they can be found on Christmas Counts fairly often. They are the commonest of our blackbirds, and the most valuable, as they subsist on grasshoppers. Although they are much diminished in recent years, a flock of a thousand is not unusual and can make a real dent in the hopper population. During a heavy grasshopper infestation my son once observed one Brewer's Blackbird eat 15 grasshoppers in 10 minutes, and then fly off to the nearest fence with its friends to preen and twitter. How often these birds might feed like this is not clear. Although the state has a statute protecting almost all birds except the magpie, the Game and Fish Department has a ruling by which all blackbirds can be shot. At times Wyoming is rather primitive, and the Game and Fish people can be just plain ignorant. Brewer's Blackbirds nest in the sagebrush of the hill country and arrive early in April. The bulk of them disappears with the grasshoppers by October.

Great-tailed Grackle—*Accidental.* On May 13, 1989, Ron Ryder of Colorado had Wyoming's first Great-tailed Grackle, at Warren Air Force Base in Cheyenne. Since this species has been steadily expanding its range northward, we had been expecting it for some time. There will surely be other records before long. In fact, Forrest Luke and others found one at Evanston on September 11, 1991.

Common Grackle—*Common summer resident.* They nest in the riparian zone along many of the larger creeks. In western Wyoming they are rare to uncommon, but eastern Wyoming has lots of them. The Great Parks, Yellowstone and Grand Teton, have very few of them, and those are in migration only. They arrive in the last week of March and leave by November.

Brown-headed Cowbird—*Common summer resident.* They are common throughout the state and are just as parasitic as elsewhere. Yellowstone National Park is perhaps the only area where they are not common. They arrive by the first of May and leave by October.

Orchard Oriole—*Common summer resident.* They are confined to the eastern edge of the state and the lower North Platte valley up to Fort Laramie. In the latter area Orchard is the predominant oriole. Over the rest of the edge-country the Northern ("Bullock's") is more common. By the time one moves west to Sheridan and Casper, the Orchard is rare and the bird seen or heard is usually the first-year male. By edge-country I mean the Black Hills, Torrington, Goshen Hole, and Pine Bluff and Cheyenne. They arrive about the second week of May and are gone by mid-September.

Northern Oriole—*Common summer resident.* Our version of the Northern is the "Bullock's." They are found statewide in deciduous trees. There are a few in Jackson Hole, but there is almost no habitat for them in Yellowstone. Occasionally, on the eastern boundary in the Black Hills and North Platte valley below Fort Laramie there are "Baltimores." The most recent ones have shown some signs of hybridization. Due to the destruction of shelter-belts we wonder if these birds might become pure again. All the earlier reports of "Baltimores" were of the pure plumage, but the "Baltimore" has always been very rare. The "Bullock's" will arrive in the second week of May; they are gone by the third week of September.

Scott's Oriole—*Rare summer resident.* They occur and nest in the southwest juniper country. Sam Fitton found the first nest in Wyoming on Powder Rim in 1982. This species has nested in the Little Firehole area for several years. Its arrival and departure dates are really not known yet.

Brambling—*Accidental.* Mary Back had one at Weltys' feeder in Dubois November 10-26, 1985, which was seen by a number of people. Helen Downing had one the same year on November 18, and again on the 30th in Sheridan. Both birds were photographed.

Rosy Finch—*Common resident.* These birds nest in the alpine zone of all our mountain ranges. In the Bighorns it is the Gray-crowned; in the west in the Tetons, Wind Rivers, and Beartooth Plateau, they are Blacks; and in the south in the Snowy Range it is the Brown-capped. They are numerous, and in spring in stormy weather one can see them on the floor of Jackson Hole until mid-June. By taking the tramway at Teton Village one can see them on their breeding-grounds. Also by going up Medicine Bow Peak in the Snowy Range one can easily see the Brown-capped. In winter they occur is sizable flocks. In fact, in the treeless country in winter any big flocks of birds are Rosy Finches until proven otherwise. In the eastern half of the state they will be Gray-crowns and in the west Blacks. The Gray-crowns roost on cliffs, particularly where there are Cliff Swallows nests which they find to be very suitable roosting-spots and will scrap interminably over who gets which one. It seems likely that these winter flocks are not local birds but probably come from farther north. Observers should pay attention to which forms they see; this birds may be split into multiple species again.

Pine Grosbeak—*Uncommon resident.* They can be found in all our higher mountain ranges such as the Tetons and Yellowstone National Park, the Bighorns, and the Grays River ranges, and Wyoming and Salt Ranges, but you are going to have to look a while to find them. The surest place to find them is Brooklyn Lake and the road up to it from Route 130 in the Snowy Range west of Laramie. I have never missed them there. In winter they spread out and often can be found in lower mountain ranges like the Laramie Range. The easiest spots would be the top of Sherman Hill west of Cheyenne and Casper Mountain, which are traversed by roads that are maintained all winter.

Purple Finch—*Very rare visitor.* The only multiple records in the state come from Sheridan and the Black Hills. They have several from spring, fall, and winter. In the early spring, however, there was one at a feeder in Casper in 1990.

Cassin's Finch—*Common summer resident.* Cassin's are probably resident some of the time. They are irregular, but very common birds. They nest in all the mountain areas of the state. They will appear at lower elevations first, often at feeders. Then when the snow melts, the birds will go up to the nesting-grounds. Usually, they show up in late February or March and will leave by December, but sometimes they are seen in the most wintery months, also.

House Finch—*Common resident.* They mostly inhabit the towns and cities of the state where they are common. Sometimes they almost outnumber the House Sparrows. They readily come to feeders. At times they can be found in the juniper country south of Rock Springs/Green River or southwest of Casper.

Red Crossbill—*Irregular common resident.* They depend on the cone crop and their numbers vary with it. Most of the time they can be found in good numbers, and somewhere in the state there will be good cones even when many mountain regions will have poor crops. Actually, they are rather common. In 44 years I have never missed them. In late July and August when the box elder seeds are ripe, Red Crossbills can be found in deciduous riparian areas, so they are not always in conifers.

White-winged Crossbill—*Rare visitor.* They are rare all over the state, but one gets the impression that they are more often seen in Grand Teton National Park than elsewhere. Yellowstone has been so inaccessible in winter that we don't know very much about their occurrence there. However, in the last few years this has changed, winter visitation via snowmobile has increased, and a few White-winged Crossbills have been observed to date. Also, one has the impression that these birds are seen more in fall and winter, but my first sighting in Casper was on June 21. Therefore, they are both rare and irregular.

Common Redpoll—*Uncommon irregular winter visitor.* They are most commonly seen in the Sheridan area. They readily come to feeders. In fact, it is a rare year when Sheridan doesn't have any. They are much more common in the eastern half of the state. About 50 percent of the time they get into the southern part of the eastern half. Usually, they come in small flocks, and they are more likely to appear when we have a good weed crop. From reading McCreary, we have fewer now than we used to have. Often, they first show up in November and can be found until March.

Hoary Redpoll—*Rare winter visitor.* Sheridan has them fairly frequently, but they are very rare farther south. In December 1975 there was an invasion of Hoaries along with many flocks of Common, and the Hoaries were seen as far south as Casper. The dates for the Hoary Redpoll are the same as those for the Common Redpoll.

Pine Siskin—*Common resident.* These must be our most common finch in the state. They are common in all mountainous conifer areas of the state. However, they sometimes nest in deciduous areas, also. They come to feeders easily and must be close to the most common bird at these winter sources of food. In winter they are in flocks and can be found where there are lots of weeds. Formerly, according to McCreary, they were rarely found in winter. Winter bird-feeders are common throughout the state in all communities. Whether this has led to more wintering Pine Siskins is not clear.

Lesser Goldfinch—*Uncommon summer resident in the southeast portion of the state.* From Cheyenne to Laramie these are regular but not common summer birds. It is presumed that they nest. They are found farther north from time to time but not regularly. They have been seen once in Sheridan and a number of times in the Casper area. They also have been seen at Glendo State Park at Glendo Reservoir about halfway between Casper and Cheyenne. They arrive in April and leave in October. They have been found occasionally as far west as southwestern Wyoming.

American Goldfinch—*Common resident in the eastern half of the state; much less common in the western part of the state.* Yellowstone National Park, for instance, has very little habitat that would interest a goldfinch. They are a weed-seed eater, and the eastern part of the state has more weeds. The small, wild sunflowers are very common and are relished by goldfinches. There are fewer goldfinches in the winter than during summer, but they come to feeders, and there are usually some around. However, they can be highly irregular in the winter.

Evening Grosbeak—*Common winter visitor.* There is circumstantial evidence that they nest in Wyoming, but no one has found a nest yet. They have been seen in almost all months throughout the state, but few in June, July, and August. They are one of the commonest birds at feeders, but are irregular even there. Some winters there are very few, such as in 1989. This is the darker western subspecies.

House Sparrow—*Abundant resident in cities and towns.* They do venture out of the inhabited areas but often not for long. They are slower to move than our native birds and thus more subject to predation. For instance, they come to my bird feeder, but shrikes and accipitrine hawks find them and catch them while the native birds escape. If this happens more than once, the flock leaves—presumably for the city, where it is safer. Where Christmas Counts cover cities and towns, they amount to about one-third of the birds seen. In rural areas they are much scarcer, particularly in winter when there are more avian predators around.

WYOMING MAMMALS

While birding in Wyoming, it is virtually impossible to miss such mammals as Moose, Elk, Buffalo (Bison), Antelope (Pronghorn), Mule Deer, or White-tailed Jackrabbit in the proper habitats. There are, however, many others as well. Here is a complete list of mammals adapted from *Mammals in Wyoming* by Clark and Stromberg. Also included is some information on range, habitats, and/or status in Wyoming.

Opossums (Family Didelphidae)
Virginia Opossum, *Didelphis virginiana virginiana*—eastern riparian areas

Shrews (Family Soricidae)
Hayden's Shrew, *Sorex haydeni*—Black Hills
Masked Shrew, *Sorex cinereus cinereus*—moist areas outside of Black Hills
Preble's Shrew, *Sorex Preblei*—extreme northwest; rare
Vagrant Shrew, *Sorex vagrans vagrans*—riparian areas, extreme western Lincoln County; uncommon
Dusky Shrew, *Sorex monticolus obscurus*—montane and alpine habitats
Dwarf Shrew, *Sorex nanus*—varied isolated populations; rare
Water Shrew, *Sorex palustris navigator*—streamsides and wet meadows in western and southeastern mountains
Merriam's Shrew, *Sorex merriami*—varied habitats; uncommon
Pygmy Shrew, *Sorex hoyi montanus*—Medicine Bow mountains; rare

Moles (Family Talpidae)
Eastern Mole, *Scalopus aquaticus caryi*—southeast; rare

Common Bats (Family Vespertilionidae)
California Myotis, *Myotis californicus californicus*—varied habitats below 1800 meters; Big Horn Basin
Small-footed Myotis, *Myotis ciliolabrum ciliolabrum*—throughout
Yuma Myotis, *Myotis yumanensis yumanensis*—drier basins
Little Brown Myotis, *Myotis lucifugus carissima*—throughout; common
Long-legged Myotis, *Myotis volans interior*—throughout; common
Fringed Myotis, *Myotis thysanodes pahasapensis*—eastern; rare
Keen's Myotis, *Myotis keenii septentrionalis*—Black Hills; rare
Long-eared Myotis, *Myotis evotis evotis*—mostly coniferous areas
Silver-haired Bat, *Lasionycteris noctivagans*—throughout
Big Brown Bat, *Eptesicus fuscus pallidus*—throughout; common
Red Bat, *Lasiurus borealis borealis*—eastern third; uncommon
Hoary Bat, *Lasiurus cinereus cinereus*—throughout; uncommon
Spotted Bat, *Euderma maculatum*—probably western; rare
Townsend's Big-eared Bat, *Plecotus townsendii pallescens*—throughout; often uses caves; relatively common
Pallid Bat, *Antrozous pallidus pallidus*—disjunct southern populations; uncommon

Free-tailed Bats (Family Molossidae)

Brazilian Free-tailed Bat, *Tadarida brasiliensis mexicana*—extreme southeastern; uses caves

Pikas (Family Ochotonidae)

Pika, *Ochotona princeps*—isolated alpine areas

Hares and Rabbits (Family Leporidae)

Pygmy Rabbit, *Sylvilagus idahoensis*—southwestern sage areas; rare
Eastern Cottontail, *Sylvilagus floridanus similis*—southeastern riparian or brushy habitats
Nuttall's Cottontail, *Sylvilagus nuttallii grangeri*—except for southeast, throughout; 1200 to 2700 meters
Desert Cottontail, *Sylvilagus audubonii baileyi*—throughout lower altitudes
Snowshoe Hare, *Lepus americanus*—mountain ranges, except Black Hills
White-tailed Jackrabbit, *Lepus townsendii*—throughout open habitats; common
Black-tailed Jackrabbit, *Lepus californicus melanotis*—eastern third at lower altitudes; relatively common

Squirrels (Family Sciuridae)

Least Chipmunk, *Tamias minimus*—throughout; common
Yellow-pine Chipmunk, *Tamias amoenus luteiventris*—western and northwestern mountains
Cliff Chipmunk, *Tamias dorsalis utahensis*—Flaming Gorge area; rare
Uinta Chipmunk, *Tamias umbrinus*—northwest mountains plus Medicine Bows and Uintas
Yellow-bellied Marmot, *Marmota flaviventris*—almost throughout, except some lower altitudes
Wyoming Ground Squirrel, *Spermophilus elegans elegans*—varied habitats in central and southern
Uinta Ground Squirrel, *Spermophilus armatus*—western fifth; common
Thirteen-lined Ground Squirrel, *Spermophilus tridecemlineatus*—throughout, except western fifth; uncommon
Spotted Ground Squirrel, *Spermophilus spilosoma obsoletus*—southeastern plains; uncommon
Golden-mantled Ground Squirrel, *Spermophilus lateralis*—southern and western; varied habitats
Black-tailed Prairie Dog, *Cynomys ludovicianus ludovicianus*—eastern; isolated populations
White-tailed Prairie Dog, *Cynomys leucurus*—western; common
Fox Squirrel, *Sciurus niger rufiventer*—eastern wooded areas
Abert's Squirrel, *Sciurus aberti ferreus*—near Harriman in southeast; rare
Red Squirrel, *Tamiasciurus hudsonicus*—conifer habitats; common
Northern Flying Squirrel, *Glaucomys sabrinus bangsi*—northwest and Black Hills

Pocket Gophers (Family Geomyidae)

Northern Pocket Gopher, *Thomomys talpoides*—throughout
Wyoming Pocket Gopher, *Thomomys clusius*—only central southern; probably common
Idaho Pocket Gopher, *Thomomys idahoensis pygmaeus*—southwest
Plains Pocket Gopher, *Geomys lutescens lutescens*—eastern quarter

Pocket Mice and Kangaroo Rats (Family Heteromyidae)

Olive-backed Pocket Mouse, *Perognathus fasciatus*—throughout, except western quarter
Plains Pocket Mouse, *Perognathus flavescens flavescens*—southeast; uncommon
Silky Pocket Mouse, *Perognathus flavus piperi*—east central
Great Basin Pocket Mouse, *Perognathus parvus clarus*—southwestern

Hispid Pocket Mouse, *Perognathus hispidus parodoxus*—eastern third
Ord's Kangaroo Rat, *Dipodomys ordii*—throughout in arid basins

Beavers (Family Castoridae)

Beaver, *Castor canadensis*—formerly throughout along wooded streams; now more restricted

New World Rats and Mice (Family Cricetidae)

Plains Harvest Mouse, *Reithrodontomys montanus albescens*—eastern; uncommon
Western Harvest Mouse, *Reithrodontomys megalotis dychei*—eastern
Deer Mouse, *Peromyscus maniculatus*—throughout; common
White-footed Mouse, *Peromyscus leucopus aridulus*—Black Hills and Bighorns
Canyon Mouse, *Peromyscus crinitus douttii*—Sweetwater County; cliffs and rock outcroppings; rare
Pinyon Mouse, *Peromyscus truei truei*—Sweetwater County; rare
Northern Grasshopper Mouse, *Onychomys leucogaster*—throughout; shrublands and grasslands
Bushy-tailed Woodrat, *Neotoma cinerea*—throughout; common
Southern Red-backed Vole, *Clethrionomys gapperi*—almost throughout in woodlands; common
Heather Vole, *Phenacomys intermedius intermedius*—western and central; cool forested ranges
Meadow Vole, *Microtus pennsylvanicus*—western and northeastern
Montane Vole, *Microtus montanus*—except for eastern third, from 1500 to 3000 meters
Long-tailed Vole, *Microtus longicaudus longicaudus*—throughout, except extreme southeastern region
Prairie Vole, *Microtus ochrogaster*—eastern two-thirds; drier habitats; common
Water Vole, *Microtus richardsoni macropus*—northwestern; rare
Sagebrush Vole, *Lemmiscus curtatus levidensis*—except for northeast, sage and related areas; uncommon
Muskrat, *Ondatra zibethicus*—throughout in wet habitats

Old World Rats and Mice (Family Muridae)

Norway Rat, *Rattus norvegicus*—mostly in cities and towns
House Mouse, *Mus musculus*—usually associated with human habitation

Jumping Mice (Family Zapodidae)

Meadow Jumping Mouse, *Zapus hudsonius*—eastern third; wet areas; rare
Western Jumping Mouse, *Zapus princeps*—western; wet areas

Porcupines (Family Erethizontidae)

Porcupine, *Erethizon dorsatum*—throughout; usually forested or riparian areas

Dogs (Family Canidae)

Coyote, *Canis latrans*—throughout
Gray Wolf, *Canis lupus*—formerly throughout, now only rare reports from northwest; endangered
Red Fox, *Vulpes vulpes*—throughout
Swift Fox, *Vulpes velox velox*—formerly common in eastern and central; rare
Gray Fox, *Urocyon cinereoargenteus ocythous*—eastern; rare

Bears (Family Ursidae)

Black Bear, *Ursus americanus cinnamomum*—throughout most mountain forests

Grizzly Bear, *Ursus arctos horribilis*—formerly almost throughout, now only northwestern; endangered

Raccoons and Allies (Family Procyonidae)

Ringtail, *Bassariscus astutus fulvescens*—southern; various habitats; rare
Raccoon, *Procyon lotor hirtus*—throughout, except northwest mountains; common

Weasels (Family Mustelidae)

Marten, *Martes americana*—mountain forests of west and south-central
Fisher, *Martes pennanti columbiana*—mostly northwest; very rare
Ermine, *Mustela erminea muricus*—throughout, though mostly coniferous areas
Least Weasel, *Mustela nivalis campestris*—Sheridan area; probably very rare
Long-tailed Weasel, *Mustela frenata*—throughout, in varied habitats
Black-footed Ferret, *Mustela nigripes*—formerly throughout non-mountainous areas, now a few probable locations; rare and endangered
Mink, *Mustela vison*—throughout; near open water
Wolverine, *Gulo gulo luscus*—mountainous western third; rare
Badger, *Taxidea taxus*—throughout
Eastern Spotted Skunk, *Spilogale putorius interrupta*—eastern quarter; usually near streams
Western Spotted Skunk, *Spilogale gracilis gracilis*—western two-thirds; usually grassland or shrub; may be uncommon
Striped Skunk, *Mephitis mephitis hudsonica*—throughout
River Otter, *Lutra canadensis pacifica*—northwestern and sometimes central; rivers, streams, and lakes; uncommon

Cats (Family Felidae)

Mountain Lion, *Felis concolor*—throughout, especially in Big Horn Basin; uncommon
Lynx, *Felis lynx canadensis*—western three-quarters in high mountains; uncommon
Bobcat, *Felis rufus pallescens*—throughout; various habitats; perhaps becoming uncommon

Deer (Family Cervidae)

Elk, *Cervus elaphus nelsoni*—throughout, especially northwest
Mule Deer, *Odocoileus hemionus hemionus*—throughout; various habitats; quite common
White-tailed Deer, *Odocoileus virginianus*—throughout, especially Black Hills
Moose, *Alces alces shirasi*—northwest

Pronghorn (Family Antilocapridae)

Antelope, *Antilocapra americana americana*—throughout, except forested and alpine areas

Bovids (Family Bovidae)

Buffalo, *Bison bison*—formerly throughout, today wild only in Great Parks
Mountain Goat, *Oreamnos americanus missoulae*—introduced to Absaroka and Teton Mountains
Bighorn Sheep, *Ovis canadensis canadensis*—northwestern mountains; formerly more widespread

REFERENCES

Clark, Tim W., and Mark R. Stromberg. 1987. *Mammals in Wyoming.* University of Kansas Press.

Dorn, Jane L. and Robert D. 1990. *Wyoming Birds.* Mountain West Publishing Company.

Downing, Helen. 1990. *Birds of North-Central Wyoming and the Bighorn National Forest.* Privately published.

Fitton, Sam D. 1984. "Wyoming's Juniper Birds". *Western Birds* 15, #2:85-90.

Fitton, Sam D. 1992. "The Distribution of Screech-Owls in Wyoming". In press.

Follett, Dick. 1986. *Birds of Yellowstone and Grand Teton Parks.* Roberts Rinehart.

Garber, Christopher S., Richard L. Wallen, and Katherine E. Duffy. 1991. "Distribution of Boreal Owl Observation Records in Wyoming". *Journal of Raptor Research* 25, #4:120-122.

Lageson, David, and Darwin Spearing. 1991. *Roadside Geology of Wyoming.* Mountain Press Publishing Company.

McCreary, Otto. 1939. *Wyoming Bird Life.* Burgess Publishing Company.

McEneaney, Terry. 1988. *Birds of Yellowstone.* Roberts Rinehart

Oakleaf, B., *et al.* 1982. *Wyoming Avian Atlas.* Wyoming Department of Game and Fish.

Peterson, Richard A. 1990. *A Birdwatcher's Guide to the Black Hills.* PC Publishing Company.

Raynes, Bert. 1984. *Birds of Grand Teton National Park.* Grand Teton Natural History Association.

NOTES

NOTES

NOTES

NOTES

NOTES

NOTES

Other Birdfinding Guides
in the
ABA/Lane Series

A Birder's Guide to the Rio Grande Valley of Texas
new format, 1991, $14.95

A Birder's Guide to Southeastern Arizona
old format, 1990, $8.95

A Birder's Guide to Southern California
new format, 1990, $14.95

A Birder's Guide to Colorado
old format, 1988, $8.95

A Birder's Guide to Florida
old format, 1989, $8.95

A Birder's Guide to the Texas Coast
new format, available in early 1993, $14.95

A Birder's Guide to Churchill (Manitoba)
new format revision due in 1993

These and many other birdfinding and bird identification
publications are available from:

ABA Sales
PO Box 6599
Colorado Springs, CO 80934-6599
Toll-free (US & Canada): 1-800-634-7736
Toll-free Fax: 1-800-247-3329

Write, call, or fax to order or to request a free copy of the most
recent ABA Sales Annotated Catalog and Pricelist containing over
400 publications and other birding-related items.

Resale inquiries invited

AMERICAN BIRDING ASSOCIATION
Membership Application

All memberships include six issues of **Birding** magazine, monthly issues of **Winging It,** ABA's newsletter, member discounts offered by ABA Sales, and full rights of participation in all ABA activities.

Membership classes and dues:

❑ Individual $30 / yr*   ❑ Family $37 / yr*

❑ Century Club $100 / yr   ❑ Library $35 / yr*

US & Canada only; all others, add $7.00

Application Type

❑ New Membership   ❑ Renewal

Member Information

Name _____

Address _____

_____

_____

Phone _____

Payment Information

❑ Check or Money Order enclosed (US funds only)

❑ Charge to VISA / MasterCard (circle one)

Account Number _____

Exp Date _____

Signature _____

(a $1.00 handling fee will be added for use of credit card)

Sent this completed form with payment to: **ABA Membership**
PO Box 6599
Colorado Springs, CO 80934

WY 1/93

American Birding Association, Inc.

Since 1969, the American Birding Association has served the North American birding community by helping birders hone their field identification skills and telling them where to find birds. This membership organization exists to promote the recreational observation and study of wild birds, to educate the public in the appreciation of birds and their vital role in the environment, to assist in the study of birds in their natural habitat, and to contribute to the development of improved bird population studies. The organization also keeps North American birders informed about bird conservation, valuable birding resources, new publications, and top-notch birding equipment.

All ABA members receive **Birding**, the official bimonthly magazine of the organization, and **Winging It,** the monthly newsletter. Both publications are chock-full of birdfinding advice, identification details, and up-to-date birding news. Members also receive discounts from ABA Sales on bird books, tapes, optical equipment, and accessories. ABA also publishes an invaluable Membership Directory, conducts biennial conventions and regional conferences, and sponsors bird-related tours of various durations to domestic and foreign birding hot-spots.

All persons interested in these aspects of bird study are invited to join. If you bird beyond your backyard, ABA membership will help you discover a whole new world of birding adventure and expertise. A membership form is included on the previous page.

American Birding Association
PO Box 6599
Colorado Springs, Colorado 80934-6599

INDEX

Fort Phil Kearny 131
Fort Steel 214

G

Gadwall 22, 41, 51, 109, 127, 129, 145, 159
Gallinule
  Purple 171
Garden Creek Falls 74, 209
Gillette 175, 208, 210
Glendo State Park 222
Glenrock 163, 171, 189
Glenrock Power Plant 161
Gnatcatcher
  Blue-gray 31, 38, 77, 200
Godwit
  Hudsonian 123, 125, 175
  Marbled 55, 176
Golden-Plover
  Lesser 39, 125, 172
Goldeneye
  Barrow's 41, 77, 84, 90-91, 96, 103, 107, 109,
    111, 114, 161
  Common 22, 161
Goldeneye Wildlife and Recreation Area 79
Goldfinch
  American 127, 222
  Lesser 222
Goose
  Canada 22, 38, 41, 55-56, 80, 101, 114, 129,
    157
  Greater White-fronted 56, 157
  Ross's 56, 157
  Snow 55-56, 157
Goshawk
  Northern 24, 68, 101, 148, 164
Goshen Hole 55, 155-159, 164, 166, 170, 175,
  182, 219
Grackle
  Common 219
  Great-tailed 219
Grand Canyon of the Yellowstone 114
Grand Teton National Park 89, 153, 156-157, 162,
  164, 167-168, 171, 174, 179, 182, 184-186,
  188-189, 191-192, 195-196, 199-201, 207,
  209-212, 215-216
Grays Lake National Wildlife Refuge, Idaho 42,
  157, 172
Grebe
  Clark's 38, 80, 85, 142, 154
  Eared 15, 22, 154
  Horned 36, 58, 83, 153
  Pied-billed 15, 129, 153
  Red-necked 104, 154
  Western 15, 22, 38, 80, 85, 130, 154
Green River 35, 38, 153, 161, 166, 192, 195,
  197-198, 200, 207-208, 210
Green River Basin 173, 214
Green River Valley 39, 207
Greybull 142, 163

Grosbeak
  Black-headed 15, 29, 44, 48, 68, 72, 135, 211
  Blue 16, 39, 59-60, 211
  Evening 222
  Pine 24, 87, 93, 97, 112, 148, 220
  Rose-breasted 211
Grouse
  Blue 44, 79, 93, 105, 107-108, 112, 117, 148,
    168
  Ruffed 44, 92, 97, 107, 109, 111, 168
  Sage 41, 43, 71, 91, 141, 169-170
  Sharp-tailed 125, 132, 134, 170
  Spruce 168
Guernsey 162, 214
Gull
  Bonaparte's 131, 147, 179
  California 15, 38, 80, 85, 87, 104, 115, 117,
    131, 147, 180
  Common Black-headed 179
  Franklin's 131, 147, 179
  Glaucous 181
  Heermann's 81, 179
  Herring 131, 181
  Mew 180
  Ring-billed 15, 38, 80, 131, 147, 180
  Sabine's 131, 181
Gyrfalcon 130, 167

H

Happy Jack Recreation Area 19
Harrier
  Northern 44, 67-68, 114, 146, 163
Harriman 184